MW00988357

# DATE DUE

The Problem of Evil
&
The Problem of God

Also by D. Z. Phillips

*The Concept of Prayer*
*Moral Practices* (with H.O. Mounce)
*Faith and Philosophical Enquiry*
*Death and Immortality*
*Sense and Delusion* (with İlham Dilman)
*Athronyddu Am Grefydd*
*Religion Without Explanation*
*Dramâu Gwenlyn Parry*
*Through a Darkening Glass*
*Belief, Change and Forms of Life*
*R.S. Thomas: Poet of the Hidden God*
*Faith After Foundationalism*
*From Fantasy to Faith*
*Interventions in Ethics*
*Wittgenstein and Religion*
*Writers of Wales: J.R. Jones*
*Introducing Philosophy: The Challenge of Scepticism*
*Philosophy's Cool Place*
*Recovering Religious Concepts*
*Religion and Friendly Fire*

THE PROBLEM OF **EVIL**
**&**
THE PROBLEM OF **GOD**

D. Z. Phillips

**Fortress Press**
Minneapolis

THE PROBLEM OF EVIL AND THE PROBLEM OF GOD

First Fortress Press edition 2005

Cover image: Lazar Vozarevic, Pieta, 1956, Museum of Modern Art, Belgrade.
Cover design: James Korsmo

The extract from *Waiting for Godot,* by Samuel Beckett, 1977, is used by permission of Faber and Faber.

ISBN 0-8006-3775-5

The paper used in this publication meets the minimum requirements of American National Standard for Information Sciences — Permanence of Paper for Printed Library Materials, ANSI Z329.48-1984.

Manufactured in the U.S.A.

09   08   07   06   05   1   2   3   4   5   6   7   8   9   10

To
Rowan Williams

We have to be careful about the level on which we place the infinite. If we put it on the level which is only suitable for the finite it does not much matter what name we give it.

Simone Weil

# Contents

# Acknowledgements

Since the manuscript for this book was read by more than one publisher at the same time, I am indebted to a number of anonymous readers for comments which led me to revise my original version. The enthusiasm of the editors of SCM Press led me to choose them from among the offers to publish the work.

As usual, I am extremely grateful for the excellent work of Helen Baldwin, Secretary to the Department of Philosophy at Swansea, in preparing my handwritten manuscript for publication. I am grateful too to my colleague at Claremont, Patrick Rogers Horn, for help with the proof reading.

In the Spring Semester of 2001 and 2003, I gave seminars on The Problem of Evil at Claremont Graduate University. I am grateful for stimulating disagreements with Stephen T. Davis with whom I co-taught the first of the semesters, and to my students, on both occasions, for their probing questions and discussions. It was these seminars which led me to the decision to put my thoughts into a book.

D. Z. Phillips
Claremont/Swansea
January 2004

# Introduction

# On Telling the Problem of Evil

## 1. Why this Book?

Philosophizing about the problem of evil has become common-place. Theories, theodicies and defences abound, all seeking either to render unintelligible, or to justify, God's ways to human beings. Such writing should be done in fear: fear that in our philo-sophizings we will betray the evils people have suffered, and, in that way, sin against them. Betrayal occurs every time explana-tions and justifications of evils are offered which are simplistic, insensitive, incredible or obscene. Greater damage is often done to religion by those who think of themselves as its philosophical friends, than by those who present themselves as religion's detractors and despisers.[1] Nowhere is this damage more in evid-ence, in my opinion, than in philosophical discussions of the problem of evil.

Most Anglo-American analytic philosophers of religion distin-guish between what is called *the logical problem of evil*, and what is variously called *the existential, practical, emotive, pas-toral or evangelistic problem of evil*. The logical problem comes from the charge that it is inconsistent to believe in the existence of an all-powerful, perfectly good God, while acknowledging the existence of evil at the same time. The existential problem is how to cope with actual evils in our own lives, and in the lives of others; something said to require more than the ability to solve abstract, logical problems.

In the present work I argue that the distinction between the logical problem of evil and the existential problem of evil is a spurious one. The 'logical' is rooted in 'the existential'. For example, anything said about evil, in the name of logic, must be answerable to the searching and challenging reality of the evils people suffer. 'The abstract', try as it will, cannot sidestep these 'particulars'. It is only by paying insufficient attention to existential problems of evil that an independent logical problem of evil can be thought to exist.

The above claim does not mean that there are no conceptual issues to reflect on in discussions of the problem of evil. It is only through such reflection that one can come to see the confusions involved in the form taken by the logical problem of evil. Concerned as it is with these and other conceptual issues, the present essay is not an exercise in religious apologetics, or anti-religious polemics. It does not seek to establish *the* proper response to the problem of evil. Philosophy possesses no criterion of its own by which this can be done, although it is concerned with the exposure of any conceptual confusion present in the responses that may be advocated. Even if all such confusions were eliminated, however, a variety of responses to the evils in the world will remain. Where one stands in relation to these is, of necessity, a personal matter. One has to speak in the first person. Philosophy is concerned with the conceptual character of such responses, and with what disagreement between them amounts to.

Having made the above assertions, I need to explain why I devote much of Part II of my essay to a particular religious response to the problem of evil. I do so because, as a religious response, it is deeply rooted. It is certainly not my creation. I do so also because it contrasts, sharply, with the philosophical discussions of the problem of evil which have dominated Anglo-American philosophy of religion. What is more, I do *not* regard those discussions, in many instances, as displaying possible responses to the problem of evil, since, as I shall argue, they manifest the kind of confusions which it is part of philosophy's task to point out. These confusions have to do, not only with central religious and moral concepts, but with the evils being discussed. They do not tell their philosophical story without betraying them.

This book is by far my most systematic attempt to discuss the problem of evil.[2] Yet, to elucidate a response to evil which I regard as religiously profound is not to advocate that response, or to provide a philosophical foundation for it. It is an attempt to clarify its character. But there are also profound secular responses to evil of which the same can be said. Even if an elucidation of the religious response is appreciated, some may recoil from what it asks of them. Others may want to combat it with responses of other kinds. What is achieved by a successful discussion of the conceptual issues involved is the creation of a situation in which there can be honest agreement and disagreement without a betrayal of suffering and affliction. With the creation of such a situation, philosophy should be more than satisfied.

Given what I have said about the profound religious response to evil discussed in Part II of my book, why is the whole of Part I devoted to discussions of the problem of evil that make up a philosophical inheritance I regard as problematic? Why not go directly to a discussion of the deeper religious response? There are two answers to this question.

First, it is true that the discussion in Part I does not begin at the best place to discuss the problem of evil, but at the most realistic place. Left to myself, as it were, I would not discuss the problem of evil in these terms. On the other hand, realism dictates that I have to recognize that, as far as the majority of contemporary philosophers are concerned, this is where we are.

Second, if I want to move philosophers from where we are, to where we ought to be, philosophically, there is little point in saying, 'You can't start from here'. Philosophically, a *path* must be shown from confusion to clarity. That is why the philosophical inheritance I regard as problematic has to be confronted. To ignore that inheritance is to ignore the very audience I hope to convince.

One of the main aims of my book, in discussing our problematic philosophical inheritance, is to show, from the outset, that a neglect of the existential problem of evil results, not only in misunderstandings of the evils that confront us, but also in misunderstandings of logic. Some of these latter misunderstandings are

linked to assumptions concerning the role of theory in the problem of evil.*

## 2. Do We Need Theories?

The claim that the distinction between the logical problem of evil
and the existential problem of evil is a spurious one will surprise
most contemporary Anglo-American philosophers of religion,
since they see a necessary connection between them. Marilyn
Adams and Robert Adams define the *practical* problem of evil as
'how to survive in such a seemingly hostile environment', and the
*existential* problem as 'how a life laced with suffering and punc-
tuated by death can have any positive meaning'. They are aware
that people have responded to these evils in different ways, but
they treat these responses as though they were problematic data
awaiting a theoretical solution. Thus, they ask:

> Should one see evils as a challenge the overcoming of which
> adds zest to life in a basically good world? Or should one see
> life as nightmarish far beyond human powers to affect? Should
> one endure it with Stoic resignation, doing what one can to ease
> the pain? Or should one rebel against it in fierce opposition?[3]

Who asks these questions? Presumably, not anyone who *already*
responds to life in any of these ways. An adherent to any one
of the responses may, of course, come to question it, so I am
not belittling the questions, but the *philosophical* setting they
are given here. Responses come to be challenged, questioned,
doubted or eroded, usually by a rival response. Or perhaps an
individual becomes sceptical of seeking such all-embracing
responses to the raggedness of human life. Large answers are no
longer sought. These do not seem to be the situations that Adams
and Adams have in mind. Their questioner seeks to ask questions
of a range of responses all at once, and one may well wonder from
what position the questions come. Perhaps they are the questions
of someone lost and bewildered among so many voices. But,

---

* Selections from Chapters 1 and 2 were presented as the Tanner-McMurrin
  Lecture at Westminster College, Salt Lake City.

again, this seems a far cry from what Adams and Adams have in mind.

For Adams and Adams, we cannot stay, philosophically, with the variety of responses, refusing to get behind them, since, for them, the responses are problems waiting to be solved. 'Their solution', they tell us, 'calls for theories about the structure of the world and the place of human beings in it, for explanations that locate the origin and/or explain the occurrence of evils, for accounts that suggest appropriate and effective human responses to them.'[4] Where are such theories to be found? According to Adams and Adams:

> Both science and religion have stepped into this role. As with all theories, their proposals have to be evaluated and reassessed against the data along the parameters of consistency, explanatory power, and (theoretical and practical) fruitfulness.[5]

This view of theory in relation to the problem of evil is extremely influential. One must disentangle the various assumptions it makes. For example, sometimes, we seem to be going in circles. We begin with various responses to the evils in life which those who make them hold to be appropriate. Then we are told that these responses are problems awaiting a theoretical solution. What is the solution meant to provide? The answer is: effective responses to the evils of life. But it is precisely those responses that we started out with. 'Not so', it may be replied, 'what we started out with are the responses which people *think* are adequate and effective. What we end up with is a response which really *is* adequate and effective, because it has been shown, theoretically, to be such. It is the response which is the most consistent, fruitful, and powerful explanation of the evils which confront us.'[6]

Given such high ambitions, we need to take a closer look at the theories that are supposed to help us fulfil them. They are said to be theories about the structure of the world and our place in it. What kind of theory is a theory about the structure of the world? If by 'the world' one wants to mean 'everything', there is no such theory. Certainly, science has no such theory, nor could it have. 'Everything' is not the name of one big thing or topic, and, therefore, there can be no theory concerning a thing or topic of this kind. To speak of a thing is to acknowledge the existence of many things, since one can always be asked *which* thing one is referring to. Science is concerned with specific states of affairs, no matter how wide the scope of its questions may be. Whatever explanations it offers, further questions can be asked about them. It makes no sense to speak of a last answer in science, one that does not admit of any further questions. Science is not concerned with 'the structure of the world', and there are no scientific investigations which have this as their subject.

According to Adams and Adams, there are not only theories about the structure of the world, but also theories about the place of human beings within it. If I think of my place in the world, the following factors come readily to mind: the country where I was born, the family into which I was born, my present immediate family, my friends and neighbours, my interests, my profession, the state of my culture and other cultures which bear on me politically, economically, morally or religiously, the state of the arts, and so on. These factors, and many more, are not theories about my place in the world, but are constitutive of the various aspects that place has.

These conclusions may be challenged by an appeal to the social sciences. How can I deny that theories abound about nations, families, professions, human relationships, social movements and cultures? My reply is that I do not deny this fact. On the other hand, it is important to recognize an essential difference between the natural and the social sciences.[7] Unlike the natural sciences, the social sciences are concerned with contexts in which *concepts are already at work* in the lives of human beings, prior to the theoretical interest that may be taken in them. The point is not to deny that the social sciences may raise questions which are not raised by the people they study, nor to deny that use may be made of technical concepts not to be found in the behaviour they study. The point to be emphasized is that if the theory claims to explain certain aspects of human activity, it must do conceptual justice to the ideas to be found in that activity. But the activity itself is no more a theory than life itself is.

Among human activities are the practices of religion. Notoriously, there have been many reductionist theories of religion which have tried to explain it away on the assumption that it is a theory whose inadequacies can be exposed.[8] But of religion, too, it can be said that it is no more a theory than life itself. We may entertain theories about all sorts of things in the course of our lives, but that fact about us is not itself a theory. We may speak of mastering a theory, of knowing its 'ins' and 'outs', of knowing our way about in it and so on. We need only try to speak of faith in God, or life itself, in this way, to begin to appreciate the difference.[9]

Adams and Adams may respond by saying that the theories they have in mind are neither the theories of the natural sciences, nor the theories of the social sciences, although their reference to 'all theories' does not help in this respect. They may say that they are referring to metaphysical theories which, typically, are theories about 'all things'.[10] It is theories of this kind that we need in order to find answers to problems such as the problem of evil.

The response I am attributing to Adams and Adams raises large issues about the philosophical status of metaphysical theories. These issues will arise, indirectly, throughout the book, but some general comments may be useful at this stage. In the revolution in philosophy that occurred in the twentieth century, there was a fundamental critique of metaphysics. In the case of Wittgenstein, the central figure in that revolution, the call was not to renounce or refute metaphysics (at least, not after 1931),[11] but to see that metaphysical propositions could not be saying what they were presented as saying. Marilyn Adams recognizes that analytic philosophers of religion, for the most part, reject the philosophical methods of Wittgenstein and ordinary language philosophers, so influential from the late 1920s to the middle 1970s.[12] Adams says:

Recall that according to this methodology, philosophers who want to find out truths about mind and body, morals, and so on, should not go about inventing philosophical theories, but should set out to analyze the concepts of mind, body, and moral goodness, and so on, implicit in our ordinary use of language . . . Many, perhaps most, analytic philosophers have abandoned the ideals of ordinary language philosophy (and rightly so, in my judgement) and resumed the traditional activity of theory construction.[13]

We are not given any details of how Adams arrived at her judgement. Her comment is more assertion than argument, and, in fairness, does not pretend to be anything else. Yet, on the face of it, it is odd to hear analytic philosophers say that they have abandoned philosophical movements which made the analysis of concepts central in philosophy. Nevertheless, if one wants to understand the relation of analytic philosophy of religion to Wittgenstein's work, or to ordinary language philosophy, 'abandonment' is the right word. It marks a contrast with 'philosophical engagement'. There has been precious little philosophical engagement on the part of analytic philosophers of religion.

The twentieth-century revolution in philosophy left mainstream Anglo-American philosophy of religion untouched. By their own admission, the problems of most contemporary philosophers of religion are still rooted in the empiricism and naturalism to be found in Locke, Hume and Reid.[14] They write, for the most part, as though Wittgenstein had never existed. As a result, there has been little engagement with his work from the direction of analytic philosophy of religion.[15] There is little sign of the situation changing. To speak of the 'abandonment' of the ideals of ordinary language philosophy is even too strong, since there was hardly an appreciation of anything to be abandoned. 'Ignored' would be a more accurate designation. In many ways this is a pity, since, as I have tried to show in my own work, engagement between these movements would raise issues of central importance in philosophy.[16]

It is worth asking whether the reluctance to abandon theory-construction in philosophy is often an obstacle of the will, rather than an obstacle of the intellect. The latter obstacle resides in the intellectual difficulty of the point being made to one, whereas, an obstacle of the will is a refusal to give up a certain way of thinking. Does the distinction apply to the commitment to theory-construction?

On the one hand, as we have seen, Adams and Adams claim that religion, as a theoretical answer to the problem of evil, must, like all other theories, 'be evaluated and reassessed against the data along the parameters of consistency, explanatory power, and (theoretical and practical) fruitfulness'.[17] On the other hand, Adams herself admits:

> Once theorizing begins, however, the hope of universal agreement in value theory is shattered, the wide-ranging extensional overlaps notwithstanding. Witness, for example, the divide in secular ethics between 'consequentialists' who assert that lying can sometimes be justified if it optimizes the consequences, and 'deontologists', who contend that lying is always wrong, no matter what![18]

We seem to have arrived at an odd situation. Having said that theories are essential to exploring how we should react to evil, we are now told that resorting to them shatters any hope of such agreement! It never occurs to Adams to ask whether the trouble lies in the conception of an all-embracing theory, which is said to determine the essence of 'the moral'. We see rival general theories in ethics stretch themselves out of all recognition in attempting to accommodate obvious counter-examples to the theory. Gradually, Aristotle begins to look like Kant, and Kant begins to look like Aristotle. There is nothing intellectually difficult in the observation that all moral convictions, actions and situations cannot be reduced to a common form. It hardly constitutes an obstacle of the intellect. What the observation confronts is an obstacle of the will, the groundless conviction that there *must* be a common form to morality behind the variety.

Think of Freud's theory of dreams. Freud asserted that all dreams are not simply products of wish-fulfilments, but are products of sexual wish-fulfilments. The suggestion that all dreams do not have a sexual origin, hardly constitutes an obstacle of the intellect, yet, Freud will not contemplate that possibility. If he could have been convinced of it, his reaction would have been, 'Well, in that case, what are *all* dreams?' Freud would not have given up the 'all', the conviction that dreams *must* have an essence. That is an obstacle of the will.

What is the effect on Adams of the theoretical failure in ethics to agree on a definition of a moral act? Instead of being rescued from essentialism, the failure to attain theoretical agreement becomes, for her, a licence for each theorist to retreat, without justification, behind the unexamined assumptions of his or her theory. Adams says:

> I am a *realist* about philosophical/theological theories in that I believe there are facts of the matter, independently of what we think, believe, or conceive of in our theories. I am a *skeptic*, however, because I believe that the defense of any well-formulated philosophical position will eventually involve premises which are fundamentally controversial and so unable to command the assent of all reasonable persons.[19]

Clearly, Adams is not saying that a philosophical theory is controversial because it does not command universal assent, but that such theories do not command universal assent because they are controversial. What does it mean to call philosophical theories 'controversial'? Apparently, it means that we cannot be sure that they put us in contact with reality. On Adams's view, how could they, since it is always logically possible that 'how things are' is quite different from how we conceive things to be. Thus, she has to conclude that, in our theories, 'the nature of reality and value is something we struggle towards via successive approximations'.[20]

Adams's licence for theory is shown in the realm of metaphysics where, she claims, what we take reality to be depends on what she calls 'our ontological commitments'. According to her, ultimate assumptions about reality and value come together in theoretical responses to the problem of evil:

different ontological commitments with their different stories of valuables widen or narrow the range of options for defeating evils with goods. Secular value theories can offer only packages of immanent goods; some religious theories posit an infinite transcendent goodness and invite relationship to it; while mainstream Christianity believes the infinite good to be personal and locates the happiness of finite persons in loving personal intimacy with the divine persons.[21]

As far as Adams is concerned, all the rival theories make 'philosophical assumptions of comparable status'.[22] The results are, therefore, '*parochial*, at best strategies that might make sense within a given framework of philosophical assumptions'.[23]

Philosophical discussions need to explore what goes unquestioned in Adams' metaphysical views; to question the intelligibility of regarding different reactions to life's evils as *theories* about them; to examine, as Adams does not, the *assumption* that they can be so regarded. What is shown, as a result, is a variety of values, religious and secular, that are not theories about anything. They conflict because of their respective contents. When philosophy is concerned with their reality, it is concerned with their meaning, not with their truth. The reason why philosophy cannot determine which response is the true one, has nothing to do with the confused assumption that each response is, at best, an approximation to reality. It is because arriving at the truth must be a personal matter.

Philosophy is not a series of theories which approximate to reality.[24] On the contrary, through philosophical discussion, we dismantle theories, so that distinctions between the real and the unreal, the valuable and the valueless, are shown for what they are. These distinctions are not hidden. They are there, like our lives. It is our pseudo-theories which make us think we can never reach them.[25] As they stand, these assertions are dogmatic. They must be given substance in our discussions of the problem of evil.

## Notes

1 Hence, the title of my last book, *Religion and Friendly Fire*, Aldershot: Ashgate 2004.

2 For my previous essays, see 'The Problem of Evil' (a symposium with Richard Swinburne) in Stuart Brown (ed.), *Reason and Religion*, Ithaca: Cornell University Press 1977; 'On Not Understanding God', *Archivio Di Filosofia*, Vol. LVI, reprinted in *Wittgenstein and Religion*, Basingstoke: Macmillan and New York: St. Martin's Press 1993; 'Theism Without Theodicy' in *Encountering Evil*, ed. Stephen T. Davis, Louisville: Westminster John Knox Press 2001.

3 Marilyn McCord Adams and Robert Merrihew Adams (eds), *The Problem of Evil*, New York: Oxford University Press 1990, p. 1.

4 Adams and Adams, *Problem of Evil*, p. 1.

5 Adams and Adams, *Problem of Evil*, p. 1.

6 As we shall see, this promise is never fulfilled. So, far from the chosen theory being held answerable to the data, we find that the data are read in the light of one's commitment to the chosen theory. See p. xx.

7 For a discussion of these differences see Peter Winch, *The Idea of a Social Science*, Second Edition, Wiltshire: Routledge 1995. For a discussion of the development in his views on this topic see my 'Beyond Rules', *History of the Human Sciences*, Vol. 13, No. 2, May 2000, pp. 17–36.

8 For a discussion of such theories see my *Religion and the Hermeneutics of Contemplation*, Cambridge: Cambridge University Press 2000.

9 For a discussion of attempts to see life as a series of games or skills that one could master, see Rush Rhees, *Wittgenstein and the Possibility of Discourse*, ed. D. Z. Phillips, Cambridge: Cambridge University Press 1998.

10 For a discussion of the difficulties involved in this notion see my *Philosophy's Cool Place*, Ithaca: Cornell University Press 1999.

11 See Rush Rhees, 'On Wittgenstein', ed. D. Z. Phillips, *Philosophical Investigations*, Vol. 24, No. 2, April 2001.

12 For a discussion of the anomalous use of 'analytic' in 'analytic philosophy of religion' when compared to the history of twentieth-century analytic philosophy, see D. Z. Phillips, *Religion and Friendly Fire*, Aldershot: Ashgate 2004.

13 Marilyn McCord Adams, *Horrendous Evils and the Goodness of God*, Ithaca: Cornell University Press 1999, p. 11.

14 I have told this story in *Religion and Friendly Fire*.

15 It may be thought that W. P. Alston's *Perceiving God*, Cornell: Cornell University Press 1991, is an exception, but his placement of Wittgenstein's work in an epistemological context, rather than in philosophical logic, means that the engagement is severely limited.

16 It could be said that the negative aspects of my work consist of a running

battle with mainstream philosophy of religion. For my reaction to early Reformed Epistemology see *Faith After Foundationalism*, Routledge 1988; Westview Press 1995. For a critique of analytic philosophy of religion in relation to the history of philosophy see *Religion and Friendly Fire*. For an exposure of the latent scepticism in the epistemologies of Alston, Hick and Swinburne, see Lance Ashdown, *Anonymous Sceptics*, Mohr Siebeck 2002.

17  Adams and Adams, *The Problem of Evil*, p. 1.
18  Adams, *Horrendous Evils*, pp. 11–12.
19  Adams, *Horrendous Evils*, p. 180.
20  Adams, *Horrendous Evils*, p. 180.
21  Adams, *Horrendous Evils*, p. 12.
22  Adams, *Horrendous Evils*, p. 178.
23  Adams, *Horrendous Evils*, p. 179.
24  See my 'What God Himself Cannot Tell Us: Realism Versus Metaphysical Realism', *Faith and Philosophy*, October 2002.
25  See my 'The Presumption of Theory' in *Interventions in Ethics*, Basingstoke: Macmillan and New York: SUNY Press 1999.

# Part One

# Our Problematic Inheritance

# I

# Logic and Omnipotence

If theism is supposed to be a *theoretical* answer to the problem of evil, then, as we have seen, it must, like all other theories, be tested for its consistency, explanatory power and fruitfulness in face of the evils it is supposed to explain. According to the logical problem of evil, theism falls at the first hurdle. It cannot be shown to be consistent with the existence of evil. This charge was well expressed by Philo in Hume's *Dialogues Concerning Natural Religion*:

> Epicurus's old questions are yet unanswered. Is he willing to prevent evil, but not able? then he is impotent. Is he able, but not willing? then he is malevolent. Is he both able and willing? whence then is evil?[1]

In recent discussions of the logical problem of evil, it is presented in the form of a problematic triad of propositions, said to be implied in Epicurus's questions. This triad owes its contemporary prominence to the discussion of it by J. L. Mackie who wrote:

> In its simplest form the problem is this: God is omnipotent; God is wholly good; and yet evil exists. There seems to be some contradiction between these three propositions, so that if any two of them were true the third would be false. But at the same time all three are essential parts of most theological positions: the theologian, it seems, at once *must* adhere, and cannot consistently adhere to all three.[2]

In the wake of Hume's formulation of the logical problem of evil, many philosophers were of the opinion that the problem was unanswerable. For example, W. T. Stace wrote:

> We have to say that Hume was right. The charge has never been answered, and never will be. The simultaneous attribution of all-power and all-goodness to the Creator of the whole world is logically incompatible with the existence of evil and pain in the world, for which reason the conception of a finite god, who is not all-powerful . . . has become popular in some quarters.[3]

Again, F. H. Bradley is clear that the reason why the logical problem of evil cannot be answered is that it is a non-problem. This is because it is self-contradictory:

> The trouble has come from the idea that the Absolute is a moral person. If you start from that basis, then the relation of evil to the Absolute presents at once an irreducible dilemma. The problem then becomes insoluble, but not because it is obscure or in any way mysterious. To any one who has sense and courage to see things as they are, and is resolved not to mystify others or himself, there is really no question to discuss. The dilemma is plainly insoluble because it is based on a clear self-contradiction.[4]

Mackie points out, however, that the self-contradiction in the logical problem of evil does not arise immediately from the triad of propositions said to be inconsistent. Mackie says that:

> to show it we need some additional premises, or perhaps some quasi-logical rules connecting the terms 'good', 'evil', and 'omnipotent'. These additional principles are that good is opposed to evil, in such a way that a good thing always eliminates evil as far as it can, and that there are no limits to what an omnipotent thing can do. From these it follows that a good omnipotent thing eliminates evil completely, and then the

propositions that a good omnipotent thing exists, and that evil exists, are incompatible.[5]

Discussion of Mackie's paper by analytic philosophers of religion has led to a major philosophical reassessment of the logical problem of evil. As a result of Nelson Pike's paper, 'Hume on Evil',[6] and the ways in which Alvin Plantinga[7] and others have built on its insights, most analytic philosophers of religion claim the problem has been solved. So successful has the solution been that, according to Stephen T. Davis, 'one rarely hears any longer the problem of evil presented as if it were a purely logical problem, as if theists are contradicting themselves'.[8]

Is this confident philosophical change of heart justified? Something intellectually momentous must have taken place to show that Hume's confidence that Epicurus' old questions remain unanswered, is misplaced; to show that Stace was wrong in thinking that the questions can never be answered; and to show contra Bradley that there is no self-contradiction in theism's answer to the logical problem of evil after all. In Part I of this book, I argue that the philosophical confidence that the logical problem of evil has been solved is misplaced, and that the views which have brought it about do not amount to anything momentous in philosophy. For these reasons, I call these views 'our problematic inheritance'.

To anticipate: if we stay *within* the terms of reference in which the logical problem of evil is usually discussed, we shall find that neither the proposition, 'God is omnipotent', nor the proposition, 'God is perfectly good', can get off the ground – and that for logical reasons. In the present chapter I argue this case with respect to the first of these propositions.

## 1. How Do We Determine the Logic of 'Omnipotence'?

What do we mean by 'divine omnipotence'? Another way of asking the same question is to ask, What is the logic or grammar of 'divine omnipotence'? How are we to go about answering these questions?

Stace says that the logical problem of evil only arises if the word 'powerful' is used in theology as it is used in ordinary discourse. Clearly, for Stace, the use of 'powerful' in theology or religion is a use in a context *other than* that of 'ordinary discourse'. But if we want to bring words back from their metaphysical to their ordinary use, we need have no such contrast in mind. The term 'ordinary' in 'ordinary discourse', is not meant in contrast to 'technical', 'scientific', 'religious' or 'figurative', etc. To ask after the meaning of a concept in ordinary discourse is to ask for its meaning in the normal context of its usage. If the concept in question is scientific or religious, the context of ordinary discourse will be scientific or religious, respectively. It follows, then, that if we want to understand what we mean by 'divine omnipotence', we need to look to the religious contexts in which it has its use. After all, it is *divine* omnipotence that we are trying to understand.

Strangely enough, the barely observed fact is that when many philosophers of religion talk of God's omnipotence, they seem to know what is meant by 'power', in this context, without any reference to God or religion at all. That is why Stace can ask whether it has *the same* use in theology. He thinks he is referring to the only sense it has. This seems to be true of Davis, too, when he says, 'It seems entirely possible that God has all the power there is. Perhaps God has the power totally to control all events and things but does not use it. This is my own view.'[9]

What does it mean to speak of 'all the power there is'? Richard Swinburne spells it out for us:

An omnipotent being is one who can do anything logically possible, anything, that is, the description of which does not involve a contradiction: such a being could not make me exist and not exist at the same instant, but he could eliminate the stars or cover the Earth with water just like that.[10]

For Swinburne, as for Davis, the meaning of 'omnipotence' is logically independent of God. In fact, Swinburne thinks it makes sense for us to imagine that we were omnipotent. He asks, 'consider what kind of world you would think it right to create if you had unlimited power and knowledge'.[11] I take it that Swinburne is not asking us to imagine that we were God. We are asked to imagine that we have a power which, as a matter of fact, only God has. But the power, the omnipotence, has a meaning quite independent of God, and Swinburne tells us what he thinks it amounts to.

This independent access to the meaning of 'omnipotence', without any reference to religion, is shared by secularists. Mackie insists on this meaning, without which, he tells us, there would be no logical problem of evil. For him, as for the religious apologists, 'omnipotence' means 'there are no limits to what an omnipotent being can do'. Some theologians do not accept this definition, but, in that case, according to Mackie, they depart from the traditional meaning of 'omnipotence'.

Is Mackie's conclusion true? Can one say that God is omnipotent and, at the same time, that there are things that God cannot do? Is it logically contradictory to say this or not? How is that matter to be settled? This question involves us in a discussion of logic and the meaning of propositions that one does not find, normally, in discussions of the logical problem of evil. But it is that problem's conception of logic and the meaning of propositions that needs to be questioned.

In the logical problem of evil, there are two conceptions of logic that need to be disentangled. In the problem, the two conceptions are thought to be interrelated. On the one hand, we have a conception of logic as that which determines whether a proposition has sense or not. On the other hand, we can ask what is the logic or grammar of a given proposition, such as 'God is omnipotent'. That is the proposition we want to understand. The question we have to ask is whether the logic of a specific proposition is determined by logic, in the more general sense, as that which determines what can and cannot be said. If the answer to this question is no, we are left with the issue of how the sense of the proposition is to be determined. Clearly, these issues are central to the question of how one is to determine the meaning of 'God is omnipotent'. I want to consider the issues first, however, in relation to familiar propositions in the literature concerning such questions, and then apply the lessons learned to 'God is omnipotent'.

What does it mean to say that logic does not allow us to say such-and-such? We are told that logic does not allow us to speak of a 'round square', or to say that 2 + 2 = 5. Once we see these words or symbols, the argument claims, we see immediately that we are trying to say something which cannot be said. We are told that the meaning of the words or symbols determines the fact that they cannot be said. If we appreciate this apparently simple truth, accepted, so often, without a second thought, we will not expect to come across a round square, or think that it will ever be possible to say 2 + 2 = 5. After all, we are told, we are dealing with logical truths, with logical necessities, not with contingent, factual matters.

These conclusions may bring a premature peace of mind to the philosopher, since further questions certainly need to be asked. For example, how is meaning related to the words and symbols? Is it a property that the words and symbols possess? If so, what kind of property is it? Is it a causal power which, when we see 2 + 2 = *makes* us write or say 4? Such a view faces insuperable difficulties. Suppose that, for some reason, seeing 2 + 2 = makes me write 2 + 2 = round square. The fact that I can truly claim that those symbols have had that causal effect on me, will not save me from the charge that what I have written is nonsense. Suppose, too, that for some reason I am able to bring about this causal effect in another. The fact that I acted with this intention, and that the causal effect intended is achieved, does not secure the meaning of 2 + 2 = round square.

We may turn from the unsupportable causal analysis of meaning to consider a psychological alternative. Perhaps symbols or words have properties that have certain psychological effects on us. When we see or hear 2 + 2 = 5 or round square, we have a feeling of inappropriateness. When we see or hear 2 + 2 = 4, we have a feeling of rightness. We might call these feelings doxastic experiences.[12] But are these of any more relevance than the causal effects already discussed? If a child appealed to a doxastic experience, a feeling of rightness, in writing 2 + 2 = 5, no teacher would accept this as an excuse for getting it wrong. The child can have as many doxastic experiences as it likes, it must still pass the examination like everyone else.

We may turn from the causal and psychological analyses of meaning, which are clearly untenable, back to the symbols and words themselves. Isn't it enough simply to say that they have the meanings they do? Clearly not, since the question of *how* they mean anything would remain unanswered. Or is the suggestion that the mere occasion of the marks or sounds guarantees their meaning?

Imagine a tribe who have no mathematics. Yet, on their walls, we find marks that we would call arithmetical. They had seen these marks on pieces of paper that had been recovered from a shipwreck. Attracted by them, they decorated their walls with them, using the marks in a variety of patterns, including 2 + 2 = 4. On the argument we are considering, the mere appearance of the marks should secure their status as an arithmetical equation. Clearly, this is not the case. The tribe have no mathematics. The marks are wall decorations.

What lesson is to be learned from this example? Surely, that to look for the meaning of the marks is not to look for any property they possess, but to the contexts, the practices, in which they have a role. Logic is not a set of abstract rules which determines what that role is. Rather, the logic of the marks is something that *shows itself in that role.*

The above conclusion can be underlined by considering the example of an alternative arithmetic in which one is allowed to say that 2 + 2 = 5.[13] Does this arithmetic contradict the one in which 2 + 2 = 4? It is tempting to say that it does because 2 + 2 = 5 contradicts the inherent meanings of the symbols, the symbols that *make* us follow 2 + 2 = with 4. But, as Rush Rhees says, arithmetic does not spring from the symbols like shoots from a bulb. It is not the symbols that give sense to the arithmetic, but the arithmetic which gives sense to the symbols. After all, without the arithmetic, we would not know that they are *arithmetical* symbols in the first place. Elsewhere, such marks may be wall decorations. Logic does not determine the form and application of our arithmetic. Rather, it is the form and application of our arithmetic that determine what is logical or illogical within it.

We can now apply the result of our discussions to propositions more generally. Logic does not determine whether propositions have sense or not. Rather, the sense is found in the logic or grammar of the propositions, and that logic is to be found in the practices in which the propositions find expression. Of course, when we see a proposition, for example, 'Caesar crossed the Rubicon', we do not consciously refer to the context in which it has its sense.[14] Nevertheless, we are taking that context for granted when we read the proposition in a certain way. That is why we are tempted to think of meaning as some kind of aura that accompanies the proposition. Not having to refer consciously to the practice, we forget how necessary it is in our understanding of a proposition. This is so obvious in the case of 'Caesar crossed the Rubicon'. Caesar is such a well-known name, historically, that we take the historical context for granted when we come across the proposition. But 'Caesar' and 'Rubicon', Lars Hertzberg suggests, might be the name of a Mafia boss and a crime syndicate. The proposition 'Caesar crossed the Rubicon' might refer to the fact that the one had fallen foul of the other. Consider the proposition, 'God is dead'. What does it mean? It means something different if said by Nietzsche, a certain theologian of the 1960s or a post-Holocaust theologian of a certain persuasion. But, using an abbreviation of a name, 'God is dead', may be a message conveying that the assassination of a Mafia Godfather has been successful. Once again, the message to be appreciated, philosophically, is that the propositions have their sense in the practices to which they belong.

It is the above message, however, that is completely ignored in philosophical discussions of the proposition 'God is omnipotent'. The meaning of 'omnipotence' is not determined by reference to the religious context implied by the proposition 'God is omnipotent'. Instead, it is laid down by what Mackie called quasi-logical rules. But where do the rules come from? They do not seem to belong to any context. Thus, we are told, in the abstract, that omnipotence means 'the ability to do whatever is not logically contradictory'. This meaning, though applied in God's case, does not depend on any reference to religion. In fact, the problematic propositional triad, in the logical problem of evil, can be generated without any reference to God. The alleged inconsistency between the propositions can be expressed as follows: 'X is omnipotent'; 'X is perfectly good'; 'Evil exists'.

Ignoring the philosophical lesson about the relation between propositions and practices leads to further confusion when we ask what is meant by saying that God can do whatever is not logically contradictory. We recall Swinburne's reply. He tells us that God can do anything 'the description of which does not involve a contradiction'.[15]

We now face the question of how we know whether a description is logically contradictory. Forgetting our philosophical lesson, we lapse back into thinking that whether this is so is conveyed immediately, in some way, by the proposition. The truth of the matter is that it is the practice in which the proposition has its home which shows whether a description we are offered is logically contradictory or not. But Swinburne offers us, not a practice, but a definition. Yet for any description we mention, we are taking for granted *some* practice in which it has its sense. The claim that God is omnipotent now becomes the claim that God can do anything which can be done in the context of any practice whatsoever, whether the practices are religious or not. The challenge to God's omnipotence would now take the following form:

1 To say that God is omnipotent is to say that God can do anything describable in any practice without contradiction.
2 There are countless activities in different practices, describable there without contradiction, which God cannot do.
3 Therefore God is not omnipotent.

If this is to be the test of God's omnipotence, isn't it clear that God fails the test? Here are just some activities within practices, describable without contradiction, which are part of the successful challenge: riding a bicycle, licking and savouring a Häagen-Dazs ice-cream, bumping one's head, having sexual intercourse, learning a language and so on and so on. All these activities are linked to surroundings that are conditions of their intelligibility. In the absence of these conditions we could not talk about them. Yet the surroundings in question are absent when we talk of God the Creator of all things. Need I elaborate? To ride a bicycle is to have a body possessing limbs, etc., and it takes a being with a head to bump it. I need a tongue and taste buds to savour ice-cream. As for sexual intercourse, need I say more? To have a language is to have acquired it. I cannot possess it 'all at once'. Even if someone thought, absurdly, that one could, or that God could, the fact would remain that the language has not been learned. As for the identity of the language in question, not even God can be Welsh, despite a popular view to the contrary in my part of the world!

We have seen the results of an appeal to Mackie's or Swinburne's quasi-logical rules for the meaning of 'omnipotence', and the abstract, context-less application of the rules to the proposition 'God is omnipotent'. It must be remembered, however, that these results only follow if we continue to discuss the problem of evil within the parameters of the logical problem of evil we have outlined. What we have seen is that if by, 'God is omnipotent', we mean that God can do any activity, whose description, in its appropriate context, is not logically contradictory, the proposition 'God is omnipotent' cannot even get off the ground.

The philosophical lesson to be learned, as we have seen, is that the meaning of 'God is omnipotent' is, of necessity, to be found in the religious contexts in which it is expressed. There are brief moments when Swinburne and Davis get close to expressing this point of view. For example, instead of saying that God can do *whatever* is not logically contradictory, Swinburne also says, 'God cannot do what is logically impossible *for him* to do – whatever the reason for that logical impossibility.'[16] Here, it seems, it is not an abstract notion of logical impossibility that determines what God cannot do, but what is meant by 'God' that determines what is logically impossible for him to do. The meaning of 'God' is found within the appropriate religious context. It is doubtful whether Swinburne meant to make this distinction. If he did, he would have to give up his abstract definition, and there is no sign of him doing so. Again, Davis says, promisingly:

> *God is omnipotent.* This statement is controversial among theists. Let me suggest that God is omnipotent if and only if for any logically possible state of affairs *such that the statement that 'God brings about that state of affairs' is coherent,* God can bring about that state of affairs.[17]

Here it is not an abstract conception of 'a logically possible state of affairs' that determines what God can bring about, but a conception of what it makes sense to speak of God doing that determines what states of affairs can be attributed to his doing. But if Davis meant to make this distinction, he would have to give up his abstract view 'that God has all the power there is',[18] of which more in the next chapter.

## 2. *Why Not Extend the Grammar of 'God'?*

It is extremely important to notice the *logical* character of the conclusions we have drawn. When we say that God cannot ride a bicycle, lick an ice-cream, or learn a language, we are not saying that, as a *matter of fact,* God does not do these things, but that, given what we mean by 'God', it *makes no sense* to attribute these activities to God.

Faced with these logical conclusions, what if someone were to say, 'We'll simply *extend* the notion of God's power, so as to include those activities that our conclusions exclude. So if a given conception of God makes it impossible to say that God can bump his head, simply change the conception. Say that God could grow a head if he wanted to, and then it makes sense to say that he could bump it.' Davis says, 'Perhaps God has the power totally to control all events and things but does not use it. This is my own view.'[19] So God can be said to have hidden powers, but simply chooses not to use them. But what is the point of saying this? Are not the proposed grammatical extensions of the grammar of 'God' simply a desperate building in the air? We will have reason to return to this topic in the next chapter, when we explore its implications for the connection between omnipotence and the will of God. For the remainder of the present chapter, I want to explore the issue of conceptual extensions in relation to miracles. The issue can be expressed as follows: We know that God and Jesus performed miracles. If God is omnipotent, he could perform any miracle that is not logically contradictory, but may have hidden reasons of his own for not doing so. The same can be said of Jesus. Again, the question is what to make of such *open-ended* readiness to extend one's conception of God. This readiness is different from developments in the idea of God which we find in the Bible; for example, the development in the idea of God after the Exile. What we are confronted by is an *open-ended philosophical or theological strategy* that is not rooted in any religious context. An example of the strategy can be found in the way one of John Perry's characters discusses omnipotence in relation to miracles.

> When we say that God is omnipotent, we mean God can perform any act or task that makes sense . . . Notice that God in fact created all sorts of stones that he *will* not in fact lift – I'm not really sure what it means for God to lift a stone . . . Take the Rock of Gibraltar. Suppose that for God to lift a stone means that he miraculously makes it rise for no apparent reason and then settle softly back where it was. God has a plan for the world, and in that plan he simply does not perform that act. He does not lift the Rock of Gibraltar . . . God *can* lift the Rock of Gibraltar, in the sense that *if* he had planned the world that way, that's what would have happened. I don't know what else it would mean, to say that God could lift it, if it wasn't that. It isn't that it's too big or heavy for him. He won't lift it, but he could. And 'he could' means that he could have created a world in which he did.[20]

God could lift the Rock of Gibraltar, but has not. By the same token, we can say that God could ride a bicycle, lick an ice-cream, bump his head, have sexual intercourse and learn a language, but has not. Notice that the argument concerning the Rock of Gibraltar has all the ingredients of our previous discussion. First, the speaker is not at all sure what it *means* to speak of God lifting a stone. Second, he *knows* what it means for the rising of the Rock of Gibraltar to be a miracle: it must rise into the air for no apparent reason and then settle back into its original place. Third, God *can* do this because the description of what happens to the Rock of Gibraltar makes sense; it is not logically contradictory. The argument moves from an abstract notion of 'what makes sense', to the ascription of an action to God, although the speaker is not at all sure of the sense of doing so. As in our previous discussion, the *religious* context for talk of God and miracles is completely ignored. It plays no part in the argument.

Perry's character has no difficulty, apparently, in understanding what a miracle is. But has he earned it? He says that the Rock of Gibraltar rises 'for no apparent reason'. By this he means that no causal explanation has been found for it rising. He does not mean that God has done it for no apparent reason, but for all he says about the religious significance of the miracle, Perry's character could be read in this way. He has no idea what it means to attribute the miracle to God. But, then, how does he know he is describing a miracle? Apparently, because he thinks it makes sense to do so. But what *sense* is that? Where does Perry's character get it from? Certainly, not from religion.

In the case of certain miracles, it is a necessary condition of so regarding them, that no causal explanation of them has been found. But although that is a necessary condition, it is not a sufficient condition. To be a miracle, the event must reveal something about God. Otherwise, what would be religious about it? Why would it be a miracle? What does the 'rising up' and 'settling back' of the Rock of Gibraltar show us about God? We are given no idea. Why, in that case, should we put it in the conceptual category of 'the miraculous'?

In the philosophical literature on miracles, they are often

spoken of as 'violations of laws of nature'. The notion of such 'violations' is problematic. Laws of nature do not compel things to happen. They describe how things happen. Explanations are sought for deviations from the laws. More rarely, in the light of conflicting evidence, the laws are modified. Some events may turn out to be inexplicable, that is, no explanation for them is found. But that is not enough to call them miracles.

Consider the raising of Lazarus. In a discussion of it, Rush Rhees says that it would be foolish to say that it *couldn't* have happened.[21] He imagines Lazarus as mostly silent for the rest of his life, bewildered as to what has happened, and especially about why it happened to *him*. Rhees says that this could be too much for a human being to bear.

Talking of his *own* reaction to the story, Rhees says that it creates an awe in him. It may also be a corrective to a hubris that thinks it can explain everything. Yet, in all this, Rhees says that he is reacting to what happened to Lazarus as a *natural* event, no matter how amazing. But why was it a *miracle*? That is what Rhees does not know. He wonders to what extent anyone does *know*. Obviously, to the writers and early readers of the New Testament, the miracles were very important. But what *was* that importance? Do we know anymore? Lessing suggests that we no longer have 'the proof of the spirit and of power' which makes such understanding possible.[22]

Peter Winch has argued that the erosion of the sense of the miraculous in our culture is not accidental.[23] The anomalous state of 'the miraculous', however, has little to do with a reluctance to admit that there can be violations of laws of nature by higher causal powers. The real anomaly is between our dominant naturalistic interest in the world, and what it asks of us by way of explanations and empirical evidence, and what acknowledging a miracle would involve. Winch considers the story of Moses and the burning bush. Moses' initial reaction to the bush which burns without being consumed, is to approach it to find out what is happening. But, in the story, it is precisely that quest for explanations that is forbidden by God speaking from the midst of the bush. Moses is told to take off his shoes, for he is on holy ground. In our culture, it has become almost impossible not to ask Moses' initial question, and to pursue it by every explanatory means at our disposal. The success of the scientific and techno-logical perspective is shown in the ironic fact that an attempt to save miracles turns God into a super-scientist. Anything we can do, he can do better. In the present chapter and the next, we see what awaits us if we go down that road.

In the discussion of a purported miracle, it seems that the only choice we have is either to explain it away naturalistically, or to establish that it is the result of higher causal powers. Now and again, however, one comes across examples that escape this stranglehold. Winch discusses the various reactions which en-sued when, in a church in a southern US state, a statue of the Virgin Mary was seen to weep from time to time.[24] The case became celebrated, discussed on television, etc. The disputants divided along now familiar lines. On the one hand were those who claimed that the phenomenon could be explained easily in terms of deception, condensation and the like. On the other hand were those who denied that there could be a naturalistic explan-ation of the weeping statue. It was being caused to weep by higher powers. Winch was disgusted with both sides of the debate. What had the considerations adduced to do with venera-tion of the Virgin? Quite apart from these disputants, however, was a woman who simply said, 'Why shouldn't the Holy Mother weep over the sins of the world?' She showed no interest in explanations. Her question is a religious response, and to under-stand it one would have to pay attention to religious categories of thought in which veneration of the Virgin plays an important part. No doubt such a woman may turn out to be too trusting. She may be fooled in many ways. But the losses or dangers are not all on one side. Those interested only in condensation, trick-ery, etc., will never see the Virgin weep; for example, weep *despite* the trickery.

It is these religious categories that are missing when Perry's character speculates about lifting the Rock of Gibraltar. To include the imagined event within the category of the miracu-lous, to *extend* that category to include it, we need a *religious* account that gives the extension its point. There is no sign of a religious context in the discussion Perry describes, hence the purely abstract and context-less discussion of whether God can lift the Rock of Gibraltar. There's no end to what God can do if we argue in this way, from making the Eiffel Tower go three times round the moon, to the humble act of riding a bicycle. But to say, in *this* sense, that there is no end to what God can do, is to say that there is no beginning to it either. The discussion bypasses the context where talk of God's miracles makes sense.

A similar bypassing of the category of the miraculous can be seen if attempts are made to extend a discussion of Jesus' healing miracles in conceptually inappropriate directions. The proposed extension occurs once we think of Jesus' miracles as something for which he had a technique that he could employ at will. As soon as we begin thinking like this, we have to face the question of why Jesus' use of his technique was so restricted. What possible reason could there be for healing some, but ignoring the majority?

Again, the questions we are led to ask trade on assumptions that ignore religious contexts. Could Jesus perform miracles at will? There seems to be good reason for saying that miracles are as much something that Jesus undergoes, as they are acts that he does. Sometimes, he testifies to feeling that an energy has left him, and there are times when he is depressed after the event because God has not been seen in the miracle. When these religious contexts are recalled, it will be seen that there is no point in an abstract discussion about miracles that Jesus *could* have performed. Such a discussion becomes a groundless attempt to extend the grammar of 'the miraculous' *in vacuo*.

A final example. It is the case that talk of 'the eye of God' has a natural place in religious discourse. We can be said to live our lives under it. From this fact, it may be thought that, as a matter of logic, we are free to *extend* our talk of God's eye to talk of his eyebrows, toenails, intestines and so on.[25] After all, what's stopping us? The answer is: nothing. The point is not that we could- *n't* speak in this way because logic forbids it. The point is that we *do* not speak in this way because, *given* the grammar of our concept of God, it makes no sense to do so. It is because philosophers ignore grammatical restraints, that they can speak of miracles, God's eyebrows, and omnipotence in the ways we have noted.

Wittgenstein asks:

'So does it depend wholly on our grammar what will be called (logically) possible and what not, – i.e. what that grammar permits?' – But surely that is arbitrary!

But he replies:

Is it arbitrary? – It is not every sentence-like formation that we know how to do something with, not every technique has an application in our life; and when we are tempted in philosophy to count some quite useless thing as a proposition, that is often because we have not considered its application sufficiently.[26]

The so-called grammatical extensions we have discussed are examples of these 'quite useless things'. They are not extensions because they have no application, no grammatical warrant.

What is the result of recognizing that the proposition 'God is omnipotent' does not mean that God can do anything that is logically possible? It is not, as Mackie and Process theologians assume, to limit God's power, or to say that limited power is all God has. To say *that*, one would have to be able to make *sense* of the notion of 'unrestricted power', and I have denied that possibility. Even analytic philosophers say that it is no restriction of God's power to say that he cannot do what is logically impossible for him to do. If it is logically impossible for God to ride a bicycle, that is, it makes *no sense* to talk of him doing so, not being able to ride a bicycle is no restriction on God's power.

In this chapter, I have begun discussing certain aspects of our problematic inheritance in the philosophy of religion. Discussions of the problem of evil, in that inheritance, have centred largely on the logical problem of evil. Analytic philosophers of religion, as we have seen, think, with some confidence, that that problem has been solved. I have argued that nothing could be further from the truth. What is needed is a logical rejection of the alleged logic of the argument. But if we stay *within* the terms of reference of the logical problem of evil, it should be seen that the first proposition in the triad – 'God is omnipotent'; 'God is perfectly good'; 'Evil exists', does not even get off the ground. In the next two chapters we shall see that a similar logical fate awaits the proposition, 'God is perfectly good'.

## Notes

1 Hume, *Dialogues Concerning Natural Religion*, ed. Norman Kemp Smith, New York: Bobbs-Merrill 1947, Part X, p. 198.

2 J. L. Mackie, 'Evil and Omnipotence' in Marilyn McCord Adams and Robert Merrihew Adams (eds), *The Problem of Evil*, New York: Oxford University Press 1990, p. 25. (Reprinted from *Mind*, Vol. 64, 1955.)

3 W. T. Stace, *Time and Eternity*, Princeton: Princeton University Press 1952, p. 56.

4 F. H. Bradley, *Appearance and Reality*, Oxford: Oxford University Press 1930, p. 74.

5 Mackie, 'Evil and Omnipotence', p. 26.

6 Nelson Pike, 'Hume on Evil' in Adams and Adams, *Problem of Evil*. (Reprinted from *The Philosophical Review*, Vol. 72, 1963.)

7 Alvin Plantinga, 'Good, Evil and the Metaphysics of Freedom' in Adams and Adams, *Problem of Evil*. (Reprinted from *The Nature of Necessity*, Oxford: Clarendon Press 1974, Chapter 9.)

8 Stephen T. Davis, 'Free Will and Evil' in Stephen T. Davis (ed.), *Encountering Evil*, Louisville: Westminster John Knox Press 2001, p. 74.

9 Stephen T. Davis, 'Critique of David Ray Griffin' in Davis, *Encountering Evil*, p. 136.

10 Richard Swinburne, *Providence and the Problem of Evil*, Oxford: Clarendon Press 1998, p. 3.

11 Richard Swinburne, 'Postscript' to 'The Problem of Evil' (a symposium with D. Z. Phillips) in Stuart Brown (ed.), *Reason and Religion*, Ithaca: Cornell University Press 1977, p. 132.

12 On such a notion see Alvin Plantinga, *Warranted Christian Belief*, Oxford: Oxford University Press 2000, p. 111.

13 I am indebted in the discussion which follows to Rush Rhees, 'On Continuity: Wittgenstein's Ideas 1938' in *Discussions of Wittgenstein*, London: Routledge and Kegan Paul 1970.

14 In the subsequent discussion, I am indebted to Lars Hertzberg, 'The sense is where you find it' in Timothy McCarthy and Sean Stidd (eds), *Wittgenstein in America*, Oxford: Clarendon Press 2001.

15 Swinburne, *Providence*, p. 3.

16 Swinburne, *Providence*, p. 126 (my italics).

17 Stephen T. Davis, 'Introduction' to Davis, *Encountering Evil*, p. ix (my italics).

18 Stephen T. Davis, 'Critique of Griffin', p. 136.

19 Davis, 'Critique of Griffin', p. 136.

20 John Perry, *Dialogue on Good, Evil, and the Existence of God*, Indianapolis: Hackett Publishing Co. Inc., 1999, pp. 39–40.

21 Rush Rhees, 'Miracles' in Rush Rhees, *On Religion and Philosophy*, ed. D. Z. Phillips, Cambridge: Cambridge University Press 1997, pp. 322–7.

22 See Gotthold Ephraim Lessing, *Theological Writings*, London: Adam and Charles Black 1956.

23 Peter Winch, 'Ceasing to Exist' in *Trying to Make Sense*, Oxford: Blackwell 1987 and 'Asking Too Many Questions' in Timothy Tessin and Mario von der Ruhr (eds), *Philosophy and the Grammar of Religious Belief*, Basingstoke: Macmillan 1995.

24 Winch, 'Asking Too Many Questions', pp. 210–11.

25 Ludwig Wittgenstein, 'Lectures on Religious Belief' in *Lectures and Conversations on Aesthetics, Psychology and Religious Belief*, ed. Cyril Barrett, Oxford: Blackwell 1966, p. 71.

26 Ludwig Wittgenstein, *Philosophical Investigations*, Oxford: Blackwell 1953, I: para. 520.

# 2

# Logic and God's Will

## *1. Sovereignty as 'All' Power*

In the last chapter, we saw what results from defining God's omnipotence as 'the ability to do whatever is not logically contradictory'. There are countless activities that it does not make sense to attribute to God. If we stick to the definition, the proposition 'God is omnipotent' doesn't even get off the ground. In the present chapter, we shall see how sticking to that definition means that the proposition, 'God is perfectly good', does not get off the ground either.

Many philosophers present us with what they call a 'robust' conception of divine sovereignty. Calling it 'robust' is meant to suggest that they are not yielding an inch with respect to what they think is the traditional belief in God's omnipotence. No one can deny that *some* aspects of power they have in mind are found in certain religious traditions. But, as we shall see, they are opposed by other religious traditions. For the moment, however, all I am concerned to show is that something called 'all power' cannot be attributed to God, since that notion is unintelligible.

Here are two philosophers who, although disagreeing about God's perfect goodness, insist on the robust conception of divine omnipotence. Stephen T. Davis writes, 'Reformed Christians – believing, as we do, in the sovereignty of God – stress God's freedom to act as God wants to act'.[1] John K. Roth writes, 'God is bound only by God's will. Ultimately, nothing except it determines what he shall do or become. All possibilities are within God's reach.'[2] It follows from these views that all power is within God's reach. As we saw in the last chapter, Davis says that God has *all the power there is*.[3]

The problem is in the conceptually unspecifiable notion of 'all power', as though 'power' referred to one thing. We have *some* of it, but God has *all* of it. This conception appears in the Bible, but so do others inconsistent with it. Problems for the view that God can do whatever is not logically contradictory ran into trouble as soon as we began specifying activities, such as riding a bicycle or licking an ice-cream. Problems for the view that God has 'all power' arise, similarly, once we start specifying the *kind* of power one has in mind. For example, despite the fact that a God of brute force is to be found in the Bible, can that *same* power be attributed to a God of compassion? Rush Rhees writes:

> If you think that the difference of God from his creatures is one of power, you will not naturally speak of compassion. (No more than Ezekiel did.) That God will destroy his enemies is more important than any idea of God's mercy. And the conception of the mercy of God is difficult . . . I grant that you have not understood much of what religion is about unless you try to recognize the disparity between God and man. But 'limitless power' gives no conception of this: you would never guess how religion could mean anything deep to anyone.[4]

Rhees argues that the appeal to 'limitless power', not only fails to give an account of the disparity between God and man, but creates a conception of God which is at variance with the belief in God most religious apologists *think* they are elucidating.

> Suppose you had to explain to someone who had no idea at all of religion or of what a belief in God was. Could you do it in this way? – By proving to him that there must be a first cause – a Something -- and that this Something is more powerful (whatever this means) than anything else: so that you would not have been conceived or born at all but for the operation of Something, and Something might wipe out the existence of everything at any time? Would this give him any sense of the

wonder and glory of God? Would he not be justified if he answered, 'What a horrible idea! Like a Frankenstein without limits, so that you cannot escape it. The most ghastly nightmare!' On the other hand if you read to him certain of the passages in the early Isaiah which describe the beauty of the world . . . then I think you might have given him some sense of what religious believers are talking about. I say *some* idea: I am talking of how you might make a beginning.[5]

For the most part, the philosophers I am criticizing have a conception of morality as a homogenous phenomenon, and of God as a member, with us, of a common moral community. If this conception were well-founded, there could not be a contrary *moral* response to God, conceived of as the possessor of 'all power'. But, clearly, there is, as shown by those in the Bible who protest *against* a God so conceived. Rhees protests too:

> If my first and chief reason for worshipping God had to be a belief that a super-Frankenstein would blast me to hell if I did not, then I hope I should have the decency to tell this being, who is named Almighty God, to go ahead and blast.[6]

It is, of course, perfectly obvious where Rhees stands, but his philosophical point in making the protest, is to mark its possibility, the possibility of its *moral* power faced by God's threats of coercion. One *kind* of power is confronted by a power of a *different kind*. The *logical* issue is the unintelligibility of combining different kinds of power in a single conception of 'all the power there is'. As Rhees says, '(As though everyone knows what "power" means, alone in its glory.) The infinite power of God.'[7] It is not enough to say with Davis, and others, that one *believes* that God has all the power there is. There is the prior logical issue of *what* one is supposed to be believing.

Is God involved in *the same* power game as the Devil, so that the issue, in advocating religion, is to get people to back the right horse? But, then, the nature of the game becomes such that *both* participants can be faced with the different power of moral condemnation:

Is the reason for not worshipping the devil instead of God that God is stronger than the Devil? God will get you in the end, the devil will not be able to save you from his fury, and then you will be *for* it. 'Think of your future, boy, and don't throw away your chances.' What a creeping and vile sort of thing religion must be.[8]

There is no way out of the difficulty of ascribing 'all power' to God, by admitting that 'power' is not being used in an unequivocal sense. This admission would involve treating 'all power' as the collection of all the different powers that exist. The claim that God is all-powerful would amount to saying that in the case of *any* power specified, God has all of that power. The insuperable logical difficulty comes from the fact that, among the powers that exist, *it does not make sense* to attribute many of them to God. For example, it makes no sense to attribute the power that belongs to the principalities of this world to God. One is supposed to *contrast* the power of God with these powers. As Rhees says, 'When Satan said that dominion over this world had been left to him, Jesus did not contradict him.'[9]

Religious apologists would admit that the distinction between worship and idolatry is extremely important in religion. The latter consists of giving God's place to that which is unworthy to be God. One form of idolatry would be to think one was acknowledging God's power, when, in fact, one was acknowledging worldly power. But if *all* kinds of power belong to God, how is the distinction between worship and idolatry to be drawn? The distinction depends on the recognition of the conceptual differences between different kinds of power. Rhees writes:

> The difference between the power of God and the power of the devil: it is difficult to understand at all clearly what this difference is (otherwise there might be no idolatry); and yet people with any religion at all will have a lively idea of it, generally. The power of God is a *different* power from the power of the devil. But if you said that God is *more* powerful than the devil – then I should not understand you, because I should not know what sort of measure you used.[10]

In the last chapter we saw that divine omnipotence cannot mean 'the power to do whatever is not logically contradictory'. At the end of the first section of the present one, we have seen that 'the sovereignty of the divine will' cannot mean the possession of 'all the power there is'. It follows that God cannot be said to be able to do anything. To see why religious apologists have thought otherwise, we need to look at some of their assumptions about 'freedom' and 'the will'.

## 2. God, Morality and Free Acts

On the face of it, the claim that God can do anything he wants is a curious one. Would anyone say that God could ask me to murder my wife, kill the innocent, deceive my friends, rob with impunity and so on? How can this be said of a God believed to be perfectly good? But if God is bounded by nothing but his will, it seems that any of these commands could come from him.

To meet these difficulties, a response may be made that we met in the previous chapter. It was said there that whereas God does not, *in fact*, ride a bicycle, lick an ice-cream or acquire a language, he *could* do so *if he wanted to*. We saw the arbitrariness and futility of such speculation. In the present context, it may be said that whereas, *in fact* God does not ask us to murder our mothers, kill the innocent, etc., he *could* do so *if he wanted to*. Does that capture our reaction if someone claimed that God had asked him to do these terrible things? We would not say, 'If God wants to issue such a command, that's up to him.' Rather, we would say that it *makes no sense* to claim that he did. God's perfect goodness rules out such commands. I am not forgetting the countless terrible deeds done in God's name, but in rejecting them it is important to note that we are rejecting that *conception* of God. We do not say of those who slaughter the innocent in God's name that God gave that command to them, but not to us. We reject the command as being God's command.

Why are religious apologists forced into the position of saying that God *could* command the slaughter of the innocent, but *chooses not to*. At the root of their difficulty is their uncritical acceptance, for the most part, of Alvin Plantinga's definition of a free act. According to Plantinga:

> If a person $S$ is free with respect to a given action, then he is free to perform that action and free to refrain; no causal laws and antecedent conditions determine either that he will perform the action, or that he will not. It is within his power, at the time in question, to perform the action, and within his power to refrain.[11]

Applying this definition to God, religious apologists have to say that God can only act freely with respect to any virtuous act if God has within him the power to do its opposite. If God helps the innocent, he has it in his power not to do so. And when he does not spare them from being slaughtered, he had the power to do so. It is this conception of what an act has to be, in order to be free, that gives rise to a certain form of the problem of evil. Roth writes:

> All possibilities are within God's reach, and so God could have created very differently . . . If God is sovereign, bound only by God's will, then apparently God chooses to be the creator and master of this universe. Although God could intervene dramatically at any point in present history, God elects to let freedom work out its own course as it lives in individuals and communities . . . It can release the worst as well as the best that is in us, and therefore the presence of this God may feel like the absence of all gods.[12]

For Roth, accepting this analysis has the consequence of not being able to call God perfectly good. I want to show that accepting Plantinga's definition of free action, with respect to God, has the same result. In fact, if we accept the definition, we cannot even account for a natural goodness that is found, sometimes, in human actions.

The root of the problem lies in a certain conception of a free moral action. Applying Plantinga's analysis, a person's compassionate act is free only if the person concerned was free to hate.

If the person was incapable of hatred, it is argued, how can the 'compassion' have any moral worth? Sometimes the requirement is made more explicit: unless a person *overcame* hatred in order to show compassion, or unless a person *made a free choice between* love and hatred, the 'compassion', logically, cannot be the virtuous act we take it to be. This logical requirement, if that is what it is, would apply to all moral agents, including God. Remember that I am arguing *within* the conceptual parameters of those who think of God as a fellow moral agent, sharing a moral community with ourselves.

Is the presence of constraint in any moral act a logical requirement of its moral worth? This seems to fly in the face of familiar judgements such as, 'He does not have it in him to hate his brother'. Is this to be analysed as, 'He was free to hate his brother, but chose not to'? What might tempt us to embrace this conclusion is the assumption that whenever we act freely, the action is preceded by an act of will, which is the 'trying' to do it. The 'trying' would provide the element of constraint which, it is argued, is logically involved in the concept of a free moral act.

Two familiar sets of circumstances can lead us to think of 'willing' as if it were an act which precedes overt action. One is the fact that there is often a temporal gap between the expression of an intention and its fulfilment. I may say that I'll meet you at six o'clock in the evening, but say this at nine o'clock in the morning. This may lead one to think that there is only a contingent connection between 'willing' and 'acting', whereas there is a conceptual relation between them. Without the reference to the later action, the intention expressed in the morning would be senseless. Nevertheless, such cases hide from us the fact that, normally, 'willing' simply is 'acting'.

A second set of circumstances that tempts us to think that 'willing' and 'acting' are separate actions is the familiar occurrence of the failure to fulfil our intentions or to succeed in our actions. But if I tell you to try to jump over the tennis net, I am not asking you to do two things: to try and to jump. I am simply indicating that it may be difficult to jump the net. When there is a temporal gap between my intentions and the time to act on them, various obstacles, or unforeseen circumstances, may prevent their fruition. Again, this does not count against a conceptual relation between 'willing' and 'acting'. Why are the explanations necessary, if not to *understand* what has happened? It would be absurd to say, 'These are simply cases where intention is not followed by action. Although not infrequent, this fact is statistically less frequent than the occasions when action follows willing.'

Samuel Beckett severs the connection between 'willing' and 'acting' in his plays, precisely to mark a breakdown in communication, or an erosion of moral expectations. In *Waiting for Godot*, one character says, 'Let's go.' Another replies, 'Yes, let's.' Neither moves. If we attempted to generalize this situation with respect to human behaviour, we would not have a series of perfectly intelligible willings, which just happen not to be followed by subsequent actions of the right kind. The notion of willing itself would be breaking down. Beckett is able to make his point only by contrast with standard cases. If a person were constantly saying that he was going, but remained; that he was going to punish someone, but rewarded him; that he was bitterly opposed to a legislative measure, but did everything possible to support it; and so on, we would not say that his willings are intelligible, whereas his behaviour was not. Lying and hypocrisy apart, we would not be able to understand the person at all. We would not know what to make of him. If we want to call this a severance of willing from acting, it is important to note that the person is no longer saying anything. He is babbling, not speaking.

Once we recognize that willing is not a separate action from acting, and that there are countless circumstances in which there is no temporal gap between intentions and their fulfilment, and no obstacle present, we will also recognize that in these cases, 'willing' is 'simply doing'. There need be no element of constraint. Natural effortless actions are as much examples of 'willing', as those actions in which I try or struggle to do something. If I am lost in the dark, or the worse for drink, I may try to find my way home. Normally, however, after a day at the university, I simply go home. But 'simply going home' is as much a free action on my part as 'trying to go home'. 'Trying' is a form of 'willing', but not all forms of 'willing' involve 'trying'. I am sympathetic to the reaction which says that to talk of 'simply doing' as 'willing' is itself a forced way of talking. The Good Samaritan was immediately moved by compassion, and Mr Jones may simply pay his bills. They just do what they do – that is what is admirable about them. Neither am I thinking of acts of 'unthinking habit' for which some would give little moral praise. The difference would be shown in the style of the actions. In talking of 'willing', I have been using the language of my opponents in these matters. In any case, my main point is that there is no ground for *denying* that the acts under consideration are free, even if the question of *whether* they are free, normally, does not arise. The main point is that the 'just doing' of the Samaritan and Mr Jones, cannot be captured in the analysis of 'free actions' I have been criticizing.[13]

This conclusion is important for an understanding of simple acts of virtue, done unhesitatingly, and for an understanding of an impressive natural goodness that some human beings possess in certain aspects of their lives.

This is shown in very simple virtuous acts, such as paying one's bills. If I am short of money, due to an unexpected financial setback, I may try to pay my bills. Normally, however, I may be a person who simply pays his bills. I do not try to pay them. It would be absurd to suggest that the honesty shown in the immediate paying of the bills, is of no moral worth if the person had not tried to pay the bills, or had not made a choice between paying or not paying the bills.

Can we say, with Plantinga, that if the person paid his bills freely, he had the power to do so and the power to refrain? What does the latter power mean if not that he had it in him not to pay his bills? But that is precisely what we do *not* want to say of the honest person who unhesitatingly pays his bills. His simple honesty could not be captured by a character reference which succumbs to Plantinga's philosophical requirement. It would read: 'Mr Jones always pays his bills, but it is within his power not to.' This would be taken, naturally, as some kind of qualification of the simple recommendation, 'Mr Jones's honesty is such that he always pays his bills.' Nor could this simple commendation be captured in a reference which said, 'Mr Jones always tried to pay his bills,' since this suggests that there are times when he fails to do so. Again, Mr Jones' simple honesty is not captured by the following reference, 'Mr Jones considers not paying his bills, but always pays them in the end,' since it imputes a hesitancy or temptation where neither is present. The conceptual inadequacy cannot be overcome by saying that the possibility of not paying his bills only occurs fleetingly to Mr Jones. Why insist, philosophically, on a second thought, when Mr Jones pays his bills without a second thought? The answer lies in the erroneous assumption that an action is free only if it is chosen from alternatives, or if the agent had the power within him to do otherwise. Thus, poor Mr Jones, whose honesty was such that he did not have it in him not to pay his bills, is defamed by philosophical theories of freedom that turn his virtue into something other than the simple thing it is.

At this point, we turn to examine the consequences of the analysis of free action we have been criticizing for the notion of a natural goodness which is sometimes found in human actions. Consider the unhesitating compassion shown by the Good Samaritan to the poor man who had fallen among thieves. It is a compassion freely shown. Must we say that the Good Samaritan had the power within him not to show compassion? That is precisely what we do *not* want to say of him. When we say that he *could not* pass by, that is a comment on his character. Given who he is, leaving the victim unaided is simply ruled out for him. For reasons which should be clear by now, we cannot capture the immediacy of his compassion by saying that he *tried* to help the victim; that he considered the alternative of not helping, however fleetingly, but decided to help him in the end. No, he simply helps. His free act knows no constraint. That is an integral part of the character of his compassion.

Did the priest and the Levite have it within their power to help the person who had fallen among thieves? What reasons do we have for thinking so? When we say that they could have helped, we are appealing to moral expectations we expect to be fulfilled.

But if the Samaritan were to say to them, 'You *can't* leave him there,' it would be a sick joke if they were to reply, 'Can't we? Just watch us walk away.' The Samaritan knows that as well as they do. 'You *can't* leave him there' is a rebuke in face of that fact; an expression of disgust at the enormity of their indifference.

For many people, certain deeds are ruled out as morally unthinkable. These are freely held views. But their 'unthinkability' cannot be captured if we describe these people as trying to hold these views, or as having arrived at them having considered the alternatives. For them, there are no alternatives where these matters are concerned. They cannot be described as having within them the power to do the things they describe as unthinkable.

An honest grocer who always gives his customers the correct change, is morally better, in this respect, than a grocer who tries to give the correct change because he is tempted not to, or to a grocer who, considering not giving the correct change, always gives it in the end. The other two grocers may succeed in overcoming their temptations, and yet long for the natural honesty of their fellow grocer. A husband who plays with his children out of a sense of duty, or because he believes it is good for them, is nevertheless different from one who is *absorbed* in play with his children. In the last case, he is not trying to play. He is absorbed in it. That is how one wants to speak of natural goodness. The agent is absorbed in it. But this cannot be captured by the analysis of free action we have been criticizing.

The consequences for our conception of God's perfect goodness should be obvious. I said that *some* human beings show natural goodness in *some* aspects of their behaviour. But no human being exhibits such natural goodness with respect to *all* the virtues *all* the time. God, on the other hand, is said to possess a perfect goodness to which we can never hope to attain. The problem is that if we apply the analysis of free actions we have criticized, to God, God can *never* in *any* of his acts exhibit the natural goodness we find, sometimes, in human beings. This is because for any free act God performs, we would have to say that he has the power within him to do it, and the power to refrain.

But the compassion of the Good Samaritan *cannot* be understood if one says of him that he had it within his power to refrain. As a result, God would never be said to possess the purity of the Samaritan's compassion.

There is an obvious connection between our criticisms of the notion of 'all power' attributed to the sovereignty of God's will, and our criticisms of the notion of freedom attributed to God's acts. 'All power' cannot be attributed to God, since some kinds of power are to be *contrasted* to God's power. 'Perfect goodness' cannot be attributed to God if to say that God acts freely entails that he has the power within him to refrain. The notion of a free act cannot even do justice to acts of simple virtue, or to impressive instances of natural goodness. As long as we stay within the conceptual parameters of the philosophical analyses we are criticizing, neither the proposition 'God is omnipotent' nor the proposition 'God is perfectly good' can get off the ground.

To anticipate the discussion in Part II of the book, we can only avoid this conceptual trouble if we see that, instead of saying that God's will (understood as 'all power') is the grammar of God's nature, we should say that God's nature (in a sense of 'perfect' goodness yet to be explored) is the grammar of God's will. Then we would see why it makes no sense to say that God could command me to murder my mother, or to betray my friends; or to say, if he doesn't, that God has within him the power to do so.

For the moment, however, I want to continue exploring our problematic philosophical inheritance with respect to God's will. In particular, I want to consider arguments which claim that, despite the fact that God has it within his power to prevent evils from occurring, the fact that he does not do so can be shown to be consistent with belief in his perfect goodness.

## 3. Can God Suffer the Consequences?

It has been argued, in response to the logical problem of evil, that belief in God's perfect goodness is consistent with the so-called robust conceptions of God's omnipotence and God's sovereign will that we have rejected. God can do or will whatever he likes and yet be perfectly good. How can this be said, given the evils that have existed and still exist? Davis replies:

> The short way with this problem, of course, is simply to point out the possibility (and that is all it takes, a mere possibility) that God has a good moral reason for allowing evil. Since that is a possibility (and free-will defenders think it is also an actuality), there is no contradiction. QED.[14]

Plantinga, to whom Davis thinks the philosophical community is indebted for this 'short way', says that 'it is only *hubris* which would tempt us to think that we could so much as grasp God's plans here, even if he proposed to divulge them to us'.[15] Richard Swinburne, on the other hand, thinks that, in the battle with atheism, it is insufficient to say 'God must have good reason for allowing bad states to occur, though we cannot see what they are.'[16] His own position is that 'There may indeed be theists who need no theodicy, but I shall be claiming that most of us do need a theodicy.'[17] A theodicy claims to know what God's reasons actually or probably are for allowing evils to exist, while defences, such as Davis's, claim that it is sufficient to believe in the possibility of an ultimate good, which redeems all evil, without knowing what that ultimate good is.

For my purposes in the present chapter, the distinction between theodicies and defences is irrelevant, since in neither case will it be possible to justify the existence of evil while saying that God is perfectly good. This will seem a bold undertaking to advocates of theodicies and defences. If, in the case of theodicies, it can be shown that God's good purposes for us can only be achieved through the evils we suffer, is not God justified in allowing such evils to exist? In the cases of defences, how can I deny that the ultimate good God has in store for us does not redeem the evils we suffer, when I admit to having no idea of what such an ultimate good could be? My objections simply seem to beg the question.

This reaction misses the point of my argument in this section. What I am going to argue is that even if we grant that things are as theodicies and defences depict them, even if the ultimate good did necessitate all the evil in the world, and even if the ultimate good somehow redeems all evil, it would still be impossible to attribute perfect goodness to God.

Before turning to my argument, it is important to emphasize that it operates within an assumption that I do not accept, but is accepted by most of those I criticize, namely, that God is a moral agent who shares a moral community with us. What I hope to do is to appeal to moral reactions that, hopefully, the philosophers of religion share with me when not philosophizing, and show them that, logically, even on their own terms, their theodicies and defences can give no account of them. The question whether God should be treated as a moral agent among others, an assumption I reject, will need further discussion.

One primary reason why advocates of theodicies and defences are blinded to common moral reactions is because of the consequentialism that dominates their arguments. We are presented with an abstract consequentalist definition of what constitutes a good act, and an equally abstract justification of why it may be good to allow bad states of affairs to exist. Thus, Swinburne writes, 'The morally best act for me to do is the one which is overall the best act, the one whose goodness overrides that of the goodness of other acts.'[18] As for God allowing bad states of affairs to exist:

> it is not always a bad act to bring about or to allow to occur a bad state of affairs. For it may be that the only way in which an agent can bring about some good state is by bringing about first (or simultaneously) some bad state, or by allowing such a state to occur.[19]

Considerations such as these are meant to show the illogicality of the assumption that 'A perfectly good being will never allow any morally bad state to occur if he can prevent it.'[20]

Since we are dealing with logical issues, it is thought that *any* example, however simple, is sufficient to overthrow the general claim that it is never right to allow a bad state to exist. But this is only so if the logic of examples is independent of their content. A consideration of different examples will show that this assumption is false.

Swinburne offers us the following example:

the only way in which a human parent can get his child's teeth repaired may be by taking him to the dentist and allowing pain to be inflicted upon him . . . But the human parent is none the less good for taking the child to the dentist.[21]

Davis offers us the following example:

Let me tell a true story. This was years ago, during my first week in junior high school . . . One day my mother made me wear a pair of pants that were embarrassingly out of the style worn by chic junior high schoolers of the day. Walking across campus, I felt conspicuous and slightly ridiculous. My fears were not assuaged when I was stopped in the hall by three mammoth ninth graders, one of whom said to me (his voice dripping with sarcasm): 'Gee kid, I wish I had a pair of pants like *that*.'

The episode was humiliating. If I could have crawled into a hole and disappeared, I would have done so.[22]

What is the point of these simple examples? Evidently, they are meant to throw light on why short-term or long-term consequences justify God in allowing evils to exist. Davis says so explicitly with regard to long-term consequences:

But here is the point: Today, many years later, I recall this event without any suffering at all. It was painful at the time, but I've grown up. I've gone on to more important things; I no longer care what ninth graders think about what I wear. That episode is now more amusing than painful.

Similarly (so I say), in the kingdom of God, when redemption is complete, all previous sufferings will pale into insignificance next to 'the glory that is to be revealed to us' . . . But given that we are dealing with infinite goods produced by a transcendent God, our inability to understand this point is just what we should expect.[23]

The attempt of the two simple examples is to produce an argument whereby an evil or bad state is compensated or redeemed by a greater good. The overall good is then to have the effect of the evil or bad state being swallowed within the overall good description of what has happened. Once this general consequentialist framework is established, *any* example can be fitted into it, including God's ultimate good for us, which is the overall goodness that swallows up, in a compensatory or redemptive act, all the evils human beings have suffered.

Once theodicies specify the nature of God's reasons for allowing evils to exist, they run into a series of insurmountable difficulties. According to Plantinga, 'most of the attempts to explain why God permits evil – *theodicies*, as we might call them – seem to me shallow, tepid, and ultimately frivolous'.[24] These reasons will be examined in the next chapter. At this moment, however, I am presenting an argument that does not depend on a criticism of those reasons; an argument that cannot be avoided by an appeal to the fact that we are ignorant of the purposes of a transcendent God. If God shares a moral community with us, *it is what we do know about moral matters*, not what we do not know, that makes Swinburne's and Davis's examples unacceptable. Further, the moral discriminations we possess, if God shares a moral community with us, have implications for what can be said of God, as they do for any other moral agent.

Let us put alongside Swinburne and Davis's examples the horrendous evil of the Holocaust. In the case of taking a child to the dentist, we may balk at Swinburne's chilling description of the parent as one who allows pain to be inflicted on the child. By talking in this way, he hopes to establish a parallel with God allowing evils to be inflicted on us. But it is a strange comparison. The parent does not feel remorse for inflicting pain on the child, and would not accept that description of what he is doing in taking the child to the dentist.

It may be thought that the above conclusion strengthens Swinburne's case. When we see God's ultimate good, it may be said, we will no longer accept 'inflicting evils on human beings' as the *overall* description of what God has done. Just like the pain at the dentist's, the evils human beings suffer will be swallowed up in a greater good.

It is precisely at this point that *what we know, morally, will not allow that comparison to be drawn.* We cannot speak of swallowing the Holocaust, as we speak of swallowing the pain at the dentist's. What is more, Swinburne knows this as well as anyone else. When not philosophizing, he does not speak of the Holocaust in the same breath as a visit to the dentist (unless they were visits to Nazi dentists!). We wouldn't know what to make of someone who did in the moral community to which Swinburne thinks God, like us, belongs. The difference emerges even when he philosophizes, for in the case of the Holocaust he has to admit that there is a case to answer. There is no case to answer for taking a child with infected teeth to a dentist. Swinburne's example serves no purpose.

Does Davis's example fare any better with its cost-effective attempt to compare his schoolboy embarrassment about his pants with the evils human beings have suffered, including of course, the Holocaust? Is not his attempt at a comparison, with its staggering 'Similarly', impossible to believe? Again, this impossibility is rooted in what we, including Davis, *already know morally.* To say, with Roth, that Davis comes 'dangerously close to trivializing suffering'[25] in his comparison, is an understatement.

Davis is both alarmed and a little annoyed at the charge of moral insensitivity. He insists, that where horrendous evils are concerned, 'I'm convinced they're just as horrendous as Phillips thinks they are.'[26] In response to Roth, Davis writes:

> I do not see how the evidence of waste in the world, massive as it is, shows that a perfectly good God could never have allowed it . . . To counter this, Roth keeps pointing out how terrible and massive the waste is. And I keep looking for an argument why this admitted amount of waste – whatever amount it is – could not have been allowed by God. He thinks I am looking at the evidence blindly; I think he is not producing an argument.[27]

Davis concludes, 'Sadly, Roth and I are at an impasse here.'[28]

The nature of the impasse between Davis and Roth is interesting. I have no doubt that, when not philosophizing, Davis does find the Holocaust to be just as horrendous as Roth and I do. He takes himself to share a moral community with us in that respect. What Davis does not see, however, is that his philosophical argument would deny him the moral attitude to the Holocaust that he says he shares with Roth and myself. What a moral attitude towards an evil is shows itself in what one is prepared to say about it. Roth and I are *not* prepared to speak about it in the way Davis does when he philosophizes. If Davis, when not philosophizing, is prepared to speak in that way, that would mark a moral difference between him and Roth and myself. We would say that such talk fails to take the Holocaust seriously. Davis may deny that. In any event, it would mark a moral difference between us. Davis, logically, cannot claim to share *the same* attitude to the Holocaust, while at the same time talk differently about it.

On reflection, going back to his example, Davis may agree on the inappropriateness of ascribing to victims and survivors of the Holocaust the kind of language he employed about himself in looking back at his schoolboy embarrassment. We must not forget that this language is meant to have a beneficial effect *now* on those who have suffered the horrendous evil. Would we speak to them like this? – 'In the eschaton you'll recall the Holocaust without any suffering at all. It was painful at the time, but you've grown up. You've gone on to more important things. You'll no longer care what was done to you in the Holocaust. The episode now is more (what?) than painful.'

If we ask what makes the above reflections of a soul redeemed unbelievable, it is what we already know of those who suffered in the Holocaust. To describe redemption in the way Davis suggests is to include in its effects a dulling of the most elementary moral reactions to horrendous evils, a result which, when not philosophizing, Davis would deplore as much as anyone else.

Roth is correct in saying that for Davis to attempt to characterize the impasse between them as 'a matter of "evangelistic

difficulty" . . . involves a conveniently limited notion of "philosophical difficulty"'.[29] On the other hand, Roth will not get to
the root of these limitations as long as he says, 'I will not contest
Davis's logical analysis.'[30] It is that analysis which needs to be
contested. Ultimately, this involves calling into question the
logical adequacy of consequentialism as a theory of moral
action. For the moment, let us grant the argument (which I do
not) that in order to achieve his purposes God had to allow evil
to exist. In other words, God did what had to be done in the
circumstances. This is an occurrence with which we are *already
morally familiar*. People often have to do what they do. We are
also morally familiar with what is said morally about them when
this happens: what is said about them by others, and what they
say of themselves. In allowing evils to exist, it is said that God
does what he has to do. So be it. But if this is so, what are we to
say of God, and what would we expect God to say of himself,
given that, like us, God is a member of a common moral community?

The evils that exist are said to be the consequences of God's
purposes. The consequences are unavoidable. That is why God
does what he has to do. The question to be faced is this: Does
God do what he has to with or without a second thought? Does
God allow that the Holocaust to occur with or without a second
thought? If we say that God allows it to happen without a second
thought, the moral community to which God is said to belong
already has a description of such an agent: even if he had to allow
it, he would still be called callous and insensitive. It follows that
God cannot share our attitude to the Holocaust if he allows it to
occur without a second thought. If, at this stage, we are suddenly told that God's ways are not our ways, this would be to abandon the basic assumption of the philosophers I am criticizing that
God is a fellow member of a moral community he shares with us.

Alternatively, we may say that God allowed the Holocaust to
happen *after a second thought*. He did what he had to do, but
gave full weight to the evil it involved. In that case, as a moral
agent, God would not absolve himself from that evil. We, seeing
what he has done, understand why this should be so. How could

it be otherwise if a morally responsible person has to answer for the Holocaust?

We are told that evil is a necessary consequence of an ultimate good God has in store for us. But whether that evil is done without or with a second thought, God has to suffer the consequences. If evil is allowed without a second thought, God is said to be callous and insensitive. If it is done with a second thought, God will recognize that he has been involved in evil. He gives that evil its proper weight. In either case, it would make no sense to speak of the perfect goodness of God.

To illustrate these logical observations, I want to consider two examples of people doing what they had to do, and what we say of them, and what they say of themselves. The first example is from William Styron's story *Sophie's Choice*. My use of it is slightly different from Roth's, but I shall quote his account of it at length.

Sophie Zawistowska was a Polish survivor of Auschwitz . . . For a time, Sophie had been a privileged prisoner, assigned to secretarial duties in the house of Rudolph Höss, the commandant of Auschwitz. Urged to use her position to assist the underground resistance movement, Sophie tried to steal a radio from Höss's house.

Sophie knew where one could be found, a small portable that belonged to Höss's daughter, Emmi. She passed the girl's room every day on her way upstairs to the office where Höss did his work. Once she tried for the radio, but Emmi caught her, and Sophie was nearly undone. Her sense of failure ran deep, only less so than the realization that she would never regain her courage to steal the radio again. Sophie learned 'how, among its other attributes, absolute evil paralyzes absolutely'.[31]

She knew the frailty of freedom not simply because of the incident with the radio, but because of the setting that surrounded it. And nothing was more important in that setting than her children, Jan and Eva. Jan was alive somewhere in the children's camp at Auschwitz. Höss had promised that Sophie could see him, and her attempted theft took place with the knowledge that she would jeopardize her chance to embrace the boy whose life gave hers a reason for going on. Sophie was not without courage – far from that – but once was enough. She could not put the radio ahead of her need for Jan.

Who could blame Sophie, especially when Eva is remembered? Eva is gone, gassed. And Sophie's freedom, or the lack of it, showed how pathetic a 'free-will defense' for God can be. Eva's life was lost because human freedom handed Sophie what the Holocaust scholar Lawrence Langer has aptly called a 'choiceless choice'.[32] As she disembarked from the stifling train that brought her and the children from Warsaw to Auschwitz, a selection took place. An SS official – Styron calls him Dr. Jerrard von Niemand – decided to make freedom real, dreadfully so, by forcing Sophie's choice. Instead of losing both Jan and Eva to the gas, which was the fate of almost all young children there, Sophie could pick one of hers to live. '*Ich kann nicht wählen!*' she screamed.[33] 'I cannot choose' . . . and then so as not to lose them both, Sophie let Eva go. Sophie's choice stayed with her. She experienced liberation in 1945, but only fully in 1947 when she gave up her own life, also by choice.[34]

When we consider Sophie's story, the distinction between first-person and third-person moral judgements is extremely important. As Roth asks, Who could blame Sophie? Who would want to make that third-person judgement? For us, Sophie is the object of pity and compassion. Yet, at the same time, it is possible to understand the personal judgement she makes in the end. As Roth says, her choice stayed with her, and she ends in taking her own life. She cannot eliminate the moral significance of letting Eva go. True, she did so as the result of a choice between Jan and Eva which is forced on her. She is involved in a moral tragedy where, whatever she did, would involve evil. That was the terrible point of forcing the choice on her. Sophie never thinks of handing Eva over as an act to be excused in the light of the total situation.

If God shares a common moral community with Sophie and ourselves, what should we say of his allowing the Holocaust to happen? Is God to be the object of pity? Is creation a moral tragedy in which God is necessarily involved in evil? And what of God's view of what he has done? Does the Holocaust stay with him? Does he think that it can be excused in the light of the greater good that made it necessary, or does he recognize he has something to answer for? It will be obvious that within these moral parameters, there is no logical space for talk of God's perfect goodness.

Consider our second example.[35] In the film *Violent Saturday*, gangsters on the run take refuge in a rural pacifist community. They terrorize its inhabitants. One of the gangsters points his gun at a young girl, and proceeds to play Russian roulette with it. Seeing this, the pacifist leader of the community, with a look of horror on his face, picks up a pitchfork and hurls it into the gangster's back.

In this example, too, the distinction between first-person and third-person moral judgements is important. As with Sophie, we can pity the leader of the pacifist sect. In killing a human being, he has broken a belief central to his whole way of life. On the other hand, he could not stand by and watch a young girl being murdered. We appreciate his dilemma. In his own eyes, he did what he had to do, but there was no unqualified right thing to do. He does not regard the killing as an act to be excused in the light of the total situation. On the contrary, he sees himself standing in need of penance.

Does God, in allowing the Holocaust, put aside the wrong of the slaughter of the innocent? Was he in some kind of moral dilemma in doing so? Does he refuse to excuse what has happened as some kind of exception? Does God feel answerable for what has happened? Can God be said to stand in need of penance? Again, if God is to suffer the consequences of what he allows, there is no logical space for the notion of God's perfect goodness.

I repeat: the conclusions I have reached only hold if, allowing that God did what he had to do in allowing evils to exist, we treat

God's moral agency as akin to our own. Once we do this, we can be reminded of familiar moral situations, in which equally familiar first-person and third-person moral judgements are made concerning actions that, in certain circumstances, morally, had to be done. Such judgements, however, if applied to God as a fellow moral agent, leave no logical space for the notion of God's perfect goodness.

Why are the circumstances I have alluded to, familiar though they are, hardly ever discussed by advocates of theodicies and defences? Is it not because, in their search for argument, they choose one which blinds them, philosophically, to central features of the moral community they want God to belong to. That argument, in ethics, is consequentialism.

## 4. Means, Ends and Morality

In the Introduction, we noted Marilyn Adams's remark about ethical theories. She said, 'Once theorizing begins . . . the hope of universal agreement in value theory is shattered.'[36] While acknowledging that consequentialism in ethics is thought to be controversial by many, the lack of theoretical agreement can lead to a complacency, philosophically, where each set of theoretical assumptions is allowed to go its own way. Thus, comparing my views with those of Swinburne's, Brian Davies says:

> It is very hard to see how we are to settle the question, for what is now at stake is a fundamental moral option . . . One side is saying that the whole attempt to justify God in terms of consequences is simply intolerable . . . The other side holds that it is not intolerable.[37]

Similarly, Davis says:

> I take it that something is instrumentally good if it is a means to, or causally contributes to, something else that is intrinsically good. Thus, as I suppose, instrumentalism in this context is understood by Phillips as the attempt to justify human suf-

fering as a means to something greater. And it is clear that Phillips finds this idea morally objectionable and untrue to the logic of moral responsibility. But I am afraid I don't, and I'm not sure what else can be said here.[38]

What I did in the previous section was to concentrate on the kinds of circumstances consequentialists like to invoke, but to show that, in perfectly familiar contexts, what Davis calls 'instrumental goods' are not excused, or fail to exact their moral demands, when they happen to be evils necessitated by a greater good. But more needs to be said because, as Davis recognizes, I hold that logical or conceptual issues are involved. In that case, everyone cannot be allowed, philosophically, simply to go their own way. I turn now to some of these further issues.

For consequentialism, morality is a guide to human conduct. Its goal, as Davis says, is that which is intrinsically good. Whether an action is instrumentally good is determined by whether it leads to what is intrinsically good. Things begin to get murky when we ask *in what sense* morality guides human conduct. Davis would surely agree that morality is not the guide to worldly success or prosperity. Some have wished it was otherwise. But the testimony that things are not so, is found in the cry that has rung down the ages, Why do the wicked prosper?[39] So if morality is not a guide around obstacles to worldly ends, is it a guide around obstacles to moral ends? But, as Peter Winch has pointed out, in that case morality is a strange sort of guide, since, without it, there would be no obstacles in the first place![40] Does morality first set up moral obstacles, and then tell us how to get round them?

The moral agent is not first confronted by a situation containing many alternatives, with morality as the guide as to which alternative to choose. Rather, if moral considerations matter to him they will be constitutive of how he will read the situation in the first place. If alternatives do face him, moral considerations do not only determine their priority, but also what is to count as an alternative in the first place. There are situations such as these confronting Sophie and the pacifist leader where what one has to do may involve evil. As we saw, that evil is not simply excused as the means to a greater good.

It is clear from these considerations that morally, means and ends are answerable to the demands of decency. However desirable the goal, it may be immoral to pursue it. On the other hand, if the goal is acceptable, it still cannot be pursued by any and every means. In morality, as J. L. Stocks has said, means are not simply assessed in terms of their efficacy in attaining an end. There is what he calls 'an additional principle of discrimination'[41] involved. It may be desirable to expand my business, and that the legal and most economic way of doing so is to put my friend out of business. But morality says, 'Not that way'.

Søren Kierkegaard asks, too, what means we employ in our occupations, and whether the means are as wholly important to us as the end. Otherwise, he says, the heterogeneous means will flow in between in confusing and corrupting fashion. Are the means we employ genuinely good? But, then, in morality, the genuine good is precisely the end.[42]

To put it in Swinburne's terms, but contra Swinburne, when evil is necessitated in terrible circumstances, the evil in the means is as objective as the good in what has to be done, and is given its full weight by the responsible moral agent. Is the Holocaust as important to God, wholly as important, as any ultimate good he may have in store for us? If not, we do not understand him to be morally serious. If he can allow it *without a second thought*, then, like Dostoyevsky's Ivan Karamazov, we respectfully return him the ticket. If he allows it *after a second thought*, God is involved in sorrows in such a way that he cannot emerge morally unscathed. In neither case can we speak of God's perfect goodness.

To repeat for one last time in this chapter, my conclusions are meant to have force against those consequentialist philosophers of religion who see God as a member of a moral community he shares with us.

What if we need to look in a radically different direction in order to understand what is meant by God's perfect goodness? That, as they say, is a totally different question.

## Notes

1 Stephen T. Davis, 'Free Will and Evil' in Stephen T. Davis (ed.), *Encountering Evil*, Louisville: Westminster John Knox Press 2001, p. 102.

2 John K. Roth, 'A Theodicy of Protest' in Davis, *Encountering Evil*, p. 13.

3 Stephen T. Davis, 'Critique of David Ray Griffin' in Davis, *Encountering Evil*, p. 136.

4 Rush Rhees, 'Natural Theology' in Rush Rhees, *On Religion and Philosophy*, ed. D. Z. Phillips, assisted by Mario von der Ruhr, Cambridge: Cambridge University Press 1997, p. 34–5.

5 Rhees, 'Natural Theology', p. 36.

6 Rhees, 'Natural Theology', p. 36.

7 Rhees, 'Natural Theology', p. 34.

8 Rhees, 'Natural Theology', p. 36.

9 Rhees, 'Natural Theology', p. 37.

10 Rhees, 'Natural Theology', p. 37.

11 Alvin Plantinga, 'God, Evil, and the Metaphysics of Freedom' in Marilyn McCord and Robert Merrihew Adams (eds), *The Problem of Evil*, Oxford: Oxford University Press 1990, pp. 84–5.

12 Roth, 'Theodicy of Protest', p. 13.

13 I owe these considerations to R. A. Sharpe.

14 Stephen T. Davis, 'Rejoinder' in Davis, *Encountering Evil*, p. 102.

15 Alvin Plantinga, 'Epistemic Probability and Evil' in Marco M. Olivetti (ed.), *Teodicea Oggi? Archivio di filosofia*, 1988, p. 562.

16 Richard Swinburne, *Providence and the Problem of Evil*, Oxford: Clarendon Press 1998, p. 14.

17 Swinburne, *Providence*, p. 17.

18 Swinburne, *Providence*, p. 5.

19 Swinburne, *Providence*, p. 10.

20 Swinburne, *Providence*, p. 7.

21 Swinburne, *Providence*, p. 10.

22 Stephen T. Davis, 'Free Will and Evil', pp. 84–5.

23 Davis, 'Free Will and Evil', p. 85.

24 Plantinga, 'Epistemic Probability and Evil', p. 558.

25 John K. Roth, 'Critique of Stephen T. Davis' in Davis, *Encountering Evil*, p. 98.

26 Stephen T. Davis, 'Critique of D. Z. Phillips' in Davis, *Encountering Evil*, p. 169.

27 Stephen T. Davis, 'Rejoinder' in Davis, *Encountering Evil*, p. 104.

28 Davis, 'Rejoinder', p. 104. Davies makes it clear that he emphatically does *not* want to equate his childhood incident with the horrors of the Holocaust. Of course he doesn't. My point is that his philosophical

perspective does not do justice to what he would say when not philosophizing.

29 Roth, 'Critique of Davis', p. 99.

30 Roth, 'Critique of Davis', p. 97.

31 William Styron, *Sophie's Choice*, New York: Random House 1979, p. 392.

32 See, for example, Lawrence L. Langer, 'The Dilemma of Choice in the Deathcamps' in John K. Roth and Michael Berenbaum (eds), *Holocaust: Religious and Philosophical Implications*, New York: Paragon House 1989, pp. 221–32.

33 Styron, *Sophie's Choice*, p. 483.

34 Roth, 'Theodicy of Protest', pp. 9–10.

35 I owe it to Peter Winch. See 'Moral Integrity' in *Ethics and Action*, London: Routledge and Kegan Paul 1972, p. 185.

36 Marilyn McCord Adams, *Horrendous Evils and the Goodness of God*, Ithaca: Cornell University Press 1999, p. 11.

37 Brian Davies, *An Introduction to the Philosophy of Religion*, Oxford: Oxford University Press. New edition 1993, p. 38.

38 Davis, 'Rejoinder' in Davis, *Encountering Evil*, p. 103.

39 For my criticisms of attempts to give moral conduct a rationale in terms of self-interest or human flourishing see my 'Does it pay to be good?' and 'On Morality's Having A Point' (with H. O. Mounce) in *Interventions in Ethics*, Basingstoke: Macmillan and New York: SUNY Press 1992.

40 Peter Winch, 'Moral Integrity'.

41 J. L. Stocks, 'The Limits of Purpose' in J. L Stocks, *Morality and Purpose*, ed. D. Z. Phillips, London: Routledge and Kegan Paul 1969, p. 27.

42 Søren Kierkegaard, *Purity of Heart*, New York: Harper and Row 1956, pp. 201–2.

# 3

# God's Morally Insufficient Reasons

## 1. Looking for God's Reasons

Does God have morally sufficient reasons for allowing evils to exist? If such reasons exist, it will be possible to believe in an omnipotent, perfectly good God, despite the existence of evil. On the other hand, it would be impossible to believe in such a God, if no such reasons exist. In *Providence and the Problem of Evil*, Richard Swinburne writes:

> Just reflect on some of the horrors that we read about in our newspapers and history books: the prolonged cruelty of parents to lonely children, the torture of the innocent, the long-drawn-out acute physical pain of some disease, and so on. If we cannot see all that as a reason for believing that there is no all-good and all-powerful being, when we cannot think of any reason why such a being should allow it all to happen, there really is something deeply wrong with *us*. We have lost our sensitivity to the good.[1]

On the one hand, Swinburne says that it is morally sensitive to search for God's morally sufficient reasons for allowing evils to exist. On the other hand, he says that he, 'can easily understand many deeply sensitive people reacting with horror at the very attempt to show that a loving God could allow humans and animals to suffer, let alone suffer some of the horrible things that happen on Earth'.[2]

Swinburne sees his book as a plea to moral sensibilities which differ from his own, but which he says he deeply respects. It may seem churlish of me not to have returned that respect in my early exchange with Swinburne. In his contribution to the symposium, Swinburne wrote, 'Now a morally sensitive antitheodicist might well in principle accept some of the above arguments.'[3] I replied, 'This conclusion is a somewhat embarrassing one since it is evident from my comments that one of the strongest criticisms available to the antitheodicist would be the moral insensitivity of the theodicist's case.'[4] I wanted then, and still want, to emphasize the extent of the gap between us. The trouble with my response, however, is that it gives the impression that that gap is simply due to a moral disagreement. As we have seen, this is how Brian Davies[5] and Stephen T. Davis[6] read our disagreement, and this was Swinburne's first response to it. He wrote, 'I hope that I am not insensitive to the evil in life, but I do not share Phillips's conviction that the evil is pointless, and I do not find enough *argument* in Phillips's paper to show that it is.[7]

What these responses miss is that I intend my objections to the theodicist's project to be *logical* and *conceptual* in character. When Wittgenstein finds such projects repellent, no doubt moral reasons are involved. But he also finds them intellectually repellent, because of what they distort and suppress. It is worth paying some attention to Wittgenstein's accusation, since it indicates the pattern of my own objections to the arguments we are offered to think that God has morally sufficient reasons for allowing evils to exist.

Wittgenstein writes, 'Religion says: *Do this! – Think like that!* – but it cannot justify this, and once it even tries to, it becomes repellent; because for every reason it offers there is a valid counter-reason.' When we are offered what is supposed to be one of God's morally sufficient reasons, something is always suppressed. As a result, Wittgenstein says, '[you] feel you were being cheated, that someone was trying to convince you by trickery'. Wittgenstein is not saying that a theodicist sets out deliberately to deceive anyone. The theodicist is as much a victim of deception as those convinced by his arguments. The deception is *in* the thoughts that attract us and hold us captive. But when one sees through the arguments, they then strike us as having not given human suffering the attention it deserves.

Wittgenstein is certainly not denying the possibility of thanking God for the whole of existence. He writes:

> Someone can be told for instance: 'Thank God for the good you receive: but don't complain about the evil as you would of course do if a human being were to do you good and evil by turns'.

But, as we saw in the last chapter, in theodicies and defences God is talked of anthropomorphically, for the most part, as though he were a moral agent with us in a common moral community. We saw the results of doing so. Wittgenstein warns us against them in what might be called his allegory of the bees:

> I can say: 'Thank these bees for their honey as though they were kind people who have prepared it for you'; that is *intelligible* and describes how I should like you to conduct yourself. But I cannot say: 'Thank them because, look, how kind they are!' – since the next moment they may sting you.[8]

The morally sufficient reasons are attempts to say of God, 'Look how kind he is', but the next minute each argument, of this kind, will sting you. In enumerating some bee-stings in the present chapter, I do not claim that every theodicy or defence exemplifies *all* of them.[9] This is almost the case, I would suggest, with respect to the confusions about 'omnipotence', 'willing' and 'perfect goodness' we have already discussed. As for the additional bee-stings I shall mention, I am content to say: to each theodicy its own.

## 2. Evil and Logical Necessity

The first morally sufficient reason ascribed to God to justify his allowing evils to exist, which I want to discuss, is the claim that if God wanted to create goods, it was logically impossible for him to do otherwise. Any good gets its sense from a contrast with an evil. To call for the absence of evil is, unwittingly, to call for the absence of good at the same time.

This claim has been disputed by secularists and religious apologists alike. J. L. Mackie argues that:

> the principle that a term must have an opposite would belong
> only to our language and to our thought, and would not be an
> ontological principle . . . the rule that good cannot exist with-
> out evil would not state a logical necessity of a sort that God
> would just have to put up with. God might have made every-
> thing good, though *we* should not have noticed it if he had.[10]

Swinburne concurs, saying:

> It might be that in such a situation, without the existence of
> contrasting bad states, the world's inhabitants would not real-
> ize that their world contained nothing bad – but it would be
> true all the same. Anyway I see no reason to suppose that the
> inhabitants could not realize that their world contained noth-
> ing bad; they could have the concept of bad (they could be born
> with an ability to recognize bad states, if they were to occur)
> without there actually being any instances of bad states.[11]

Mackie and Swinburne underestimate the logical difficulties
involved. Mackie wants his description of things in the world as
'good' to be *correct*, while the same can be said of the states
Swinburne says would be recognized as bad. But in order for
their claims to be correct, there must be some standard, *independent of them*, to determine this. But Mackie and Swinburne
want to bypass the logical necessity of such a standard and make
their claims correct by, what Wittgenstein aptly calls, 'a baptism
of meaning'. What Mackie and Swinburne do is to presuppose
the standard they think unnecessary in their very descriptions of
the situations they ask us to envisage.

Certain examples of moral purity may lead us to think that an
appeal to wider standards is unnecessary. We may appeal to the
generosity of thought seen in certain saints, where its opposite
simply does not occur in them. Even so, this description of them
cannot be cut off from its wider surroundings. It is not self-

authenticating. We are impressed by their generosity of spirit because it is possessed by them in a world in which it is all too easy to think of human beings in a very different spirit. Generosity, kindness, loyalty, truthfulness, etc., can only have their identity in a world in which meanness, cruelty, disloyalty and lies also have purchase.

Moral standards develop and have their sense in our reactions to human behaviour. Consider a simple example of how a child may begin acquiring a notion of selfishness. Its arm may be pulled back as it reaches for its third cream bun, and the child is told, at the same time, that other children at the table have not had one yet.

It may be suggested that a disdain for the immoral could be taught by means of hypothetical cases without anything immoral actually taking place. For example, a child may be told that if human beings were killed as animals are killed, this would be a bad thing.[12] The difficulty in this suggestion, is that there is a difference in our moral reactions to what has *actually* happened from our reactions to what could happen. For agents and spectators alike, there is a difference in that to which one is answerable, in what judgements can be made and in what reparation, if any, is possible. Such distinctions, which are so central to moral perception, can only develop in the context of actual, not hypothetical, events. Of course, one can hypothesize about events, but then 'the hypothetical' trades on 'the actual'.

Swinburne rejects the possibility of God creating a world in which people only seem to be harmed, on the grounds that God would be guilty of a great deceit.[13] The difficulty with this suggestion is not moral, but logical. The notion of someone *seeming* to be in pain is logically parasitic on the notion of someone *being* in pain. If everything is said to be a 'seeming', nothing is. The metaphysical claim ceases to affect anything that actually happens. We will go on making our usual distinctions between 'what seems to be the case' and 'what is the case'. Swinburne's God, in this context, suffers the same fate as Descartes's malignant demon. The threat of a world of 'seemings' is no more successful than the threat to deceive us all the time.

If we now look back at Mackie's and Swinburne's claim that God could have created a world in which human beings are naturally good, we can see that whoever these beings would be, they would not be human. Human beings live the lives they do with a knowledge of good and evil. How could it be otherwise?

At this point, the reader may wonder what has happened to any argument *against* the claim that God is justified in allowing evils to exist, because it is logically impossible for him to do otherwise if he wants to create goods. I seem to be giving that morally sufficient reason stronger support than Mackie and Swinburne! That is how my argument struck John Hick, who wrote:

> where Swinburne argues that God could not have done such-and-such because this would have been incompatible with the value that he is said to put upon the existence of free creatures, Phillips says that God could not have done that same thing because it does not make sense to speak of its being done – it is logically undoable. Swinburne's theodicy gains either way. For if Phillips is right, he has supplied an even stronger argument for Swinburne's conclusion.[14]

Hick's reaction misses the logical implications of the argument I'm presenting. It is precisely by recognizing the *logical* character of the distinctions I have been insisting on that we see why they cannot be used as *justifications* of the existence of evil in either global or specific contexts.

Let us turn to the global context first. Freedom of the will, it is said, entails the ability to choose between good and evil. Freedom of the will is an undeniable good. It is better for us to have it, than not to have it. Therefore, a world containing freedom of the will must be a world that contains some evil.

The problem with the argument comes from thinking of the deprivation of freedom of the will as such, as though it were akin to being deprived of a specific mental or physical capacity. But lacking freedom of the will as such is not a larger scale defect than, say, being brainwashed or becoming insane. When we speak of freedom of the will in general, we are not referring to a specific condition human beings may be in, by contrast with some *other* condition in which human beings might have been created. As Hick says, 'to say that God should not have created beings who might sin amounts to saying that God should not have created people'.[15] To ask whether it is better for people to have free will or not is to ask whether it is better for people to be as they are or to be in a state called 'non-people'. The latter alternative is not a worse one for *us*, for who would the 'us' be? In that case, the former alternative cannot be said to be a *better* one for us either. That being so, it cannot be used as a *justification* of the evils in human life.[16]

When we turn to the specific contexts in which actual evils are experienced, it is difficult to see how the logical point that there are conceptual interrelations between 'good' and 'evil' can act in any way as a *justification* of the existence of the *actual* evil one is confronting. W. Somerset Maugham has expressed the matter succinctly:

> It may be that courage and sympathy are excellent and that they could not come into existence without danger and suffering. It is hard to see how the Victoria Cross that rewards the soldier who has risked his life to save a blinded man is going to solace *him* for the loss of his sight. To give alms shows charity, and charity is a virtue, but does *that* good compensate for the evil of the cripple whose poverty has called it forth?[17]

Clearly, for God's morally sufficient reasons for allowing actual evils to be found, an attempt would have to be made to forge a *logical* link between the requirement that *some* evils have to exist if goods are to exist and the *actual* evils which do exist. Nelson Pike admits in 'Hume on Evil',[18] as do Adams and Adams in the introduction to their collection,[19] that the attempt to forge such a link is highly problematic. I would venture to say that it is as problematic as attempting to move from the necessity of a distinction between sense and nonsense to a justification of the actual forms that distinction takes in our discourse.

Plantinga has suggested what the link might be, albeit in a very general way. He writes:

> The world, after all, contains a *great deal* of moral evil; and what we have seen so far is only that God's existence is compatible with *some* evil. Perhaps the atheologian can regroup, arguing that at any rate God's existence is not consistent with the vast amount and variety of evil the universe actually contains.

Plantinga's answer is to posit *the mere possibility* that the actual evils in our world, rather than any others, are logically necessary for God to achieve his purposes. As Marilyn Adams has pointed out:

> With startling candor, Plantinga actually commends his generic and global approach on the ground that it enables us to avoid specific consideration of evils, so appalling and so horrifying that we not only do not know why God permits them, we cannot even conceive of any plausible candidate reasons . . . At the same time, Plantinga seems to want to respond to the concrete and not merely the abstract problem of evil.[20]

Recall, too, that when theodicists have ventured to produce reasons as to why God has permitted specific evils, Plantinga finds most of them to be 'shallow, tepid, and ultimately frivolous'.[21] As we look at other reasons that have been offered as God's morally sufficient reasons for allowing evils to exist, we shall see whether they merit Plantinga's description.

## 3. Evils as Opportunities for Character Development

A second morally sufficient reason ascribed to God for allowing evils to exist is that the evils are part of God's plan for our character development. That development makes the presence of evils logically necessary, since it cannot occur without them.

Some theodicists are dissatisfied with Plantinga's defence. At best, what it provides is the logical *possibility* that the evils which exist are logically necessary for the realization of God's purposes. This leaves open, of course, the logical possibility that the evils which exist are not logically necessary. Why believe one possibility rather than the other? More is needed to convince atheists. They must be shown that God has good reasons for allowing evils to exist.[22] The appeal to the conditions for character development is one of these. To want a world without evil is to want at the same time, albeit unwittingly, a world without character development.

We are told that in allowing evils to exist, God is providing the conditions needed to give us the choice of moulding our characters in one direction or another.[23] This offer of God's morally sufficient reason suffers from a fatal objection. *To make the development of one's character an aim is to ensure that the development will not take place.* This is because the endeavour so conceived is self-defeating: *it lacks character.*

We act in a variety of ways. Some of these ways may show character, but not because the agents thought about their characters. Character is shown in the ways we deal with *other things.* If seeing someone yielding to cowardice, someone urges, 'Come on, show some character', he is being urged not to think about himself, about his character, but, rather, being urged to be brave. Even if one did act bravely, without a second thought, but later revelled in the thought of one's character, the figure one must have cut and so on, for many that would detract from the moral worth of the action. It seems to be both a logical and moral truth that to seek one's character development is to lose it.

It may be said that my criticisms are misdirected. This is because the morally sufficient reason being discussed is God's reason for acting, not ours, and thus was never advanced as a thesis about human moral motivation.[24] Two responses can be made to this objection. First, if God's reasons are confused and morally objectionable, this would have the unhappy consequence, for the theodicist, of making God inferior to human beings. Second, however, one need not accept the view that the issue of our own moral motivation is not involved in God's morally sufficient reason for allowing evils to exist. After all, it is we who want to know that reason, when those evils threaten our belief in God's perfect goodness. Theodicies are for our benefit, not God's. We are told that the evils exist as opportunities for our character development. If we understand the evils in these terms, this will obviously determine what we think we are doing when we respond to them, namely, that we are developing our characters. In this way, God's morally sufficient reason clearly affects our own motivation.

There is a fatal instrumentalism in the conception of character development we have criticized, namely, the conceptual incoherence it suffers from. The analysis of a character that should show itself, in the main, in the way we behave towards others, gives us instead a picture of an indulgent concern with oneself. As we shall see, this instrumentalism, and concentration on the self, appears again and again in the morally sufficient reasons, advanced by theodicists, to explain why God permits the existence of evil.

## 4. *Evils as Opportunities for Moral Responsibility*

A third morally sufficient reason ascribed to God, to explain why he allows evils to exist is that they afford the opportunities for people to be morally responsible in reacting to them. To want a world without evils is to want unwittingly, at the same time, a world without moral responsibility which, logically, cannot exist without them.

Swinburne makes the case as follows:

A world in which no one except the agent was affected by his evil actions might be a world in which men had freedom but it would not be a world in which men had responsibility . . . the price of possible passive evils for other creatures is a price worth paying for agents to have great responsibilities for each other. It is a price which (logically) must be paid if they are to have those responsibilities. Here again a reasonable anti-theodicist may see the point.[25]

Contrary to Swinburne's hopes, a reasonable response to this theodicy should see the incoherence it suffers from. The very logical claim it advances is illogical. From the logical truth that we cannot be responsible unless we are responsible to someone, or for something, it by no means follows that that 'someone' or 'something' can be regarded as an *opportunity* for us to be responsible. As in the previous section on character development, Swinburne's analysis leads to the vulgarization of the concept being analysed. It would make it possible for the Good Samaritan to say, on coming across the victim of the robbers, 'Thank you, God, for another opportunity to be responsible.' It does make it possible for Swinburne to say of sufferings such as rape, abortion and marriage breakdown:

> And when we have not ourselves had such experience we can freely choose to seek out those who have before coming to form a view about the moral principles involved. The suffering becomes the tool which we use for our growth of moral understanding, and so in yet another way the sufferer is of use to us in helping us so to grow.[26]

These remarks make it obvious how the sufferings of others are made instrumental to the self. Our moral growth is presented by Swinburne as the justification of those sufferings which he treats as the means of achieving it. We cannot speak of moral growth in this way. In fact, we are in the grip of its opposite.

Swinburne's instrumentalism worsens when he tries to justify the existence of horrendous evils, by saying that we need them in order to grow deeply in responding to them. Apparently, God knows this as well as we do, and wants to separate the men from the boys. Swinburne tells us that 'a creator who gave them only coughs and colds, and not cancer and cholera would be a creator who treated men as children instead of giving them real encouragement to subdue the world'.[27] But would the world not be better off without such attitudes to the sufferings of others, attitudes that are a denial of the very moral concepts they claim to be elucidating?[28] Here is a clear instance where a theodicy, in the very language it employs, actually adds to the evils it seeks to justify.

Because Swinburne does not appreciate the logical and conceptual aspects of the criticisms, he simply sees them as premature conclusions, which could be corrected if the benefits he has mentioned could be explored in greater detail. He writes:

> The argument must go on with regard to particular cases. The antitheodicist must sketch in detail and show his adversary the horrors of particular wars and diseases. The theodicist in reply must sketch in detail and show his adversary the good which such disasters make possible . . . Interfere to stop the evil and you cut off the good.[29]

Swinburne does not see that the objections are not to the details of his calculations, but to his readiness to think of human sufferings in terms of such calculations in the first place. Swinburne says, in passing, 'Now obviously it would be crazy for God to multiply pains in order to multiply compassion.'[30] But according to the logic of his argument why should this be so? Is not 'multiplication' the name of the game?

## 5. Physical and Mental Evils as Causal Initiatives

A fourth morally sufficient reason ascribed to God to explain why evils exist is that God allows certain physical and mental evils to occur because, when they are not the result of intentional actions, they act as a spur to rectify them, so bringing about, in this initiative, a character development that is not imposed on us by God. The difficulty in the argument lies in its false assumption that something called 'the spur to change', caused by the evils, can be assessed *independently* of the character of the agent who experiences the evils.

Swinburne attempts to make the case for the assumption, with respect to physical evils, as follows:

> An itch causally inclines a man to do whatever will cause the itch to cease, e.g., scratch, and provides a reason for doing that

action. Its causal influence is quite independent of the agent –
saint or sinner, strong-willed or weak-willed, will all be
strongly inclined to get rid of their pains (though some may
learn to resist the inclination). Hence a creator who wished to
give agents some inclination to improve the world without
giving them a character, a wide set of general purposes which
they naturally pursue, would tie some of the imperfections of
the world to physical or mental evils.[31]

The problem lies in the attempt to link 'the causal spur' with
'some inclination to improve the world', and the assumption that
this is achieved as easily as it is to say that itches cause us to
improve the world by scratching so that they cease. First, the itch,
then no itch – what could be simpler? But the simplicity of the
conclusion depends on the simplicity of the example. The thesis,
however, is a general one, and must be tested by other cases.

Consider the example of Kierkegaard's calculating lecher. He
discovers that his lechery has led to a disease. As Swinburne
would say, this causes him to seek a remedy for it. The doctor
warns him of the consequences. Kierkegaard informs us of the
result: 'Indeed, fear of the body's infirmities has taught the
voluptuary to observe moderation in debauchery . . . but it has
never made him chaste.'[32] Is Swinburne going to say that the
lecher has been spurred to improve the world by curing his disease? But what if one added: in order to continue in debauchery?
Is one going to say that he was spurred to improve the world in
moderating his debauchery? But what if one added: in order that
he might practise it longer? Aren't these speculations besides the
point, as far as morality is concerned, since whether the physical,
causal spur can be linked to 'an inclination to improve the world'
will depend on considerations concerning the moral character of
the agent? For example, suppose a person's policy relating to
whether he acts morally or immorally is determined, whenever
possible, by gauging, in each case, the likely effect of such conduct on his health. Such a policy, though activated by the desire
to improve health, would be described, morally, as thoroughly
servile.

Similar conclusions may be drawn about Swinburne's attempts
to illustrate his assumptions in the case of mental evils:

> Many mental evils too are caused by things going wrong in a
> man's life or in the life of his fellows and often serve as a spur
> to a man to put things right, either to put right the cause of the
> particular mental evil or to put similar things right. A man's
> feeling of frustration at the failure of his plans spurs him either
> to fulfill those plans despite their initial failure or to curtail his
> ambitions. A man's sadness at the failure of the plans of his
> child will incline him to help the child more in future. A man's
> grief at the absence of a loved one inclines him to do whatever
> will get the loved one back. As with physical pain, the spur
> inclines a man to do what is right but does so without impos-
> ing a character – without, say, making a man responsive to
> duty, or strong-willed.[33]

Once again, too much is taken for granted, or left out of consideration. In the case of physical pains, the analysis only worked
in simple, straightforward cases, such as a toothache. If a person
has toothache, normally, it will spur him on to get it attended to.
It may be lavish to say that he has improved the world thereby,
but, at least, he has improved a tooth. But it would be naïve to
suggest that mental evils stand to subsequent behaviour as having toothache stands to the search for a remedy. Even in the
physical cases, we saw the difficulty of forging a direct conceptual, or causal, link between the physical pain and the description
of the reaction to it as 'an inclination to improve the world'.
Similarly, it is equally, if not more, difficult to forge such links
between mental pains, on the one hand and, on the other hand,
the description of an attempt to get rid of it as an 'inclination to
do what is right'. This is so if only because what a mental evil
spurs one to do to get rid of it may not be a case of doing the right
thing at all. It does not even follow that it is always right to try to
get rid of mental evils.

In Tolstoy's *Anna Karenina*, the husband, Karenin, is in mental anguish over the loss of his wife, Anna, to her lover, Vronsky.

He is frustrated at the failure of his plans that the loss entails. The anguish and frustration spur him on to get her back, but not to do the right thing. His character, his emphasis on himself, are such that he can only think of what Anna owes him. He heaps shame and degradation on her relentlessly. Had he not tried to get rid of his anguish, but reflected on it, he might have acted differently.

For every example Swinburne brings to show how physical and mental evils act as a spur to developments which are good, there are counter-examples, which show how such evils act as a spur to developments that are not only evil, but often a far greater evil than those which prompted it. If one emphasizes only the former examples to support a *general* thesis, one will be contradicted constantly by the counter-examples one is suppressing or failing to recognize. We have already met this feature of theodicies and are about to meet it again in the sections that follow.

## 6. Admirable Responses to the Sufferings of Others

A fifth morally sufficient reason ascribed to God to explain why he allows evils to exist is that the evils suffered by others give us the opportunity to be shown at our best in the ways we respond to them. Our discussion of 'character development' and 'moral responsibility' will recall one difficulty that such a view invites immediately. As in the other cases, it involves the objectionable instrumentalism in which the sufferings of others are treated as an opportunity for me to be shown at my best. Ironically, if I think of their sufferings in this way, I am shown at my worst. But I shall not dwell on this aspect of the position in this section. Instead, I want to comment on a second difficulty from which it suffers. Even within its way of thinking, it suffers from a fatal generality. If the sufferings of others sometimes prompt the best in us, they often prompt the worst.

In his earlier expression of this point of view, Swinburne writes:

A world without evils would be a world in which men could show no forgiveness, no compassion, no self-sacrifice. And

men without that opportunity are deprived of the opportunity
to show themselves at their noblest. For this reason God might
well allow some of his creatures to perform evil acts with passive evils as consequences, since these provide the opportunity
for especially noble acts.[34]

In his later view, Swinburne's perspective is modified somewhat:

> A particular natural evil such as pain makes possible felt com-
> passion – one's sorrow, concern, and desire to help the sufferer
> ... But of course, the objector will say, even if pain is better for
> the response of compassion, better still that there be no pain at
> all ... But I suggest that a world with some pain and some com-
> passion is at least as good as a world with no pain.[35]

This latter position is not enough for a theodicy, especially for
one that takes pride in its reliance on probability. Philo's first
major criticism of Cleanthes in Hume's *Dialogues*[36] is that he is
not permitted to infer more of God than the mixed evidence
allows. Mixed evidence concerning responses to human suffering
can never justify belief in God's perfect goodness. And the evidence is certainly mixed. Theodicies need to be reminded of that
fact. It is one that can be illustrated with a range of examples,
ranging from light home truths to the darkest deeds imaginable.
Let us begin with Jonathan Swift's comic reminder:

> DEAR honest *Ned* is in the Gout,
> Lies rackt with PAIN, and you without:
> How patiently you hear him groan!
> How glad the CASE is not your own![37]

In a darker expression of the same thought, one of Roche-
foucauld's maxims declares, 'In the adversity of our friends, we
find something which doth not displease us.'
Further, the sufferings of others may be viewed as false moves
on their part in the highly competitive game of life; death being
the worst move of all. Consider the attitude to Ivan Ilych's death

by his colleagues in Tolstoy's short story, *The Death of Ivan Ilyich*. When Peter Ivanovich goes to sympathize with the widow, he meets another of his colleagues, who winked at him as if to say, 'Ivan Ilyich has made a mess of things – not like you and me.'[38]

It is an obvious fact, of course, that knowledge of the nature of suffering is what motivates the form taken by an attack on others. Again, examples range from the simplest infliction to the most horrendous evils. On seeing a little boy hitting a little girl in a schoolyard, a teacher reprimanded him and asked, 'Don't you know you're hurting her?' The little boy replied, 'Yes miss.' What the torturer knows about suffering entered into the form taken by the horrendous degradations inflicted on the victims of the Holocaust. Terrence Des Pres writes:

> The fact is that prisoners were *systematically* subjected to filth. They were the deliberate target of excremental assault. Defilement was a constant threat, a condition of life from day to day, and at any moment it was liable to take abruptly vicious and sometimes fatal forms.[39]

Des Pres emphasizes how the form taken by torture depended on knowledge of its effects on the soul:

> . . . conditions like these were not accidental, they were determined by a deliberate policy which aimed at complete humiliation and debasement of prisoners. Why this was necessary is not at first apparent, since none of the goals of the camp system – to spread torture, to provide slaves, to exterminate populations – require the kind of thoroughness with which conditions of defilement were enforced. But here too, for all its madness, there was method and reason . . . The SS could kill anyone they happened to run into. Criminal *Kapos* would walk about in groups of two and three, making bets among themselves on who could kill a prisoner with a single blow. The pathological rage of such men, their uncontrollable fury when rules were broken, is evidence of a boundless desire to

annihilate, to destroy, to smash everything not mobilized within the movement of their own authority. And inevitably, the mere act of killing is not enough; for if a man dies without surrender, if something within him remains unbroken to the end, then the power which destroyed him has not, after all, crushed everything. Something has escaped its reach, and it is precisely this something – let us call it 'dignity' – that must die if those in power are to reach the orgasmic peak of their potential domination.[40]

## 7. Admirable Responses to Our Own Sufferings

A sixth morally sufficient reason ascribed to God to explain why he allows evils to exist is closely related to the fifth we have just discussed. This time, however, the emphasis is on the evils we suffer ourselves, and how these afford us an opportunity to show ourselves at our best in the ways we bear them. Swinburne writes:

> Without a significant amount of natural evil, we simply would not have the opportunity to show patience . . . on the heroic scale required for us to form heroically good characters. It is a great good for us to be able, through free choice over time, to form such characters.[41]

The individualistic voluntarism in Swinburne's argument is linked to his conception of life as a moral obstacle course that God has designed as a means for character development. Some have called it 'the outward-bound school of theology'. In this respect, it is similar to Hick's conception of life as 'a person-making process' designed by God. Hick argues that human beings are born at an epistemic distance from God. They are born immature, subject to the radical contingencies of human life. The hope is that they emerge mature from the person-making process. Such a theodicy, Hick argues, 'appeals to the principle that virtues that have been formed within the agent as a hard-won deposit of right decisions in situations of challenge and temptation are intrinsically more valuable than ready-made virtues created within her without any effort on her own part'.[42]

Hick says that the principle to which he appeals 'expresses a basic value judgement that cannot be established by argument but which one can only present, in the hope that it will be as morally plausible, and indeed compelling, to others as to one-self'.[43] But Hick does not need an appeal to a basic moral judgement to make his point. The notion of a 'ready-made virtue' is unintelligible, as we shall see in the next chapter. Neither should it be confused with the notion of natural goodness discussed in the previous chapter. This is not the objection Hick needs to fear. That is to be found in both Swinburne's and Hick's one-sided diet of examples, and the way they suppress or ignore obvious examples of the disastrous effects suffering has had on human beings; the ways in which it has marked them. I am simply going to present reminders of some of them. Some philosophers react with impatience to my examples, saying, 'Do you think we don't know that such things can happen? We know all about that.' To which I reply, 'In that case, why do you forget it all when you philosophize?' Consider, for example, Settembrini's comments to Hans Castrop in Thomas Mann's *The Magic Mountain*:

> You said that the sight of dullness and disease going hand in hand must be the most melancholy in life. I grant you, I grant you that. I too prefer an intelligent ailing person to a consump-tive idiot. But I take issue where you regard the combination of disease with dullness as a sort of aesthetic inconsistency, an error in taste on the part of nature, a 'dilemma for the human feelings', as you were pleased to express yourself. When you professed to regard disease as something so refined, so – what did you call it? – possessing a 'certain dignity' – that it doesn't 'go with' stupidity. That was the expression you used. Well, I say no! Disease has nothing refined about it, nothing dignified. Such a conception is in itself pathological, or at least tends in that direction . . . Do not, for heaven's sake, speak to me of the ennobling effects of physical suffering! A soul without a body is as inhuman and horrible as a body without a soul – though

the latter is the rule and the former the exception. It is the body, as a rule, which flourishes exceedingly, which draws everything to itself, which usurps the predominant place and lives repulsively emancipated from the soul. A human being who is first of all an invalid is *all* body; therein lies his inhumanity and his debasement. In most cases he is little better than a carcass.[44]

Consider also W. Somerset Maugham's recollections of what he saw in hospital wards as he trained for the medical profession, and how they contrast with the generalities theodicies offer us. Maugham addresses the specific morally sufficient reason ascribed to God that we are discussing.

At that time (a time to most people of sufficient ease, when peace seemed certain and prosperity secure) there was a school of writers who enlarged upon the moral value of suffering. They claimed that it was salutary. They claimed that it increased sympathy and enhanced the sensibilities. They claimed that it opened to the spirit new avenues of beauty and enabled it to get into touch with the mystical kingdom of God. They claimed that it strengthened the character, purified it from its human grossness and brought to him who did not avoid but sought it a more perfect happiness . . . I set down in my notebooks, not once or twice, but in a dozen places, the facts that I had seen. I knew that suffering did not ennoble; it degraded. It made men selfish, mean, petty and suspicious. It absorbed them in small things. It did not make them more than men; it made them less than men; and I wrote ferociously that we learn resignation not by our own suffering, but by the suffering of others.[45]

The point of quoting Mann and Maugham is not, of course, to replace one generality by another, but to try to end the evasion in theodicies of the hard questions which need to be asked. It is such evasion that leads Rush Rhees to ask:

What is the value of suffering like that in *King Lear*?
What was the value of the *degradation* that belonged to the

sufferings in the concentration camps? When, for instance, a man is going to pieces morally and knows it. 'Joyful acceptance'??? . . . If I could put my questions more strongly, I should do so. For I think that religious apologists have generally been irresponsible and frivolous in writing about this matter. They have deceived both themselves and others by such phrases as 'suffering for Christ', 'joyful sacrifice', etc.[46]

There are, of course, examples of moral and religious survival from the midst of degradation. What made it possible for some can be found, for example, in the questions Primo Levi put to himself in the filth of the concentration camp, and in the answers he was able to give to them at that time.

Why should I wash? Would I be better off than I am? Would I please someone more? Would I live a day, an hour longer? I would probably live a shorter time, because to wash is an effort, a waste of energy and warmth . . . But later I understood . . . In this place it is practically pointless to wash every day in the turbid water of the filthy washbasins for purposes of cleanliness and health; but it is most important as a symptom of remaining vitality, and necessary as an instrument of moral survival.[47]

When Levi speaks here of washing in filthy water '*as an instrument* of moral survival', this is a far cry from the instrumentalism of theodicies. Levi is speaking of a moral necessity, not something which he would dream of citing as a *justification* of the horrendous evils which made it necessary. *That* latter suggestion has a horror of its own. Levi continues:

So we must certainly wash our faces without soap in dirty water and dry ourselves on our jackets. We must polish our shoes, not because the regulation states it, but for dignity and propriety. We must walk erect, without dragging our feet, not in homage to Prussian discipline but to remain alive, not to begin to die.[48]

When Rhees asks what good came out of the degradation of the concentration camps, he should not be taken as denying anything of which Levi speaks. Rhees is referring to people who were falling apart morally in horrific circumstances. Granting the survivals of the kind Levi speaks, would anyone in their right mind say that these showed that the Holocaust was justified? Those who survived it would not dream of speaking in this way. The most ardent supporter of the founding of the state of Israel would not speak in this way either.

I say that 'no one in their right mind' would speak in this way while knowing that many philosophical religious apologists do. But my language registers my amazement at that fact. I have found the same amazement among non-philosophically minded people, believers and non-believers alike, who have asked me why I'm writing about the problem of evil. When I outline the arguments I'm opposing the most common response is, 'Good God! They don't say that do they?' No doubt the response to this anecdote will be to say that I've obviously been talking to the philosophically unsophisticated. My reaction is one of relief to find that my reaction is not the oddity it appears to be in the eyes of many theodicists. My amazement is not captured by protests that may seem, at first, to be close to mine. For example, Roth notes that 'Eschatological hopes hinge on some version of an instrumental view of evil.'[49] His objection to such instrumentalism, however, misses the mark. Roth argues that it faces us with a dilemma. If we believe that God *had* to allow the actual evils which have occurred, we deny his freedom. If we grant God's freedom, on the other hand, who can deny that the alternative he has chosen has caused too much waste? Roth's conclusion is that we cannot 'rationally justify God's economy as purely cost-effective in pursuing goodness . . . such a wasteful God cannot be totally benevolent'.[50] Had God's economy been *less* wasteful, would it have been justified? One child's death was too high a price for Alyosha Karamazov.

Roth is using *the same* criterion as the theodicist in appealing to the fact that there has been too much waste. My objection is to this whole way of speaking; an objection to speaking of human beings as 'waste' in the economic sense. Roth says, 'Theodicy must reckon with God-as-economist, and the question posed above deals with God's waste.'[51] My objection is to thinking of God in this way at all. Philosophers of religion, for the most part, do not pause to consider whether *the logic* of economic management, the calculus of gain and loss, should be introduced into discussions of human suffering. Swinburne certainly does not. For him, the Holocaust simply presents another circumstance, albeit a challenging one, that requires him 'to argue . . . for the greater good which allowing . . . such horrible things to occur makes possible'.[52] His justification consists of, first, pointing to the centuries of freely made bad choices that led to the Holocaust. Second, he points to the opportunities for heroism it provided, and the way in which it has served to stir the consciences of so many. We, as human beings, of course, would never be justified in permitting the Holocaust to occur. Only God can be so, because his purposes are so much larger than ours. Overall, he sees that a world in which people have freedom to make decisions, good or bad, is better than a world devoid of such freedom.[53] To have such a world, even the Holocaust is not too high a price to pay.

It will be obvious from this section, and discussions in previous sections, why I am opposed to instrumentalism in ethics. To rescue sufferings from degradation by employing cost-benefit analysis, is like rescuing a prostitute from degradation by telling her to charge higher fees.[54] To the theodicist who argues in this way, refusal to do so will strike him as a refusal to argue, since he sees no alternative. He invites us to calculate our way down a road we shouldn't have turned into in the first place. This issue will reappear in the next section.

## 8. Evils and Bad Choices

A seventh morally sufficient reason we are offered to explain why God allows evils to exist is that many evils are the results of freely made bad decisions. As we saw in the last section, the justification consists of saying that a world with freedom to choose, is better than one devoid of that freedom. Further, it is good that we are given an opportunity to behave responsibly in facing the bad consequences of our bad decisions, thus having an opportunity to put things right.

To maintain such a view, the theodicist must adhere to a voluntarism which believes that, no matter what the circumstances, people retain the freedom to decide in one way rather than another. The problem is whether this is credible in all circumstances. Swinburne is aware of the problem:

> The theodicist says that a good God could allow men to do to each other the hurt they do, in order to allow them to be free and responsible. But against him the antitheodicist . . . says that in our world freedom and responsibility have gone too far – produced too much physical and mental hurt. God might well tolerate a boy hitting his younger brother, but not Belsen.[55]

Swinburne admits that it would be a telling criticism against his theodicy if there were many circumstances in which people are so crushed that it makes little sense to ascribe freedom of choice to them. After all, it is such freedom that is supposed to justify why God allows the evil consequences of bad choices to stand. But what if the evil can't be accounted for by such choices? Swinburne says that this question does not admit of a quick answer, but, as he looks around him, he does not think we can conclude that this is so. He gives two reasons for this view.

Swinburne's first answer is that there are situations where it is difficult to ascertain the facts. This is shown in his response to one of my examples which reads as follows. It concerns the fate of a jazz musician's wife as related by Billie Holiday.

> I can tell you about a big-name performer who had a habit and a bad one. There were times when he had it licked. And other times it licked him. It went around that way for years. He was well known, like me, which made it worse. He had bookings to make, contracts to fulfil. In the middle of one engagement he was about to crack up and go crazy because he had run out of stuff. There was no way in God's world that he could kick

cold turkey and make three shows a day. There wasn't a doctor in town who would be seen looking at him. His wife gets so scared that he'd kill himself that she tried to help him the only way she knew – by risking her own neck and trying to get him what he needed. She went out in the street like a pigeon, begging everyone she knew for help. Finally she found someone who sold her some stuff for an arm and a leg. It was just her luck to be carrying it back to her old man when she was arrested.

She was as innocent and clean as the day she was born. But she knew that if she tried to tell that to the cops it would only make her a 'pusher' under the law, liable for a good long time in jail. She thought if she told them she was a user, and took some of the stuff in her pocket to prove it, they might believe her, and feel sorry for her, go easy on her. And she could protect her man. So that's what she did. She used junk for the first time to prove to the law she wasn't a pusher. And that's the way she got hooked. She's rotting in jail, right now. Yes siree bob, life is just a bowl of cherries.[56]

Later, Billie Holiday sums up her own experience, 'If you expect nothing but trouble, maybe a few happy days will turn up. If you expect happy days, look out.'[57] Swinburne's reaction to the example marks something of a contrast:

I cannot see that the production of this example of evil settles anything. To start with, we just don't know some of the crucial factors involved – could the 'performer' have resisted his 'habit'? And could his wife have resisted the temptation to use 'junk' on occasions subsequent to the first? If the answers to these questions are yes, clearly the performer and his wife have some share in the responsibility for her troubles.[58]

The point of the example was not so much to settle anything, but to put forward the possibility that things could be as Billie Holiday says they were. Further, if Swinburne pleads ignorance of the facts, must he not admit that the answer to his question could be 'yes' or 'no'. In the case of the latter, what are the implications for his thesis concerning the connection between evils and bad choices? Would not one be that, as far as the performer's wife is concerned, the availability of free choice cannot be invoked to justify the evils which befell her? Curiously, Swinburne does not tell us whether he thinks those evils are justified by the free choices she certainly did make, such as the decision to try to help and to save her husband.

The real reason for Swinburne's appeal to ignorance has little to do with contingent ignorance about the facts. Rather, it has to do with our alleged necessary ignorance as to whether people are free to resist in horrendous circumstances, until science and philosophy solve the free-will problem. When I said that, in individual cases, God seemed to have sent too much suffering, and freedom to choose is crushed, Swinburne replied:

> which one? presumably one who has collapsed morally under the suffering – God 'has gone too far for him'. But that follows only if we know that he couldn't help collapsing, that he hasn't given in to forces which he could have resisted – and that's just what we don't know until philosophers and scientists together have solved the free will problem.[59]

This answer simply will not do. Our common understanding of when people's burdens have been too great for them, is not dependent on scientific or philosophical theories. It comes from informal standards of what people are capable of which play a crucial role in the making of such judgements as, 'He could have resisted', 'He couldn't have resisted', 'He was crushed, and didn't stand a chance' and 'It's hard to say whether he could have resisted or not.' What Swinburne does is to give the latter a metaphysical status as a general answer to a question that, in practice, admits of many answers, including the one Swinburne sublimes. Some of the circumstances about which we are asked to judge may be such that it is impossible to imagine anyone *not* being crushed by them. Consider the following:

For six years the captured Gallic general Vercengetorix was kept shackled, solitary, in total darkness, except on one day of each year when he was brought out in his chains and exhibited for the scorn and ridicule of the Roman mob. Do you honestly think *anybody* would be ennobled by that? Or: if he 'joyfully accepted it' how long would he keep this up – remember that he never spoke to anyone from one year's end to the other. Take any saint you like and try to imagine it.[60]

Behind Swinburne's reluctance to concede that there are such situations is his voluntarism with respect to ethics. A picture begins to emerge in which people are free to make good or bad decisions. Responsible people make the former, while irresponsible people make the latter. Consequences can be pretty bad, but, then, they are the result of bad decisions. It is good that irresponsible people should face up to the consequences of their bad actions, because that gives them the opportunity of putting things right, including changing the direction of their character development. Such a world is one that is overall better than one without these features.

The irony in Swinburne's voluntaristic picture is that it is a perfect picture of Christianity's conception of the worst of all sins – the sin of pride. Rhees comments on the misplaced confidence it exhibits: ' "They could have refused." Could they? ("We who have not fallen" – the fall that there is in *that*. Circumstances by which people are defeated.)'[61]

Even when theodicies recognize that hard decisions have to be made, it is always with a view to claiming that it is just such decisions we need in order to have the moral fibre our characters need. Recall again Sophie's exclamation at the terrible decision she was forced to make: *'Ich kann nicht wählen!'*

As we saw at the end of the previous section, Swinburne actually tried to justify God's allowing the Holocaust to occur partly in terms of the bad decisions that led to it. We saw the same attempt in his reaction to Billie Holiday's story. At least, in the latter case, the decisions he appealed to were taken by people directly involved in the story she told. But, on his own account, bad decisions leading to the Holocaust stretch over centuries. But what have these to do with the victims of the Holocaust? The decisions referred to were the decisions of others, not their own! Some of the most momentous decisions, for example, to implement 'the final solution', were taken in their time. What have these to do with the victims of that solution? No doubt some made bad decisions to stay when they could have fled? What is that supposed to justify? Some made decisions to stay with others, knowing what this meant. Does that justify what happened to them?

To turn from the unease these questions cause, the theodicist turns from the particular to the general, and appeals to the overall goodness of a world in which free decision is possible, and in which their consequences are the price, often a high price, that has to be paid for it.

For reasons that are obvious by now, this appeal to a higher consequentialism has to be resisted. It corrupts central moral and religious concepts, and vulgarizes human relationships. Swinburne, however, reacts to what he sees as an irrational attempt to stop enquiry taking its natural course:

> It is indeed often the case in life that we have to make decisions in the light of the evidence as we have it and of the moral judgements which we are initially inclined to make. There is often no time to consider the moral issues further, for if we did we should fail to take the action which we ought morally to take instantly. Here indeed delay is the sign of a corrupt mind. But that is not our situation today. We are not delaying essential action by insisting on moral theorizing. We are doing philosophy. And, when we are doing philosophy and are justified in doing so (as I hope that we are now), it is *never* a 'sign of a corrupt mind' to be open-minded about things.[62]

Swinburne is confusing open-mindedness with a priori consequentialism. The open-mindedness, within those narrow parameters, is simply the readiness to weigh the pros and cons concerning what the consequences are. Where the open-mindedness is missing is in the unreadiness to consider the conceptual inadequacies of consequentialism. There is an unreadiness to consider examples where the moral perspective involved is one which says that doing, or allowing, certain evils for the sake of a greater good is ruled out.

I do not deny Swinburne's observation that there are situations in which moral judgements have been hasty. Why does Swinburne give no attention to situations where they have not? I do not deny that there are situations in which initial moral judgements are revised. Why does Swinburne pay no attention to situations where they are not? On whose side is the a priori assumption and the lack of open-mindedness? Emphasizing certainty in one context (we were too hasty), Swinburne denies its logical possibility in another. This tendency will reappear in the next morally sufficient reason to be discussed.

## 9. *Things are Not as Bad as They Seem*

An eighth morally sufficient reason ascribed to God to explain why evils are allowed to exist is that the evils that God does allow are not as bad as they seem to us. To have its effect, this morally sufficient reason should not be thought of as standing alone, but as one of a cluster including those we have already discussed.

Faced by horrendous evils, the theodicist asks us not to be too hasty in our judgements. For example, Swinburne argues, 'if we saw a man sawing off another's leg . . . our initial moral indignations might have been quite misplaced – maybe the man was doing his utmost to save another's life, removing a wounded leg in the absence of anaesthetics'.[63] Swinburne's advice to suspend judgement depends on the presence of unfavourable circumstances for judgement. One might see the event through a window, not knowing what was happening. But Swinburne's full example depends on his invoking a certainty, that a doctor was trying to save a patient's life. He cannot, therefore, rule out examples where the certainty goes in the opposite direction. If we saw a doctor sawing off a patient's leg, our initial admiring

assumption that he is trying to save a patient's life without anaes-
thetic may prove to be quite mistaken. The doctor is in the service of the patient's captors, who have ordered his mutilation.[64]

Theodicies cannot rely on a one-sided diet of examples. They
argue that things are not as bad as they seem. The irony comes in
the realization that they can be, and can be even worse.

There are circumstances in which we would not know what it
would mean to say that things may be other than they are. Not
even God could persuade us otherwise in using this possibility to
explain why he does not intervene to rescue the situation.
According to Swinburne, God

> may know that the suffering that A will cause B is not nearly
> as great as B's screams might suggest to us and will provide
> (unknown to us) an opportunity to C to help B recover and
> will thus give C a deep responsibility which he would not
> otherwise have. God may very well have reason for allowing
> particular evils which it is our bounden duty to attempt to stop
> at all costs simply because he knows so much more about them
> than we do.[65]

There are screams and screams. In some cases, it would be
meaningless to think that the evil is not as bad as the screams suggest. Just try applying Swinburne's argument for suspended
judgement to the Holocaust.

## 10. God Never Sends Us Unlimited Suffering

A ninth morally sufficient reason ascribed to God to explain why
he allows evils to exist is that God does this for good reasons, and
among them is that he never allows suffering to be unlimited.

Swinburne describes '[t]his world-order [as] a very dangerous
and costly experiment'.[66] As we have seen, it is difficult to make
sense of God's finishing school for the development of human
character. Ever since our discussion of the development of character and moral responsibility, we have noted a fatal instrumentalism that runs through it. We can see this instrumentalism at

work in the account Swinburne gives of why God allows human beings to harm each other: 'Only agents who can do this have real responsibility.'[67] Nevertheless, Swinburne wants to avoid the following objection: 'It would, I believe we would all judge, be morally wrong for a very powerful being to give *limitless* power to one agent to hurt another.'[68] But that is exactly what God does not do. He does not allow limitless suffering.

> Giving to agents the power to kill is giving vast power of a qualitatively different kind from other power: but it involves the end of experience. It is very different from a power to produce endless suffering.[69]

Swinburne is treating death as a limit. Since we are all subject to this limit, it seems to follow that we cannot experience limitless suffering. He combines this point with the claim that people can only stand a certain amount of suffering at any given time.

> There are limits to the amount and degree of evil which are possible in our world. Thus there are limits to the amount of pain which a person can suffer – persons live in our world only so many years and the amount which they can suffer at any given time (if mental goings-on are in any way correlated with bodily ones) is limited by their physiology . . . So the theodicist can certainly claim that a good God stops too much suffering – it is just that he and his opponent draw the line in different places.[70]

Swinburne seems to be commending God for something, but it is difficult to understand what for exactly. Swinburne and I may disagree about whether anyone is visited by too much suffering, but, in any case, Swinburne wants to distinguish between this and the notion of limitless suffering. Even if Swinburne agreed that a given person, who dies, was crushed by circumstances, he would not say that the person had suffered unlimited suffering. The person died, the sufferings have a limit, therefore they cannot be called 'unlimited'. Swinburne's argument seems to amount to this: God cannot send unlimited suffering to anyone, since there is a limit to what anyone can stand.

What exactly has God not done? Would it be odd if someone were to say of a torturer, who had inflicted limitless, endless sufferings on his victim, that this could not be so because his victim died? For Swinburne, the proposition, 'Endless sufferings were inflicted on him until he died', expresses a contradiction. Yet, what is said seems perfectly intelligible. It only seems otherwise to us if we succumb to Swinburne's understanding of 'limitless'.

Swinburne's use of 'limitless' seems to be borrowed from arithmetic. The infinite series 2, 4, 6, 8 . . . has no end, no limit, because it makes no sense to speak of the last number in the series. The infinity of such a series has to do with its grammar, not with its length. A written finite series may be longer, for example, 2, 4, 6, 8, 10, 12. The other series is infinite, meaning that the instruction '+ 2' can always be obeyed with respect to it. To say that the length of a piece of wood can be divided to infinity is to say, for example, that the instruction '÷ 2' can always be obeyed. It does not follow at all, of course, that the piece of wood has an infinite number of parts, for it does not make sense to speak of dividing it, physically, to infinity. Imagine, for some reason, that I am annoyed at the fact that someone has chopped up the piece of wood. Would it be of any comfort if someone were to reply, 'Well, at least it wasn't chopped up to infinity'? It would not, for the simple reason that in order to be comforted thus, what did not happen must have been a possibility. But it does not make sense to speak of the wood being chopped up to infinity. So what substance does the comfort have?

It looks as though Swinburne is comforting us with the thought that a good God stops limitless suffering. But this reassurance only has substance if the notion of 'limitless suffering' makes sense. I can, in the abstract, for any number of sores mentioned, keep obeying the instruction '+ 2'. But I cannot say this of the actual sores from which Job suffered. What would it mean if a comforter were to say to Job, 'It could have been worse. You could have always suffered from more'? But that is not true. As

Swinburne recognizes, there is a physical limit to human suffering. What Swinburne does *not* see, is that since the abstract 'X sores + 2 to infinity' has no application or sense in relation to human suffering, this can be no reason for calling God good. He cannot be called good for not doing something it makes no sense to speak of anyone doing in the first place.

When we turn from the inappropriate arithmetical analogy to the actual sufferings of human beings, people may still speak, without confusion, of the endless pains we bear, and of the limitless troubles that crushed a person in the end.

In God's finishing school, everyone is finished in one way or another. Either, if certain theodicists are to be believed, they are well finished, mature, responsible, shaped by surviving the obstacle course, or they are finished off completely by it, as very many obviously are, whether it's God's fault or not. If the 'finishing off' were done by someone who is solely the bringer of death, then, in certain circumstances, he could be described as the bringer of welcome release. But this is not true of the God of theodicies or defences. Since the bringer of death is also the bringer of affliction, the one who devised the whole fiendish obstacle course, we cannot even attribute to him the compassion with which a dog may be put out of its misery. As each candidate fails to make the grade, it is more appropriate to say, with Thomas Hardy, that thus God has ended his play. We should hurry from this scene.

## 11. Compensation or Redemption After Death

A tenth and final morally sufficient reason ascribed to God to explain why he allows evils is that after the travails of this life are over God will either compensate us for, or in some way redeem, all the evils we have suffered in this life.

When we look back at the features of human life we have mentioned in discussing the nine other morally sufficient reasons ascribed to God, the radical contingencies, the vast evils in evidence, the lack of correlation between evil, virtue and suffering, can we really sustain the idea of the kind of order and rationale that theodicists invite us to find there? Our discussions give us reason to say that we cannot. Theodicists need to remember again that 'When Satan said that dominion over this world had been left to him, Jesus did not contradict him.'[71]

Theodicies are marked by their ideas of order, optimism and progress. The world is presented as a God-given setting in which human beings are given an opportunity to exercise rational choices that mould their character, and determine the kind of people they are to become. As I have tried to show, this is neither a world we know or live in. If moral concepts admitted of the analyses given of them by many theodicists, the world would be even worse than it is. Our relationships with others, with all their joys and sorrows, are a better story than their instrumentalism would make it. No great literature or music could emanate from the narrow parameters of the theodicist's world.

When I say that ours is a world in which disasters of natural or moral kinds strike without rhyme or reason; where, if much can be done to influence character, there is far more over which we have no control; where character lies as much, if not more, in reacting to the unavoidable, than with choosing between rational alternatives; some theodicists look at me with amazement, and I look back amazed that they should do so. I do not know what it would mean to speak of life, as human life at all, without the features of it which I have mentioned. To think that, at our best, we would behave according to theodicy's ideal, is to envisage us as *less* than human. Hardy refers to such ideas of rational progress at the close of *Tess of the D'Urbervilles*, and contrasts them with the contingencies by which his 'pure woman' has ended up a murderess:

Nature does not often say 'See!' to her poor creature when seeing can lead to happy doing; or reply 'Here!' to a body's cry of 'Where?' till the hide-and-seek has become an irksome, outworn game. We may wonder whether at the acme and summit of the human progress these anachronisms will be corrected by a finer intuition, a closer interaction of the social machinery than that which now jolts us round and along; but such completeness is not to be prophesied, or even conceived as possible.[72]

The nine objections I have considered should help us to resist secular and religious attempts at rationalizing human life. As Hardy says, 'why so often the coarse appropriates the finer . . . the wrong man the woman, the wrong woman the man, many thousand years of analytical philosophy have failed to explain to our sense of order'.[73] Hardy, of course, is not looking for this explanation, and notes that the trouble comes from extending a proper sense of order to contexts where it simply does not apply. He would have agreed with the comments of one of Beckett's characters, 'you're on earth, there's no cure for that'.[74]

In one sense, our theodicists agree. With one voice, joined by the framers of defences, they say, 'There's *got* to be more than this.' They do not settle for life. They want more of it. What we seldom find, however, is very much discussion of the implications of their reactions for their own theodicies and defences. At best, it would make curious reading. Don't forget all the preamble about God's plan for human beings, the divinely designed moral obstacle course for the development of human character. Don't forget all the talk about how we are created immature, to be developed during life's trial in the direction of perfection. If we don't forget all this, the question facing such a scenario is obvious: what went wrong? The site of the obstacle course is strewn with corpses and casualties, and, even among those who cross the line, no one has a perfect score. What was all this for? Anyone who bought this packet surely has an obvious claim for compensation. Theodicists agree. There *must* be something more than life. And, suddenly, like the small print in advertisement material, an addendum is added to the story: there's a second instalment – we are to live again after death.

What does this addendum tell us about the moral obstacle course? Not that it was tried and found wanting, since God does not try out a game on players who are independent of it. He created both game and players. So if we speak the language of theodicy, God invents a test for human life that he knows will

not work. Or, if the shadow of determinism threatens, God takes
a risk in creating a game that, after a very short time, he knows is
not going to work. He had standards the plan was meant to fulfil,
but God didn't have to wait for Hick to come along to tell him,
'Clearly the enormous majority of men and women die without
reaching such levels.'[75] Things didn't look too good from the
start. But God ploughed on. What must he have been thinking
about? How did he convince the investors in the plan, faced, as
they were, with 'the slaughter-bench at which the happiness of
peoples, the wisdom of states, and the virtue of individuals have
been sacrificed'?[76] Well, I suppose he inspired some to write
theodicies on his behalf, but, while the products satisfied some,
they horrified far more. But even his apologists should spend
*some* time wondering about the point of the plan in the first
place, for they know, some later than others, that the plan for
development in life simply does not work in the very life it was
supposed to be designed for. We find Davis admitting from the
outset that, for him, the problem of evil 'can only be solved . . .
from a perspective that makes use of Christian doctrine, especially Christian soteriology and eschatology'.[77] Hick admits,
'Without such an eschatological fulfilment, this theodicy would
collapse.'[78] One of the differences between Swinburne's early
and later views is the decreased optimism in the latter, given his
recognition that God's experiment has been costly indeed, and
that life after death has to answer many unanswered questions as
death, for many, brings that experiment to a merciful end. All in
all, then, a huge apologetic weight is placed on the hope of survival after death.

This is not the place for a full-scale discussion of the intelligibility of the notion of life after death, and the issue of whether it
is to be identified with the notion of eternal life.[79] It is a huge
negation of the hopes I have mentioned, of course, if the notion
is unintelligible. I am going to concentrate on questions that raise
that issue, but in relation to the nine objections that have already
emerged in our discussion. Central to my argument is the problematic task of showing the sense in which life after death is
meant to be some kind of solution to the unfinished business left

on life's shores by theodicies and defences. Two difficulties are involved in the theodicies and defences on offer: one involves the nature of the compensation or redemption that is supposed to occur after death; the second involves the nature of the creatures, after death, to whom all this is supposed to occur. But I shall preface these discussions with the admission that I do not think that the notion of life after death does make sense. This issue will return in Part II of this book. For now, as no more than a prefatory remark, I want to endorse the following remarks by Rhees:

> 'There can be nothing after death' is wrong in one obvious sense, of course; for all sorts of things will still go on after I am dead. People will try to clean up the mess I have left behind, etc.
>
> A rather stupid theology student once asked me, 'What do you think is going to happen to you when you die?' In one sense certainly nothing will 'happen to me' after I have died – whatever may happen to my body. If I could suffer or be inspired I should not be dead. 'I won't know anything after I am dead' can be confusing if it be thought of as parallel to 'when I am asleep' or 'when I am unconscious' – as though 'when I am dead' meant 'when I am in a certain state' – as 'when I am unconscious'. I shall not be in any sort of state. I shall not be at all.[80]

My endorsement of these remarks is important, otherwise, the remainder of my discussion will give the impression that I am allowing, after all, the possibility of survival after death in being prepared to ask questions about who the survivors are, how they are to be compensated or redeemed, etc. My questions are meant to be indications of logical difficulties *within* the general charge of unintelligibility.

Given the nature of many of the evils human beings undergo, it would make little sense to speak of compensations for them after death. It does not even make sense to speak of compensation, in this life, with respect to many of our losses – the loss of a child, the end of a friendship, various forms of injustice which

create harm, a harm done to someone who dies before any resti-
tution can be made and so on. In some of these circumstances,
the law decrees financial compensation, but one almost always
hears those who receive it say, 'Nothing, of course, can compensate for . . .' Faced with this undeniable fact, the picture cannot
change by changing the landscape from an earthly to a heavenly
one. The loss is a human loss, and nothing from an allegedly different realm can compensate for *that*. It is no surprise whatever,
therefore, to find theodicists and framers of defences retreating
into ignorance when asked *how* human sorrows are to be compensated or redeemed. Hick, for example, says that

> the very fact that we cannot see how the extent of evil in the
> course of the world is going to be engulfed by the limitlessly
> good end that is gradually being achieved is itself a necessary
> aspect of the cognitive distance that creates our freedom in
> relation to God.[81]

A similar reaction is made by Davis in face of the paucity of
details regarding how our evils are to be redeemed: 'So the fact
that there are mysteries in theodicy and that many of the relevant
truths are quite beyond our ken is not a last-ditch attempt to save
a theology from criticism but rather exactly what that theology
should lead us to expect.'[82]

Even taking these responses at their word, they can still be
accused of confusing religious mysteries, whose *positive* contents
are meant to be food for the faithful, with epistemological mysteries, which offer at best an empty space, a vacuity where one
would expect religious or theological vision. If, after travelling
the long road, with all the evils we have noted hitherto, having
been told that however bad it gets, it is all for some greater glory,
we ask for some indication of what this glory is, are we really to
believe that the only resource within religion, is the answer, 'We
don't really know'? This may not be an attempt to evade criticism, but it is surely an indication of the erosion of religious
discourse that Beckett satirizes so brilliantly. Imagine, in the
following excerpt, the prayer being directed for some revelation

regarding the point of God's costly experiment with human beings:

| | |
|---|---|
| *Vladimir*: | Let's wait until we know exactly where we stand. |
| *Estragon*: | On the other hand it might be better to strike the iron before it freezes. |
| *Vladimir*: | I'm curious to hear what he has to offer. Then we'll take it or leave it. |
| *Estragon*: | What exactly did we ask him for? |
| *Vladimir*: | Oh . . . nothing very definite. |
| *Estragon*: | A kind of prayer. |
| *Vladimir*: | Precisely. |
| *Estragon*: | A vague supplication. |
| *Vladimir*: | Exactly. |
| *Estragon*: | And what did he reply? |
| *Vladimir*: | That he'd see.[83] |

As though difficulties concerning compensation were not enough, we have to ask to whom these indescribable compensations or redemptions are supposed to happen? Who are the creatures who are said to survive death? If there is to be continuity with those human beings who have run the obstacle race, those who survive, to reap the rewards at last, *must* be human beings. But there are severe logical objections to what we are told by theodicists and defenders, which make it impossible to see how this can be so.

For Hick, the life after death is one of continued development. It is a development, however, of a rather special kind, since it is not the survival after death of 'the present conscious self that lives again but a deeper element of our nature, which is expressed in a new personality each time'[84] through many lives. Hick would not be worried, as Davis is, that these speculations are not rooted in the Bible. He'd respond:

Frankly, I don't mind if it's unbiblical. To my mind the biblical eschatology, in for example the Book of Revelation, is itself speculative, as indeed are all conceptions of the final end. The question is, what speculation seems most probable?[85]

This raises the question of whether what we find in the Bible is speculation *about* religion, or religious viewpoints which we either accept or reject. At *that* level, is 'the language concerning the end' Hick offers us an *advance* on the language of the Bible? Is it not rather an example of an arbitrary attempt to extend conceptions of eschatology, such as the attempts we discussed in the second section of Chapter 1? The answer to that question is a matter of *religious* judgement.

We are still left with the question of what development *means* after death. If it is to be related to that development which, according to Hick, human lives are for, it must be a matter of the development of men, women and children, fathers and mothers, brothers and sisters, friends, lovers, neighbours and so on. After all, it is *these* people who have suffered. But if these relationships are to develop, I do not see how they can do so in relation to my parents, unless I am their son (all the things I now wish I'd said, but didn't); I do not see how they can do so in my relation to my wife, unless I am her husband; in relation to my children, unless I am their father; in relation to my lover, unless I am her lover; in relation to my neighbours, unless I am their neighbour. Yet, no one pretends that the contexts in which these relationships *have their sense* survive death. This logical issue cannot be avoided. No wonder the apologists plead ignorance.

As we have seen, Hick says that what survives is not ourselves, as we know ourselves now, 'but a deeper element of our nature'. It seems that human life is no more than the occasion for the development of this 'deeper element' as will be the successive lives it will live. In that case 'the deeper element' (whatever that means) is not a human being. So all the suffering was for something 'not human' after all, despite the fact that the whole rationale of Hick's theodicy is premised on the assumption that the development of human beings is the point of the story. Again, as Rhees shows, the logic of the situation cannot be evaded by appeals to ignorance.

If you try to think of an individual as something abstracted from the process of generation and flourishing and perishing, then there is the question of whether you are thinking of anything at all. If I say my father survives, I mean someone who had that history, who is historical in that sense. And so I mean too, someone who died. If I referred to some 'part' of him that did not die, those could not have any characteristic I could recognize. (It would not be something that came to be and matured and declined and got sleepy or offended or happy, as everything else that I know about him did.) It would not be something that had *parents*, for instance; that is important.[86]

Hick's theodicy, for all its emphasis on human beings, does not treat *human life* seriously enough. But does Davis fare any better? Sceptical of Hick's emphasis on our moral development after death, Davis says, 'the evidence of how people behave here and now does not give me much hope that the human race will gradually improve till all are the God-conscious "persons" God intended'.[87] Davis's own view is that 'at a decisive point in history God will seize the initiative and will give those who say yes to him a new "heart of flesh" (Ezek. 11: 19-20). God will, in short, suddenly transform us into "new persons" '.[88] I agree that is pretty short. In fact, it's downright magical. So short that 'transform' has been robbed of content. What is the relation of the transformation to the long journey through God's moral obstacle course? Failing an answer, what does 'transformation' come to?

Similarly, what is the relation of the new persons after death to those familiar folk Rhees talked of, part of whose history is that they have died, been burned or cremated? Obviously the resurrected body will be a different one. Davis may think that God can then provide it with the right memories, but that is something not even God can do. Memories are not self-authenticating mental images. I can have images of myself walking on the pier at Mumbles or San Clemente, but unless I *did* walk on those piers, those images, logically, cannot be memories. Whatever new bodies God creates, they would not be us. As Rhees said – they

wouldn't have parents, even if other new bodies had images of
having them, and that is important.

Theodicists and defenders may think I am too fussy about the
details, but the trouble is precisely the fact that they are not. They
do not, I repeat, treat human life seriously enough.

In *Waiting for Godot*, the tramps, to relieve their boredom
suddenly consider the possibility of repentance.

| | |
|---|---|
| *Vladimir*: | Suppose we repented. |
| *Estragon*: | Repented what? |
| *Vladimir*: | Oh . . . (*He reflects*) We wouldn't have to go into details. |

But I'm afraid we do. Take away the surroundings, take away the
details, and one would be left with nothing. One cannot strip
'repentance' of its surroundings and call whatever remains
'repentance' all the same. That is the point of Beckett's conceptual joke and, at the same time, an exposure of the etherealiza-
tion of religious language. Talk of a deceptively solid 'new body'
after death does not escape the charge. Stripped of all its surroundings the new body cannot be myself, my father, my friend
– cannot be any human being, in fact.

As in Hick's case, so in Davis's, if these other creatures cannot
be 'us', how are they related to our long human story, one which
has witnessed so many evils for which compensation or redemption was promised? I do not believe in these new creatures for a
moment, but supposing I did. When all is said and done, our
story is offered another, of a world to come, occupied by creatures who are not human beings. Then I would ask, What do
they know about us?

### Notes

1 Richard Swinburne, *Providence and the Problem of Evil*, Oxford:
  Clarendon Press 1998, p. 23.
2 Swinburne, *Providence*, p. xiii.
3 Richard Swinburne, 'The Problem of Evil' in Stuart Brown (ed.), *Reason
  and Religion*, Ithaca: Cornell University Press 1977, p. 100.

4 D. Z. Phillips, 'The Problem of Evil' in Brown, *Reason and Religion*, p. 118.

5 Brian Davies, *An Introduction to the Philosophy of Religion*, Oxford: Oxford University Press, new edition 1993, p. 38.

6 Stephen T. Davis, 'Rejoinder' in Stephen T. Davis (ed.), *Encountering Evil*, Louisville: Westminster John Knox Press 2001, p. 103.

7 Richard Swinburne, 'Postscript' in Brown, *Reason and Religion*, p. 129.

8 Ludwig Wittgenstein, *Culture and Value*, Oxford: Blackwell 1980, p. 29.

9 I make this qualification given the reaction of my fellow symposiasts to my previous attempt to enumerate the bee-stings. John K. Roth identified himself with my criticisms, saying, 'Phillips inclines to agree with me that none of them could be completely satisfactory' ('Critique of D. Z. Phillips' in Davis, *Encountering Evil*, p. 171). David Ray Griffin also agreed with the criticisms of traditional theodicies, but exempted Process theology from them ('Critique of D. Z. Phillips', in Davis, *Encountering Evil*, p. 164). Stephen T. Davis was untouched by the bee-stings, saying, 'Most of them sound like powerful arguments against somebody (maybe Hick or Swinburne), but not me' ('Critique of D. Z. Phillips' in Davis, *Encountering Evil*, p. 169). John Hick identified the 'somebody' with Swinburne, but absolved himself, 'Most of Phillips's "bee-stings" are directed against this theodicy; and I have also criticized it for much the same reasons. In doing so I also agree with Phillips in rejecting Swinburne's concept of God' ('Critique of D. Z. Phillips' in Davis, *Encountering Evil*, p. 162). From my point of view, it is encouraging to see bee-stings being recognized in the same theodicies and defences, at least.

10 J. L. Mackie, 'Evil and Omnipotence' in Marilyn McCord Adams and Robert Merrihew Adams (eds), *The Problem of Evil*, Oxford: Oxford University Press 1990, pp. 29–30.

11 Swinburne, *Providence*, p. 8.

12 This suggestion was put to me by Joseph L. Cowan.

13 See Swinburne, *Providence*, pp. 138–9 and 'The Problem of Evil', p. 90.

14 John Hick, 'Remarks' in Brown, *Reason and Religion*, p. 123.

15 John Hick, *Philosophy of Religion*, third edition, Englewood Cliffs: Prentice-Hall 1983, p. 41. Unfortunately, this early insight does not prevent Hick from thinking later that 'God could, without logical contradiction, have created humans as wholly good, free beings' (John Hick, 'An Irenaean Theodicy' in Davis, *Encountering Evil*, p. 43). There is quite a different question philosophers may want to ask, namely, whether the world would be a better one if human beings were free of conceptions of 'God' and 'sin'. Wittgenstein says that certain religious pictures have caused great harm. It is obvious from my criticisms that I

think this is true of theodicies. My claim, however, is that theodicies and defences distort certain fundamental religious beliefs to which they seek to give expression.

16 I am indebted for this argument to Ben Tilghman's paper, 'Free Will Defences and Foundationalism' in John H. Whittaker (ed.), *The Possibilities of Sense*, Basingstoke: Palgrave 2002.

This 'short way' should not be taken as a criticism of the possibility of feeling gratitude for life as a whole, or as a denial that people may be driven to say that it had been better had they never been born. My argument is that these real issues are being distorted in a metaphysical context such as the one being discussed.

17 W. Somerset Maugham, *The Summing Up*, Collected Edition. London 1948, p. 259.

18 In Adams and Adams, *The Problem of Evil*, p. 47.

19 Adams and Adams, *The Problem of Evil*, p. 4.

20 Marilyn McCord Adams, *Horrendous Evils and the Goodness of God*, Ithaca: Cornell University Press 1999, p. 25. For Plantinga's admission see his 'Self-Profile' in James E. Tomberlin and Peter Van Inwagen (eds), *Alvin Plantinga*, Dordrecht: D. Reidel 1985, pp. 34–5.

21 Plantinga, 'Epistemic Probability and Evil', p. 558.

22 See Swinburne, *Providence*, p. 15, fn. 8.

23 Swinburne, *Providence*, Chapter 5. See also Chapter 8, p. 143 f.

24 This objection was put to me by H. D. Lewis in the Swinburne–Phillips symposium in Brown, *Reason and Religion*.

25 Swinburne, 'The Problem of Evil', pp. 87–8.

26 Swinburne, *Providence*, p. 168.

27 Swinburne, 'The Problem of Evil', p. 100.

28 I wish I could say these views are purely theoretical, but I know a mother who was told that her extremely deformed child, now living a less than animal existence in his forties, had been given to her to make her an exceptional parent.

29 Swinburne, 'The Problem of Evil', p. 100.

30 Swinburne, *Providence*, p. 161.

31 Swinburne, 'The Problem of Evil', pp. 96–7.

32 Søren Kierkegaard, *Purity of Heart*, New York: Harper & Row 1956, p. 81.

33 Swinburne, 'The Problem of Evil', p. 98.

34 Swinburne, 'The Problem of Evil', pp. 90–1.

35 Swinburne, *Providence*, p. 161.

36 Hume, *Dialogues Concerning Natural Religion*, ed. N. Kemp Smith, New York: Bobbs-Merrill 1947, Part V.

37 Jonathan Swift, *The Complete Poems*, London: Penguin 1983, p. 486.

38 Leo Tolstoy, *The Death of Ivan Ilyich and Other Stories*, Signet Classic, New American Library 1960, p. 97.

39 Terrence Des Pres, *The Survivor*, New York: Oxford University Press 1976, p. 57.

40 Des Pres, *The Survivor*, pp. 59–60.

41 Swinburne, *Providence*, p. 169.

42 Hick, 'An Irenaean Theodicy', p. 43.

43 Hick, 'An Irenaean Theodicy', p. 43.

44 Thomas Mann, *The Magic Mountain*, Harmondsworth: Penguin Books 1965, pp. 98–100.

45 Maugham, *The Summing Up*, p. 62.

46 Rush Rhees, 'Suffering' in Rush Rhees, *On Religion and Philosophy*, ed. D. Z. Phillips, assisted by Mario von der Ruhr, Cambridge: Cambridge University Press 1997, p. 304.

47 Primo Levi, *Survival in Auschwitz*, New York: Collier 1969, p. 35.

48 Levi, *Survival in Auschwitz*, p. 36.

49 John K. Roth, 'A Theodicy of Protest' in Davis, *Encountering Evil*, p. 5.

50 Roth, 'A Theodicy of Protest', p. 7.

51 Roth, 'A Theodicy of Protest', p. 7.

52 Swinburne, *Providence*, p. 107.

53 Swinburne, *Providence*, p. 151. See also Chapter 12.

54 This analogy was suggested to me by remarks of Simone Weil. See 'Human Personality' in *Selected Essays 1934–45*, ed. Richard Rees, London: Oxford University Press 1962, p. 18.

55 Swinburne, 'The Problem of Evil', p. 89.

56 Billie Holiday, with William Dufty, *Lady Sings the Blues*, London: Abacus, Sphere Books 1975, pp. 183–4.

57 Holiday, *Lady Sings the Blues*, p. 187.

58 Swinburne, 'Postscript', p. 129.

59 Swinburne, 'Postscript', p. 132.

60 Rhees, 'Suffering', p. 304.

61 Rhees, 'Difficulties of belief', in Rhees, *On Religion and Philosophy*, p. 149.

62 Swinburne, 'Postscript', p. 130.

63 Swinburne, 'Postscript', pp. 130–1.

64 For an account of the co-operation of doctors in the Holocaust see Robert Jay Lifton, 'This World Is Not This World' in John K. Roth and Michael Berenbaum (eds), *Holocaust: Religious and Philosophical Implications*, New York: Paragon 1989.

65 Swinburne, 'The Problem of Evil', p. 92.

66 Swinburne, *Providence*, p. 249.

67 Swinburne, *Providence*, p. 213.

68 Swinburne, *Providence*, p. 213.

69 Swinburne, *Providence*, pp. 213–4.

70 Swinburne, 'The Problem of Evil', pp. 89–90.

71 Rhees, 'Natural Theology', in Rhees, *On Religion and Philosophy*, p. 37.

72  Thomas Hardy, *Tess of the D'Urbervilles*, London 1912.

73  Hardy, *Tess of the D'Urbervilles*, p. 91.

74  Samuel Beckett, *Endgame*, London: Faber and Faber 1976, p. 44.

75  Hick, 'An Irenaean Theodicy', p. 51.

76  G. W. F. Hegel, *Reason in History*, Indianapolis: Bobbs-Merrill 1953, p. 27.

77  Stephen T. Davis, 'Free Will and Evil' in Davis, *Encountering Evil*, p. 73.

78  Hick, 'An Irenaean Theodicy', p. 51.

79  For my discussion of these issues see my *Death and Immortality*, London: Macmillan 1970, and the chapter on Feuerbach in my *Religion and the Hermeneutics of Contemplation*, Cambridge: Cambridge University Press 2001.

80  Rush Rhees, 'Death and Immortality' in Rhees, *On Religion and Philosophy*, p. 206. These remarks by Rhees are not a prelude to dismissing such notions as 'eternal life' or 'the Last Judgement'. On the contrary, he proceeds to elucidate the sense of these notions, in one of the finest essays on the subject since Kierkegaard.

81  Hick, 'Rejoinder' in Davis, *Encountering Evil*, p. 69.

82  Davis, 'Free Will and Evil', in Davis, *Encountering Evil*, p. 88.

83  Samuel Beckett, *Waiting for Godot*, London: Faber and Faber 1977.

84  Hick, 'Rejoinder' in Davis, *Encountering Evil*, p. 71.

85  Hick, 'Rejoinder', pp. 68–9.

86  Rhees, 'Death and Immortality', pp. 209–10.

87  Davis, 'Critique of John Hick' in Davis, *Encountering Evil*, p. 59.

88  Davis, 'Critique of Hick', p. 59.

# 4

# The Free-Will Defence

## 1. Free Will and the Logical Problem of Evil

It would be a mistake to think that we arrive at a consideration of the free-will defence only at this stage of the book. It has been with us in different ways, some more explicit than others, from its outset. It would be surprising if it were otherwise, since it is one of the main themes of theodicies. Alvin Plantinga has expressed the essence of the defence as follows:

> A world containing creatures who are sometimes significantly free (and freely perform more good than evil actions) is more valuable, all else being equal, than a world containing no free creatures at all.[1]

The global reference in the definition is important, despite the many criticisms made of it in the previous chapter where we saw ten philosophical difficulties from which theodicies suffer. This is because it asks us to consider the possibility of the following reaction to them:

> I know all the evils to which you draw my attention as well as you do, but religion still offers me a way of being grateful for existence despite them; a way of thanking God for life as a whole.

This reaction is of great importance. It is difficult to imagine Judaism or Christianity without it. As always, the conceptual task is in appreciating how it is to be elucidated. In the first section of the present chapter my argument is that the logical problem of evil is not the context in which we should try to do so.

At the outset, we should recall an objection to using free will as a good, in a global way, which we discussed in the second section of Chapter 3 on 'Evil and Logical Necessity'. The objection is to treating free will as though it were a great good, on the same scale as lesser goods; as the prerequisite of the other goods. There would be the same objection to treating the complete absence of free will as a loss, far greater than any other loss.

In the case of genuine gains and losses, they are thought of as such in relation to *us*. But who are the creatures we are asked to imagine who have no free will at all? Us? These creatures would not be human beings at all. The free-will defence, which, after all, is an appeal to *us*, would then take a curious form. It would ask us whether a world in which we are human beings is better than a world in which we are not human beings! Obviously, the latter alternative fails to refer to us at all. But, in that case, so does the former. It *may* be said that the species to which *we* belong need not have developed in the way it has. It could have lacked rationality and free will. All that shows, however, is that 'human being' is not a purely biological concept. Those creatures would not be us.

The consequence of the above argument is that we cannot speak of free will *in vacuo* as a good that we possess, any more than one can speak of 'human being' as a good that human beings possess. Of course, this is not to deny that it is a terrible thing when a person loses his faculties, but that is because he ceases to be a human being in the normal sense. Insanity gets its sense by contrast with sanity. It is a limiting case. It still would make no sense to say that God chose to give human beings the good of creating them sane rather than insane. Insanity presupposes our world. It is not a human alternative to it.

What we talk of as good or bad are the actual choices we make, and actions we perform. The discussion of the free-will defence usually moves quickly into that context. At this point, a number of logical issues are raised concerning those free acts, none of which, in my opinion, actually address the existential problem of pain. It will be said that all they are meant to further is the logical problem of evil. Precisely. The difficulties that emerge illustrate further the folly of separating the problems.

Even granting that it makes little sense to argue that God has done good to creatures by creating them as people, rather than as creatures who would not be people at all, it still makes sense to ask whether God could have created human life containing less evil than our own. This question has taken two forms within the logical problem of evil, one of which we have already discussed. In Chapter 3, section 2, on 'Evil and Logical Necessity', we discussed Mackie's and Swinburne's contention that God could have created naturally good creatures in a world containing no actual evils. This suggestion was rejected as incoherent.

In the present section of this chapter, I want to discuss a slightly different suggestion, namely, that God could have created human beings who choose freely between good and evil, but who, in fact, always choose the good. The difficulty is to see what can be meant by saying that God could ensure, or see to it, that this is so. The difficulty has two aspects. The first concerns the metaphysical level at which God's 'ensuring' or 'seeing to things' is said to take place. The second concerns the more general issue of what it could mean to speak of seeing to, or securing, the formation of human character.

What do we mean by the *metaphysical* character of God 'ensuring' or 'seeing to things' in the free-will defence? Our characters are affected by countless events and action. People are affected in different ways. Even when they are affected in the same way, the effect may itself affect other aspects of their lives in different ways. Sometimes, it will be extremely difficult to distinguish between what an event is, and how it is taken up into a person's life, since the latter will include, often, how the event is read.

By contrast, with the complexities referred to above, talk of wanting to ensure or fix a person's character suggests something akin to post-hypnotic suggestion. Although a person 'obeys a command', and even 'gives reasons' for doing so, as the result of such a suggestion, we would not say that 'obedience' or 'giving reasons' had really taken place. There would be features of the behaviour that would make us withhold those descriptions. Of course, on a given occasion, we may fail to detect these. A person may be angry as a result of post-hypnotic suggestion when anger is the appropriate response anyway. The logical point is not that the difference is always detected, but that there is a difference to be detected. Of course, we may have direct knowledge about the hypnosis. But in God's case, what is to be the criterion by which we could determine whether God had seen to something or not? The difficulty is in locating a discernible difference in human affairs that would confirm or refute the speculations concerning God.

Those who want to say that God could see to it that free human beings always make the right decisions do not want to think of God as the divine hypnotist. On the other hand, the way God would 'see to it' would not be a discernible phenomenon in some circumstances, but not in others, since God is supposed to see to it that we *always* make the right decisions. The suggestion about what God has seen to, is meant to have the force of a particular 'ensuring', which would be discernible as a *distinct* event. On the other hand, its generality is such that such force is logically ruled out for it.

If we try to give God's 'seeing to it' a more determinate character, as in certain popular readings of predestination, it is difficult to see how any notion of 'free action' can be retained at all. Human beings would simply be determined to act in a certain way from the outset. The result would be a kind of natural necessity without any logical room for notions of freedom or responsibility.[2] To ensure the outcome of free action is a logical contradiction.

When we turn from the metaphysical context to that of ordinary life, does the notion of 'ensuring' that human characters are of such-and-such a kind *make sense*? If not, then not even God could avail himself of *that* opportunity of doing so. For Swinburne, the notion poses no difficulty. He simply thinks it would be a bad thing to do, just as it is a bad thing for parents to do.

The creator could help agents toward right actions by making these reasons more effective causally: that is, he could make agents so that by nature they were inclined (though not perhaps compelled) to pursue what is good. But this would be to impose a moral character on agents, to give them wide general purposes which they naturally pursue, to make them naturally altruistic, tenacious of purpose, or strong-willed. But to impose a character on creatures might well seem to take away from creatures the privilege of developing their own characters and those of their fellows. We tend to think that parents who try to forcibly impose a character, however good a character, on the children, are less than perfect parents.[3]

Some might argue from the same parental facts to an opposite conclusion concerning God. A parent who wants to ensure, or see to it, that his child has one sort of character rather than another, it may be said, is not necessarily interfering with the freedom of the child. If we do not regard such measures as an interference with freedom, despite all our ignorance and the many mistakes we make, why should a logical or moral limit be drawn on God, who is not ignorant, nor liable to error, in seeing to it that human beings freely develop in the right way?[4]

I do not want to enter a dispute over which parental attitude to children is right or wrong. My difficulties are logically prior to any such disagreement. They have to do with the intelligibility of what is being envisaged.[5] I am not denying that measures taken by parents may influence the development of their children in the way hoped for by the parents. I speak deliberately in the subjunctive mood, and speak of hope, since I think it is important to distinguish between the retrospective judgement, 'I influenced the development of my child's character' or 'I did what I could', with the claim, 'I ensured or saw to it that my child's character developed in a certain way'. Almost as if there were a method. Measures taken in hope, on the other hand, recognize that they are taken in contexts where a great deal lies out of the control of the agent. A wise parent will recognize that this is not contingently so. That parent would not know what it would mean if someone wanted to speak of parental influence on the development of a child's character in any other way. Greater control would begin to point us in the direction of coercion, which would not be included in talk of *development* at all.

The wise parent may say, 'I thank my lucky stars that I was able to help in the development of my child's character', or, 'I thank God I was able to help my child.' The references to God or lucky stars are not references to agencies that *did* ensure the outcome. On the contrary, they are a recognition of the luck or the grace involved in that outcome. It is ironic that the debate over whether God can ensure, or see to, the development of character uproots talk of things 'being in God's hands' from one of its natural religious contexts. If those contexts were recognized, one would no longer ask whether God could ensure, or see to it, that we act freely in certain directions.

## 2. *Counterfactuals and 'Those Others'*

We may be convinced that it makes little sense to think that God could ensure, or see to it, that we would always freely make the right decisions, and yet feel that things need not be as bad as they are or have been. This has led to the following worry: Could God have created another world in which human beings would have caused less evil than there is in our own? God's omniscience is such that he would know whether this is possible. If it is possible, God is not justified in creating our world.

This issue has rekindled a debate which, as Robert Adams points out, occurred in theology in the sixteenth and seventeenth centuries.[6] It concerned whether it is possible for God to have what was called 'middle knowledge': This is the sort of knowledge 'of what every possible free creature would freely do in any situation in which that creature might possibly find itself'.[7] The possibility of middle knowledge depends on knowing the truth of certain counterfactuals, namely, the truth about what certain creatures would have done freely had they been created.

The issue of the relation of the problem of middle knowledge to the problem of evil should not be confused with the question of whether, in creating our world, God has created the best of all possible worlds. Most philosophers question the intelligibility of this latter notion, since, as Aquinas said, 'God could make other things, or add other things to those he has made, and there would be another and better universe.'[8] Nevertheless, the relation of middle knowledge to the problem of evil does pose the question of whether God could have created a possible world better than his actual creation. There are difficulties that arise within the terms of reference of the problem. I shall consider these first. The deeper problems are only recognized when the terms of reference themselves are questioned as they should be.

In order for the possible world God could have created to be better than the one he did create, we would have to know that the possible creatures in that possible world would create less evil than there is in our world. Adams says that it is difficult to see how the truth of the counterfactuals involved is to be determined. Yet, if it is a question of comparing amounts of evil, it is difficult to see how the problem of truth can be avoided. Plantinga could reply that the notion of conditional truth is sufficient in this context. In order to defeat the logical problem of evil, Plantinga does not have to claim to *know* that the evil in the world God created is less than that caused by any possible creatures in any possible world. All he needs to show is that this is *possible*, and, hence, that it makes sense to believe it. There would then be no inconsistency between the fact of evil in our world, and belief in an all-powerful, all-good God.

I am not content to leave the disputants on this issue where they are, however, because we need to question the terms of reference that, allegedly, give the dispute its sense. In particular we need to look at what is attributed to God's omniscience. God is said to know every possible move every possible creature will make. One need not go into the realm of possibility to uncover the logical difficulties involved in this claim. They are present if God is said to know these things about us. The confusion can take different forms.

When God is said to know, not only every move we have made, and are making, but every move we will make, a certain picture of the future may hold us captive. We may think of the future as something unseen, but which already exists. The past may be thought of as part of a reel of film that has already been seen, while the present may be thought of as that part of the film being seen at the moment. The future is then thought of as part of the film that is there to be seen, although it has not yet appeared on the screen. Mortal sight is limited, but God, who seeth all things, can see the future, and therefore knows its content before it actually happens. But since 'the future' is not a 'something' that exists at all, not even God claims to know it. An omniscient God cannot read the future, since there is no future to be read.

Problems of knowledge of the future, or of middle knowledge, need not be the product of the above confusion. To understand the kind of knowledge of the future God has, we need only think of an analogy of a grandmaster in chess, playing five ordinary players at the same time. While they ponder their moves, he responds with alacrity with his own as soon as they are made. The chess master's ability to do so does not mean that the other chess players do not make their moves freely. Nor does it mean that their moves exist in some realm called 'the future' before they make them, and that the chess master has some means of reading them before they are activated. All it means is that the grandmaster, with his greater knowledge of chess, is predicting the moves the other players will make. We are players in God's game. If powerful predictions are possible for a mortal grandmaster, so the argument runs, think of the knowledge an omniscient God has of us. Isn't he said to know our very frame? Since all created creatures have to play God's game, God can simply imagine a possible creature and know, thereby, all the possible moves that creature would make. Yet, with creatures both actual and possible, their actions would be free.

Where does the incoherence in this way of thinking lie? In the confused conception of the future, the incoherence consisted in thinking of the future as an existing 'something' which is there to be seen. The second incoherence lies in thinking of a person's life as 'all possible moves', and that this pseudo-collectivity is something God could be said to know or predict.

In the chess example, the notion of 'all possible moves' has sense because of the formal parameters of the game. The fact that we are talking about a game is important. The thought is that we could extend this example until it includes 'everything', the one big game which is our lives. But if life is not a game with formal parameters, or not even a game at all, then the notion of 'all the possible moves' within it becomes vacuous; a supposed 'something' which, in fact, not even God could tell us anything about.

Famously, Wittgenstein said in his *Philosophical Investigations* that language was a family of language games. He did so in revolt against his earlier view in the *Tractatus* that the form of language is akin to the form of a calculus. He had felt that 'saying something' must always come to the same thing, otherwise it would be an arbitrary matter. He looked for the general form of the proposition. Logic determined what *can* be said, and all possible propositions were thought to be determined by the basic constituents of logic. What *can* be said is a function of the possible combinations of those constituents. This is one root of the notion that it makes sense to speak of 'all the possible things we could say'. There was thought to be a correspondence between the structure of language and the structure of the world – all the possible things that could be done.

Rush Rhees has pointed out that despite major changes in his view of logic, the analogy with the calculus continued to influence Wittgenstein's later view of language, at least in Part I of the *Investigations*. On the surface, nothing would seem further removed from that analogy than the description of us as engaged in a family of language games. Yet, the analogy between speaking a language and playing a game has obvious limitations of its own. The many games we play do not make up one big game, whereas the language games we engage in are said to belong to *the same* language. The issue of what the identity of a language amounts to (by which one does not mean the fact that it is English, Welsh, German, etc.) remains to be explored. Rhees argues that making the notion of conversation central, the dialogical character of discourse, will help us to appreciate that identity and also to appreciate what 'saying something' amounts to.

The relevance of these issues for the kind of knowledge attributed to God's omniscience, with respect to us, can be seen by noting that our discourse with each other is not illuminated by the
analogy with playing a game. Rhees notes that Wittgenstein's
emphases on 'following a rule', 'continuing a series', 'going on in
the same way' have their natural home in the context of playing a
game or operating within formal systems. They are not at home,
on the other hand, if we think of our innumerable daily conversations with each other. What rules are we following in a conversation? How does one 'go on in the same way' within it? Our conversations go as they go. They do not have a formal structure that
determines 'all possible' things that could be said in them.

Where games are concerned, we can speak of someone mastering a game, knowing all the moves and so on. Talk of being a
grandmaster in chess is a case in point: being able to think of
more ingenious moves, within the rules, in reaction to the moves
others have made. But one cannot speak of mastering conversation in this way, any more than one could speak of mastering life.
And when we take part in a conversation, we are not usually
countering moves made by the other speaker (though sometimes
we may be). We are saying something to another human being.
In the conversation people are speaking to each other. In fact
when a conversation has been a matter simply of countering
moves, that is a sign of failure. ('You can't have a natural or
decent conversation with him.')

What I say may depend on what the other says, or I may initi-
ate a new topic in the conversation. This new topic may itself be
occasioned by what someone else said to me yesterday, by what
is in the morning paper, by something in a book I am reading and
so on. And then there is the style of what is said within a culture,
its humour, its sarcasm, with variants of their own. There are the
individual traits of families, with the differences within them too.
They are the factors that are intertwined with the language; factors belonging to music, literature, politics, religion. Need we go
on? How remote all this is from the idea of 'all possible things' an
individual can do and say, as though any such notion could be
generated by a prior insight into something concerning him. One

need only ask prior knowledge of *what*, given the considerations I have adduced, to see how vacuous that notion becomes.[9] Yet, it is precisely a notion such as this which is needed to give credence to the view that an omniscient God knows all the possible moves that every possible creature could make, or would make. Since this notion of 'all possible moves' is itself an illusion, there is nothing for an omniscient God to know in these terms. We go as we go.

The notion of 'omniscience' that appears in the philosophical discussions of middle knowledge and the problem of evil is reminiscent of similar discussions of 'omnipotence' which we discussed in Chapter 1. Theodicists defined 'omnipotence' as 'the power to do whatever is not logically contradictory' and then applied the definition to God. The analysis was confronted with the awkward fact that God can't ride a bicycle. If one had started with a *religious* notion of omnipotence, who would have talked of God in that way in the first place? Yet, despite the acknowledgement that God cannot ride a bicycle, we are assured that God knows everything there is to know about bicycles.[10] If we began with religion, we wouldn't talk in that way either, with its picture of countless propositions lying about inert in the divine mind. What has any of this to do with religion?

In the present context, too, we begin with a definition of omniscience which is then applied to God. Hence our problems with 'knowledge of every possible move by every possible creature'. If we began with religious notions of omniscience, we would concentrate on contexts that give such talk its point; contexts in which believers say that no one can hide from God who knows the secrets of our hearts. These contexts have little to do with the problem of middle knowledge, and the truth of counterfactuals. A failed philosophical joke of mine in an attempt to illustrate the differences between the contexts will no doubt fail again. I pointed out that the Bible expresses the way we are known by God, a knowledge we cannot escape, by saying that, with God, even the hairs of our heads are numbered. 'Of course', I said, 'this doesn't mean that we could ask God what the number is, treating him as weight-watchers treat the scales – 'How many today?' The philosopher replied, 'Of course you could, since he knows the number.' I should have known better. This is but another example of the context-less improper extension of concepts we discussed in Chapter 1, section 2.

### 3. *Free Will and God's Non-Interventions*

The free-will defence has been used in many ways. One of these is the attempt to limit God's responsibility for the evils in the world. God created human beings and gave them freedom. The use made of it may be good or bad. Evil is the result of bad use of the God-given freedom. Therefore, God cannot be said to be *directly* responsible for the evils in the world.

This use of the free-will defence simply leads to further questions. Hasn't God given us too much freedom? Why couldn't he curtail it from time to time when there is an obvious need to do so? Such curtailment would show no lack of respect for human freedom. We may have the greatest respect for the freedom and independence of others, but we would not hesitate to intervene to save a person from impending disaster. Often, it is the least we could do. Why doesn't God do the same? This challenge has been well expressed by Roth:

> Is it clear . . . that moral freedom is or must be indivisible, or that such indivisibility is all that good? The moral fabric of human existence, for example, depends on intervention, on stopping people from doing certain things. On the other hand . . . vaunted indivisibility allows freedom to make all hell break loose. Apparently God will not intervene to stop this waste, but that fact does little to enhance the plausibility of God's limitless love and goodness – unless 'limitless' implies something very strange in this case. Rather the waste of permissiveness, God's and ours, in allowing freedom to be indivisible augurs against God's benevolence.[11]

John Hick has attempted to reply to this challenge:

> It seems to me that once you ask God to intervene to prevent some specific evil you are in principle asking him, or her, to

rescind our human freedom and responsibility. Was God supposed to change Hitler's nature, or to have engineered his sudden death, at a certain point in history? But the forces leading to the Holocaust ramify out far beyond that one man. God would have had to override the freedom not only of Hitler and the Nazis, but all participants in the widespread secular anti-Semitism of nineteenth- and twentieth-century Europe, which itself was rooted in nearly two thousand years of Christian anti-Semitism. Further, having prevented this particular evil, God would be equally obliged to prevent all other very great human evils . . . Where should a miraculously intervening God have stopped? Only, it would seem, when human free will had been abolished.[12]

This is a curious answer. Hick does not deny that God could do all these things. He simply thinks he would face problems if he tried to do so. Apparently, on Hick's view, if God tries to do something of the kind envisaged, he has to do everything. But that is precisely what Roth is questioning. True, God would have his problems. He would have to decide where to draw the line. Doing so may confront God will all sorts of dilemmas, but so what? But who would accept the following defence, 'I can't save everyone, so I'll save no one'? What is true, as we saw in Chapter 2, section 3, whether God faces up to the dilemmas or ducks them, is that he cannot emerge as perfectly good. This is simply a consequence of treating God as a moral agent like ourselves.

The above conclusion can only be avoided if Hick, like Swinburne, argues that free will is a good of such overriding importance that God wants us to develop in relation to the results of our free choices. In that case, we have to consider the *particular* goods that facing up to the consequences of our choices are supposed to bestow on us. That takes us back to the ten difficulties described in the previous chapter.

Davis's answer to Roth's challenge is very different from that of Hick or Swinburne. He simply pleads ignorance:

In my . . . theodicy, there is just one question that I admit I cannot answer, viz., why God allows certain terribly evil events to occur, or certain terribly evil people to exist. The general answer, of course, is that God's policy in creating this sort of world, with these sorts of natural laws and this degree of human freedom, will turn out best in the long run. But I do not know why God did not step in to prevent African slavery or destroy Hitler at birth. But no other contributor to this book (with the possible exception of Griffin, whose God is largely powerless to do such things) can adequately explain this either.[13]

Within the conception of theodicies and defences, Davis's answer is the only possible one, but not in the sense he intended. One would be driven to it, *conceptually*, as an uncomprehending ignorance. Davis wants to say that waiting for a final answer, without knowing what it is, can be an uplifting experience.[14] But as with the eschatological expectations discussed in the last section of the previous chapter, Davis's response seems theologically and religiously thin as an attempt to capture what is supposed to be, after all, part of the consummation of all things. It is not that 'waiting on God' is unimportant, but it is surely something other than the 'waiting in ignorance' which it is often turned into in our problematic inheritance.

## 4. *The Importance of the Free-Will Defence*

Given the criticisms I have made of the free-will defence, it may be thought that I see nothing of importance in it. This is not so. I do think that the use made of it in our problematic inheritance is profoundly confused. On the other hand, in insisting on certain features of the relation between belief in God and human life, I think that the free-will defence is profoundly right. First, it is profoundly right in emphasizing the freedom without which life would not be recognizably human at all; a freedom with all its attendant opportunities, risks and dangers. Second, it is profoundly right in emphasizing that religious belief is the response to that life *as a whole*. What we have seen, however, is the mess we get into by thinking that that response must be a consequentialist justification of human life, a kind of religious utilitarianism. But what is the alternative? That question marks the transition between Parts I and II of the book.

The question is not one that can be avoided by saying that all God did was to create free beings, and that everything thereafter is their responsibility. Roth, for example, responds by saying:

> It is irresponsible to assign responsibility inequitably. God must bear God's share, and this share is not small, unless God could never be described as One for whom all things are possible. God's responsibility is located in the fact that God is the One who ultimately sets the boundaries in which we live and move and have our being. True, since we are thrown into history at our birth, we appear in social settings made by human hands, but ultimately those hands cannot account for themselves. To the extent that they are born with the potential and the power to be dirty, credit for that fact belongs elsewhere. 'Elsewhere' is God's address.[15]

Where is 'elsewhere', and what is the nature of the God who lives there? If no adequate answer can be found within our problematic inheritance, where do we go from there?

## Notes

1 Alvin Plantinga, 'Good, Evil, and the Metaphysics of Freedom' in Marilyn McCord Adams and Robert Merrihew Adams (eds), *The Problem of Evil*, Oxford: Oxford University Press 1990, p. 85.

2 See Ludwig Wittgenstein, *Culture and Value*, Oxford: Blackwell 1980, p. 81e.

3 Richard Swinburne, 'The Problem of Evil' in Stuart Brown (ed.), *Reason and Religion*, Ithaca: Cornell University Press 1977, p. 96.

4 This view was put to me in a discussion by Renford Bambrough.

5 I am indebted to Peter Winch, in the discussion referred to in the previous footnote, for suggesting that the unintelligibility lies in this direction.

6 See Robert Merrihew Adams, 'Middle Knowledge and the Problem of Evil' in Adams and Adams, *The Problem of Evil*.

7 Adams and Adams, 'Introduction', *The Problem of Evil*, p. 14.

8   Aquinas, *Summa Theologiae* Ia 25 6 and 3.

9   I have been giving the merest sketch of issues explored in depth by Rush Rhees in *Wittgenstein and the Possibility of Discourse*, ed. D. Z. Phillips, Cambridge: Cambridge University Press 1998.

10  George Mavrodes, 'Omniscience' in Philip L. Quinn and Charles Taliaferro (eds), *A Companion to Philosophy of Religion*, Oxford: Blackwell 1997, p. 237.

11  John K. Roth, 'Critique of Hick' in Stephen T. Davis (ed.), *Encountering Evil*, Louisville: Westminster John Knox Press 2001, p. 64.

12  Hick, 'Rejoinder' in Davis, *Encountering Evil*, p. 70.

13  Davis, 'Rejoinder' in Davis, *Encountering Evil*, p. 101.

14  Davis, 'Free Will and Evil' in Davis, *Encountering Evil*, p. 83.

15  Roth, 'A Theodicy of Protest' in Davis, *Encountering Evil*, p. 8.

# Interlude

# Where Do We Go From Here?

# 5

# God Unmasked

## 1. Retrospect

At the end of Part I, it is not difficult to see why it was called 'Our Problematic Inheritance'. Yet, that inheritance still dominates contemporary philosophical discussion of the problem of evil. In the first chapter, serious objections were raised against the intelligibility of defining 'omnipotence' as 'the ability to do whatever is not logically contradictory'. *Within* the tradition that thinks of God in this way, the refutation of his omnipotence is a simple matter. It proceeds as follows, to give but one example: If God is omnipotent he can do whatever is not logically contradictory. 'Riding a bicycle' is not logically contradictory. God cannot ride a bicycle. Therefore, God is not omnipotent. One may respond to the objection, a response that can be repeated in countless examples, by saying that it simply so happens that God cannot ride a bicycle, and that he could will all the changes necessary to make this possible. But the objection asserted that it *made no sense* to speak of God riding a bicycle. If 'sense', in relation to God, is to be extended to cover any absurd suggestion, the extension has no contextual warrant of any kind. It is quite unlike biblical religious developments in the idea of God. We are simply confronted with 'building in the air'. No one would actually inhabit these philosophical castles.

In the second chapter, we explored further the confusions in the abstract notion of 'all power'. There is no such power, and therefore it cannot be attributed to God. There are different kinds of power, including the power of evil. Is this power to be included in the power God has? Is God *more* powerful than the

Devil. If so, what measure of comparison are we using? Failure to distinguish divine power from other kinds of power leads to confused notions of God's will. We are told that God can will anything he chooses, including the most heinous crimes. Again, it will not do to say that God could ask us to commit such crimes, but chooses not to. It makes no sense to attribute such things to God's will. Behind the readiness to do so is the confused notion of a free act, which assumes that, in any act, the agent was free to do the action from which he refrains. God's good deeds have worth, on such a view, only if God has chosen not to do evil, or was free to do that evil. The evil alternative need only be before his mind fleetingly, but if this were not so, the good act would not be a free or a moral one. The result of this confusion is that God becomes incapable of that natural goodness, seen in simple and extraordinary deeds, where its character depends on the virtuous deed being done immediately, without a second thought. One will not appreciate this if one thinks that all 'willing' involves 'trying'. This assumption has far-reaching consequences for what one is to say of the horrendous evils, not to mention the others, that God is said to allow. Does God allow them to happen with or without a second thought? If God does so without a second thought, he is callous and insensitive. If he does so after a second thought, he does so by resolving a moral dilemma, or he simply does what has to be done. In any event, God could not be called perfectly good.

The logical difficulties encountered in the first two chapters come from an abstract view of logic that is imposed on religion. This can be seen in the abstract conception of omnipotence, which leads to the view that God is 'sheer will'. God's will is then said to determine God's nature. If, by contrast, we began with religious contexts in which talk of God has its sense, we would see that God's nature is the grammar of God's will. What ought to be said is not that God can do whatever is not logically contradictory, but that God can do whatever is not logically contradictory for God to do. That gives primacy to religious sense, not to an abstract conception of 'omnipotence' that has no application.

Unfortunately, in our problematic inheritance, either an abstract concept of logic prevails, or the emphasis is on an anthropomorphism that attempts to treat God as though he were a fellow moral agent in a moral community he shares with us. Even the latter emphasis turns out to be *less* than one could hope for, when the motives for allowing evils to exist, which are attributed to God, turn out to be the negation or denial of the very moral concepts they are meant to illustrate. In Chapter 3, this embarrassing result is illustrated by reference to ten difficulties involved in various theodicies. We see that the fact that 'good' is often contrasted with 'evil', in the logical sense that its intelligibility depends on the contrast, cannot be used as a justification of the evil in question. We see, too, that making character development or moral responsibility an aim, in an instrumental way, contradicts the nature of those notions. Also, an appeal to the way physical and mental pains stimulate action cannot itself be regarded as a good, until we see in which direction action is stimulated. One general tendency in religious apologetics is to offer a one-sided diet of examples. Were the counter-evidence produced, the general thesis being advanced could no longer be maintained. We see this, again and again, in the ways theodicists appeal to the fact that evils afford opportunities for admirable reactions to our own and other people's sufferings; to the fact that evils are the results of bad choices people needn't have made; to the fact that things are not as bad as they seem and that God never sends anyone unlimited suffering. Finally, despite the divine design of the moral obstacle course we have all had to run, theodicists have to admit that only a small minority, if any, fulfil the purposes for which it was intended. So the course needs a back-up programme in the form of some kind of compensation or redemption after death. After we saw, however, the context in which this is supposed to happen, the nature of the compensation or redemption on offer, and the nature of the creatures after death to whom they are supposed to be offered, all lack intelligibility. It seems that the conceptual bankruptcy of these notions is hidden by an appeal to our ignorance concerning God's ultimate purposes.

In Chapter 4, the final cluster of difficulties in our problematic inheritance was discussed in relation to the free-will defence. These difficulties concern, first, the attempt to regard free will, as such, as a general good for *us*, as though we could have been in some non-free state; second, difficulties about the suggestion that God could ensure that human beings had characters of a certain kind; third, difficulties relating to the supposition that God could have created a possible world in which, he knows, its possible creatures would have caused less evil than we have done in our world; fourth, difficulties relating to the question why God has not intervened to prevent evils when any decent human being would. In the last case, if we are given reasons, they tend to be those that suffer from the difficulties discussed in Chapter 3. Alternatively, we are confronted by the appeal to ignorance. Nevertheless, despite these difficulties, the free-will defence is right to emphasize two central aspects of the problem of evil. One is the freedom in human life without which that life would not be called human. The other is the fact that religion is some kind of response to that life as a whole, since it purports to account for the boundaries within which that life is lived. The question with which we are left, at the end of Part I, is what sense can be made of those boundaries given the difficulties we have noted. My complaint has been that religious and theological accounts of the boundaries have been extraordinarily thin, given that they are supposed to herald what is purported to be the culmination of life's journey.

## 2. *Questioning God*

John Roth writes:

> Most people want a totally good God or none at all. In religious circles, then, putting God on trial has not been popular. For centuries, human beings have taken themselves to task in order to protect God's innocence, and not without reason . . . Life is simpler that way. And so theology puts Father in the right and his children in the wrong.[1]

Given the vast amount of evil in human life, Roth cannot accept what is for him a simplistic dichotomy between sinful human beings and a perfectly good God. God has to share the blame. That being so, from where we are now, we should not be prepared to speak of God as perfectly good. That attitude has to be earned. In claiming that God is 'sheer will', Roth wants that to include a readiness to change on God's part. That has struck some as an odd hope. For example, Griffin writes in response:

> . . . the traditional doctrine that God's will is not necessitated by anything outside of God did not entail that God's basic character or will could change. For example, Luther, an extreme voluntarist if ever there was one, said that '[God's] will is eternal and changeless, because His nature is so' (quoted in my *God, Power, and Evil*, p.103). It seems a rather desperate hope that, assuming that God has had a mean streak for not only the past 15 billion years but from all eternity, our protests in the next century or so will bring about a change. Even if we were to assume that, by analogy with human beings, God could in principle undergo a moral conversion, the basis for expecting such an occurrence would be missing. Moral conversions in human beings usually involve coming to adopt a larger perspective on things, but God by definition already has an all-inclusive perspective.[2]

In response, I could well imagine Roth invoking the fact that there is a long tradition, certainly in Judaism, of questioning God. Although Roth says that it is not popular to put God on trial, he might have been thinking more of Christian apologists and theodicists. But in the Bible, as in the Hebrew Bible, we have examples of arguments with God, even chidings of God's proposals, and of God seemingly changing his mind as a result. I confess to finding this tradition difficult to understand, and I am ready to be corrected in what I am about to say. Although the quarrels are certainly quarrels with God, for the most part, they are not akin to the quarrels with God one expects from authors of the Prometheus Press. They are not exercises in philosophical humanism or atheism. But they are protests through which, it is hoped, things will change. The difficulty, as Griffin says, is in understanding this hope. The questioning, to my mind, is less an attempt to get an unchanging God to change, than a matter of questioning what the unchanging nature of God is. The prophetic protest 'You can't do that' is a matter of saying, 'You can't *be* that'. It is a struggle for a more adequate understanding of God *within* an essentially believing relationship to God. But I do not want to tidy things up too much. I said that the quarrels with God do not come from the perspective of a convinced atheism, but the discussion between belief and unbelief is not a sharp one. If the questions go far enough in a certain direction, they will lead, not to changes within the relationship with God, but to the end of that relationship. But this is difficult for theodicists to grasp: the questioners are not accusing theodicists of not being careful enough in their assessments. Rather, they are rejecting *in toto* the very conception of assessment they offer. To put it bluntly: the God of the theodicists is their Devil.

The conceptual gap I have in mind can be appreciated, to some extent, by contrasting the following comments by Hick and Roth. First, Hick:

> God has set us in a world containing unpredictable contingencies and dangers – in which unexpected and undeserved calamities may occur to anyone – because only in such a world can mutual caring and love be elicited. As an abstract philosophical hypothesis, this may offer little comfort. But translated into religious language it tells us that God's good purpose enfolds the entire process of this world, with all its good and bad contingencies, and that even amidst tragic calamity and suffering we are still within the sphere of God's love and are moving towards the divine kingdom.[3]

Roth replies:

> Hick's theodicy is just too good to be true . . . Waste will waste away. Evil will be transcended, rendered inconsequential, for-

gotten so that neither God nor humanity is in any way permanently soiled. There shall be pie in the sky by and by – a whole one, not just a slice. This theodicy is nice. Its plausibility, however, must be judged in terms of how nice life seems to be.[4]

Roth's challenge is one within a continuing relationship with God, whereas others have pressed their questions further. What if the very *conception* of such a relationship comes under threat? Is it not easy to see how this can come about? Suppose one holds a certain covenantal conception of that relationship, in terms of which God is said to keep his promises if people behave in a certain way. Confronted by the radical contingency of human life, the horrendous evils that have occurred and still occur in it, the correlation between God's promises and our fate, the covenant, collapses under their weight. On the other hand, for many, it seems, without a correlation of that kind, life seems devoid of purpose; we become historical accidents who have their brief day and disappear without trace.

For people who think in this way, there appear to be only two alternatives: first, the kind of order theodicists try to find in the world, or ultimate meaninglessness, a world without God. We will have reason to question the exclusivity of these alternatives, but, for the moment, I want to concentrate on the fact that this situation can come about as a result of realizing the unintelligibility of certain conceptions of the God of the Covenant, for example, his alleged exercise of rewards and punishments in history. For example, is the Holocaust to be regarded as God's punishment on the Jewish people? I realize that some people have held (and perhaps still do hold) this view. Some Jewish thinkers have seen it as a consequence of unfaithfulness to God, while some Christian theologians have seen it as punishment for crucifying Jesus. I am suggesting that to read history in this way, one would have to sever the notion of divine punishment from the notion of desert, since the horrors seem to fall on people indiscriminately. There is the further question of why God would inflict *that* horror on anyone. The same difficulty was involved, as we saw, in Swinburne's rationalization of the Holocaust as the result of bad choices, but a result that gives people an opportunity to show themselves at their best in response to it.[5] The commitment to theological consequentialism, which asks us to be open-minded about the possibility of a balance for good being on the side of allowing the Holocaust, is itself a corruption of the notion of open-mindedness.[6] These matters are worth emphasizing in order to understand that the terms 'meaningless' and 'absurd' are not used *in vacuo*, as general philosophical stances, but as terms to express the most violent rejection and negation possible of the *kind* of 'meaning' and 'order' offered by the theodicist-like conception of God's covenant with his people. After all, as the Book of Job shows, such a reaction is not unknown in the Bible.

Job is confronted by a theodicy in which he can find no sense, but which those who try to comfort him urge him to accept. By the end of the book, God rebukes the comforters for the *kind* of comfort they have offered Job. It is interesting to find Swinburne saying:

> The Old Testament contains several meditations, subsequent to that of the Book of Genesis on theodicy, the best-known of which is that of the Book of Job. But exactly what is the final conclusion of that enigmatic book is much disputed. In any case, it is a pre-Christian conclusion.[7]

Despite finding some consequentialist arguments in the New Testament, Swinburne admits that it 'contains no systematic treatment of the source of all the world's bad states'.[8] He sees theodicists, like himself, as filling out the details in this otherwise uncompleted task. It is clear from my arguments that I regard this as a disastrous assumption. Not only is it odd that if a system is what we really need, the Bible does not give us one, but that characterizing what it says as the beginning of a system to be completed in a theodicist fashion, turns out to be the *negation* of what it has to say about central religious beliefs. Bringing out what it has to say, depends on emphasizing continuities, not discontinuities, between books like the Book of Job and Christian revelation.

What does Job find out about God? I want to consider this question *within* the context of the conception of God offered him by his comforters. As Herman Tennessen has argued in a provocative essay on the Book of Job, we meet, in Job:

> a man with profoundly personal knowledge of pain, of violent passions and with a lucid power of reason . . . a man with a fanatic will to intellectual honesty and a poet.[9]

Urged on by those who seek to comfort him in his affliction, Job tries to reason with God, but realizes, unlike anthropomorphizing theodicists, how difficult this 'reasoning' is going to be: 'For he is not a man as I am, that I should answer him, and we should come together in judgement' (Job 9.32). How different this is from the kind of end-of-term report theodicists give of why God deals with us in the ways he does. We are asked to look at the world and to ask, 'Isn't this what you would expect from a being of high moral excellence?' After a few detours to explain the evils, horrendous and otherwise, that might bother us, the breathtakingly confident answer is, 'Yes'. As a result, there is not the slightest indication that their systems might be met by the divine response, 'Who is this that darkeneth counsel by words without knowledge?' (Job 38.2). This is not surprising, because if one is being told that one's very conception of light and reason is, in fact, darkness, how great is that darkness! While in it, how can the confusion be acknowledged? Job is silent when asked, 'Where wast thou when I laid the foundations of the earth? declare, if thou hast understanding' (Job 38.4). Not so our present day theodicists. In effect, their books and articles reply: 'It is true that we were not there, and that you haven't exactly given us full details, but we know exactly what it must have been like and why you did it.' I confess to finding this one of the most comic spectacles in contemporary philosophy.

### 3. *Is God Fit to Plead?*

God is questioned, according to Tennessen, within two distinct contexts. First, he is treated as most theodicists treat him, as a fellow moral agent who shares a moral community with us. We have seen already, in the section on 'Can God Suffer the Consequences?', in Chapter 2, that if God allows evils with or without a second thought, he is either callous or indifferent, or is someone caught in a moral dilemma or who does what he has to do, respectively. But Job's questions show that those conclusions are too charitable, since they assume that we know what we are talking about. The point is that the whole account of God's governance, presented as a paradigm of rationality is, in fact, senseless. Even in the earlier argument, it must be remembered that its outcome was that it *makes no sense* to speak of God's perfect goodness.

As we have seen, when the going gets tough, as the result of treating God as a moral agent like ourselves, an appeal is made to the inscrutable will of God which is beyond our comprehension. But one cannot have it both ways. Either God is to be treated as a member of a moral community we share with him, or he is not. One cannot opt in and out of this perspective. Tennessen is adamant on this question:

> And neither shall we tolerate that swindle which the believers are guilty of when they call an act 'a most shameful crime', 'a most irreparable infamy', as long as it is done by a man, but an 'act of inscrutable love' if God is its author. Either one or the other: the same law and the same sentence for both, or separate laws and different sentences. If we are to accept the direction of the Universe as something just, claims Job . . . then this must mean: just by human standards. Otherwise God may be as 'just' as he pleases, in his own language.[10]

It is extremely difficult to get theodicists to appreciate the radical character of this *conceptual* challenge. Its first aspect is that if God is weighed in the scales of human justice, he is found wanting. What is the consequence of this verdict? Tennessen replies:

> The human demand for order and reason is leaping towards the heavens like a flame; Job is hammering away at the ear of

his God, hoping to strike a chord of human fibre. If you are inquiring about my sins and misdeeds, there exists comprehensible contact on at least one single point, then a single common principle must sustain your evaluations as well as mine. Then there must be something commensurable in our apprehensions and judgements; and this similarity must also include my sense of justice, a sense you have created along with all other things.[11]

Yet, when we apply what I regard as ordinary understandings of a concern with character, moral responsibility, evidence of evil and so on to theodicies and the kind of God Job's comforters are asking him to believe in, the results are the kind of difficulties listed in Chapter 3. In the same way, Job cannot make *sense* of what he is told to believe about God. He is asked to believe that his predicament is due to sins that he is unaware of or has forgotten. But this suggestion lacks credibility. No such easy correlation can be established. So why is he punished for something he hasn't done? It robs 'desert' and 'punishment' itself of their familiar meanings. Alternatively, it is suggested to him that his affliction is due to the sins of his ancestors, his family or his people. But when Job makes comparisons, *in these terms,* no sense can be made of the standards of desert, proportion or correlation which should still operate in this wider context. It follows that no *sense* can be made of his situation in terms of justice. As Tennessen says:

It is in the interest of elucidation, for the sake of the problem *per se,* that he scrutinises his conduct. He wants to know what they *mean* by sin when they build their entire argument on the premise that the wicked will perish and the righteous will triumph.[12]

What *kind* of understanding can be achieved on this basis? Theodicists claim that their systems make God's ways understandable to us. But the understanding we achieve by examining what they say is to see how destructive it is of moral responses to suffering. It seems, then, that God can be found, not only to be guilty (the lesser verdict), but also to be unintelligible (the deeper verdict), if we try to understand him both as a moral agent like ourselves *and* in the terms theodicies offer us.

At this point, Tennessen argues, there is a change of direction in Job's questioning. He realizes that the unintelligibility he has arrived at by means of his previous questions is no accident. It is a direct result of trying to argue with God as though he were a fellow member of a shared moral community; the direct result of trying to apply common standards to God. In the second context of Job's encounter with the God of the comforters, Tennessen argues, Job realizes that these moral standards cannot be applied to God. He had been mistaken in trying to locate 'a chord of human fibre' in God and a commensurability between human and divine judgements. Job comes to see that he had not taken his own admonition seriously enough, 'For he is not a man as I am, that I should answer him, and we should come together in judgement' (Job 9.32). Job discovers that if God resides beyond morality, the creature to be found there is certainly not a man. The problem is, however, that God is now seen as a creature who occupies the logical space we reserve for 'the monstrous'. God is characterized, not by justice, but by sheer power – by the notion of 'omnipotence' that we met in Chapters 1 and 2. Tennessen writes:

> We can easily imagine Job's boundless astonishment at this tangible appearance by Jehovah. Here Job has been sitting, attaching the most profound and central importance to the problem, in the belief that he was dealing with an opponent who would convince him at the point of mortal embarrassment as soon as his tongue touched the burning issue – a god of such holiness and purity that even his indictment would release exultation! Only to find himself confronted by a ruler of grotesque primitivity, a cosmic cave dweller, a braggart and a rumble-dumble, almost congenial in his complete ignorance about spiritual refinement.[13]

Tennessen reads the Book of Job as a piece of existential blasphemy, so successful in its irony, that believers have been fooled by it.

> Through the interpolations of believers, this book of frenzied execrations has been included among those rocks of faith on which men, even men of today, build their metaphysical consolation.[14]

God's conceptual fate, within the conceptual parameters offered by most theodicies, ends in the monstrous.

We do not have to accept Tennessen's rather fanciful view of the ironic purpose of the Book of Job, to appreciate the negative points in his analysis. The problem is that Tennessen wants to extend his reading to parts of the Book of Job where it does not fit very naturally. But we can still learn even from Tennessen's depiction of Job's repentance in dust and ashes as ironic.

> Job is now speaking to the Lord in the placative manner one would employ were one to address a mentally deranged person. He has fought against the Lord on completely erroneous premises . . . The new thing for Job is not God's quantitative greatness; he had realized this in advance . . . his discovery lies in God's qualitative smallness . . . By capitulating in this manner he inflicts the worst conceivable of indignities on the tyrant, Jehovah: that his opponent is not even worthy of a battle![15]

The final outcome of examining a God of theodicies, is not that God is immoral. If *that* were the verdict, God *would* be a fellow moral agent with ourselves, subject to the same standards of criticism. But any attempt to make sense of God in these terms leads, as we have seen, to the unintelligible. Confronting the unintelligible, as far as morality is concerned, is like facing the monstrous, for it knows no moral bounds.

We have had similar suggestions from Hume in response to Cleanthes' attempt to build an order out of the contingencies of human existence. Even if we allow that the world arose from something like design,[16] Philo argues:

> . . . beyond that position he cannot ascertain one single circum-
> stance, and is left afterwards to fix every point of his theology,
> by the utmost licence of fancy and hypothesis. This world, for
> aught he knows, is very faulty and imperfect, compared to a
> superior standard; and was only the first rude essay of some
> infant Deity, who afterwards abandoned it, ashamed of his
> lame performance; it is the work of some dependent, inferior
> Deity; and is the object of derision to his superiors: it is the
> production of old age and dotage in some superannuated
> Deity; and ever since his death, has run on at adventures, from
> the first impulse and active force, which it received from him .
> . . I cannot, for my part, think, that so wild and unsettled a
> system of theology is, in any respect, preferable to none
> at all.[17]

It is difficult for theodicists to accept the God who emerges from all these deliberations. For Tennessen, the God who emerges from the Book of Job is a cosmic cave dweller, a brag-gart, a rumble-dumble. In Hume, God could turn out to be a doodling infant, ashamed of his efforts; an incompetent God; or a senile God after whose death we have been left unattended. Hume calls these 'wild and unsettled hypotheses'. Yet, aren't such hypotheses more in accord with life's contingencies than the order theodicies attempt to impose on them? There is one high price to pay, however: the God who emerges from this picture is equally wild and unsettled. But, then, perhaps he is. This is what we mean when we say, so often, that things are in the lap of the gods. Some say this God does not exist. Tennessen rebels against him. In any event, he cannot be put in the dock for purposes of moral scrutiny. This God would be found unfit to plead.

## Notes

1 John K. Roth, 'A Theodicy of Protest' in Stephen T. Davis (ed.), *Encountering Evil*, Louisville: John Knox Press 2001, p. 7.
2 David Ray Griffin, 'Critique of Roth' in Davis, *Encountering Evil*, p. 26.
3 John Hick, 'An Irenaean Theodicy' in Davis, *Encountering Evil*, p. 50.
4 John K. Roth, 'Critique of Hick' in Davis, *Encountering Evil*, pp. 62–4.
5 See the close of the section 'Evils as Bad Choices' in Chapter 3 and the section, 'Things are Not as Bad as They Seem'.
6 See close of Chapter 3, section 8: 'Evils as Bad Choices'.
7 Richard Swinburne, *Providence and the Problem of Evil*, Oxford: Clarendon Press 1998, p. 41.
8 Swinburne, *Providence*, p. 41.
9 Herman Tennessen, 'A Masterpiece of Existential Blasphemy: the Book of Job', *The Human World*, No. 13, Nov. 1973, p. 1.
10 Tennessen, 'Masterpiece', p. 5.
11 Tennessen, 'Masterpiece', p. 5.
12 Tennessen, 'Masterpiece', p. 3.
13 Tennessen, 'Masterpiece', p. 8.
14 Tennessen, 'Masterpiece', p. 2.
15 Tennessen, 'Masterpiece', pp. 8–9.
16 I am far from meaning that this assumption is unproblematic. See my 'From World to God' in *Recovering Religious Concepts*, Basingstoke: Macmillan 2000, pp. 45–62.
17 Hume, *Dialogues Concerning Natural Religion*, ed. Norman Kemp Smith, Indianapolis: Bobbs Merrill 1947, Part V, p. 169.

# 6

# Goodbye God?

## *1. Death by Ridicule?*

If we accept the conclusions of the previous chapter, God, it seems, has not been argued to death in the traditional positivistic way, but has been ridiculed to death. The God who remains is one found to be unfit to plead; one who could be aptly assigned to the company of Hume's infantile, incompetent or geriatric gods. Nevertheless, it may be thought, whatever the means of God's demise, the desirable result is the same, namely, that we should finally turn aside from a religious mode of explaining human affairs which must end in ridicule. When human beings were at the early stages of their development, looking for religious explanations was a natural tendency for the enquiring mind, but, now, we are without excuse for doing so. We have had opportunities enough to heed the warnings of enlightened minds which have shown us the way ahead without religion.[1]

Sometimes, it seemed that thinkers did not deny the gods, but, rather, proclaimed their irrelevance for human life. But such qualification was no more than a stay of execution. The fate of the gods was never in doubt. This can be seen, for example, in Lucretius' challenge to explain how human misdeeds are to be correlated with the thunderbolts that the gods were thought to send as punishment for them. Lucretius asks a number of questions, not because he expects answers to them, but because he knows none can be given. Roth hopes that through protesting against the waste in God's plan, a deeper conception of God will be arrived at, one that will not attempt to explain the waste away. Roth says, 'If will does go that way, then God's nature remains in the making'.[2] But this does not take account of how deep the incoherence in the conception of the divine is said to be. It cannot be resolved *within* the tradition in which Roth struggles to retain a footing. When Lucretius seeks alternative explanations for the wastage incurred by the gods, what he offers is as humorous as Hume's wild hypotheses. Once again, God or the gods are being ridiculed to death.

> But if Jupiter and other gods shake the shining regions of heaven with appalling din, if they cast fire whither it may be the pleasure of each one, why do they not see to it that those who have not refrained from some abominable crime, shall be struck and breathe out sulphurous flames from breast pierced through, a sharp lesson to mankind? Why rather does one with no base guilt on his conscience roll in flames all innocent, suddenly involved in a tornado from heaven and taken off by fire? Why again do they aim at deserts and waste their labour? Or are they then practising their hands and strengthening their muscles? And why do they suffer the Father's bolt to be blunted against the earth? Why does he himself allow this, instead of saving it for his enemies? Why again does Jupiter never cast a bolt on the earth and sound his thunder, when the heaven is clear on all sides? Does he wait until clouds have come up, to descend into them himself, that he may be near by to direct hence the blow of his bolt?[3]

Lucretius' inference is clear: once we understand the real origins of thunderbolts, we will no longer relate them to human affairs via the notion of supernatural activity. On the other side of ridicule is the clarity of scientific explanation. Henceforth, we will look to human resources for the solution of human problems. The irrelevance of God or the gods is simply the concealed announcement of their demise.

If the course of the present argument is embraced, one form of explanation takes the place of the other, except that the 'other', the religious explanation, is thought never to have been a real explanation in the first place. In any case, progress is going to be made: where religion mystified, secular explanations will make

plain. As Flannery O'Connor has pointed out, 'Since the eight-
eenth century, the popular spirit of each succeeding age has
tended more and more to the view that the ills and mysteries of
life will eventually fall before the scientific advances of man.'⁴
To question this conclusion, in certain circumstances, is itself to
become the object of ridicule; a just fate, it is thought, for those
who still worship a ridiculous God. If it has been shown, intellectually, that, at best, the divine is indifferent to us, we can
afford to be equally indifferent to the divine. It need no longer be
part of our thinking, or of our world.

## 2. *Limiting Questions*

If scientific explanations are to *replace* religious explanations of
the evils in human existence, there seems to be an implicit appeal
to a common measure that will show why one set of answers is
*better* than the other set. The difficulty is that when one looks for
this common measure, it proves difficult to find. As Rhees says:

> When we speak of a progressive enlightenment, we take for
> granted a common measure where we cannot even imagine
> one.
>       Suppose it were said that science has freed us from subjec-
> tion to fate. And suppose we asked *how* science has done this.
>       As though men had spoken of fate because they knew no
> better. As though the reasoned beliefs of science could *replace*
> any thought of fate.⁵

Rhees is not denying the possibility that an individual, or even a
people, may not think any longer in terms of fate, because that
way of thinking has been eroded by emphases of a different kind.
People may give up asking certain questions. After all, not everyone asks them now and, perhaps, at no time did everyone do so.
But these eventualities are different from the claim that scientific
answers have *replaced* religious answers, as though they were
competing solutions within a *common* system of explanation.
That assumes that they are asking *the same* questions, and that is
what Rhees disputes.

Suppose there has been an earthquake, and geologists now give an explanation of it. This will not be an answer to the woman who has lost her home and her child and asks 'Why?' It does not make it easier to understand 'what has befallen us'. And the woman's question, though it may drive her mad, does not seek an answer. 'It was fate' may some day come to take the place of asking.

A man whose son is in danger of death may say, 'The outcome will be whatever is fated to be'. And he is not predicting anything. Or if he says, 'Whatever happens will be the will of God' – this cannot *mislead* us about what is going to happen.[6]

If the questions asked are not ones which have answers, in the form of explanations, what kind of questions are they? They can be called *limiting questions*. Not everyone asks these questions, or responds to them in the same way. They are questions born of bewilderment at the contingencies of life: 'I thought I had the strength to see that through, but . . .'; 'I thought I could rely on that relationship and then . . .'; 'We had worked hard, the worst seemed to be over and then look what happened'; 'He had everything to live for, and yet'; 'Something really worthwhile could have been achieved, but for the chance presence of deep malice in a person', and so on. The thought 'If only . . .' keeps resuming. 'If only it hadn't happened just at that time when I was ready to . . . wanted to . . . seemed able to'; 'If only I'd been born twenty years earlier when there was an opportunity to . . .'; 'Why was I born into the family just when those problems occurred?'; 'Why are conditions such that my energies are expended just in avoiding friction?'; 'Why are times such that lies win the day when truth should be so plain to see?' These are the limits of space and time, and the questions asked of them are limiting questions.

As we have seen, theodicies make the mistake of thinking that, faced by the limits of human existence, what is needed is some kind of super-explanation of them. When the explanation is provided, as we have seen, it runs into familiar difficulties. If the transcendent divine plan refers to a future state of affairs after death, continuous, in some sense, with this life, which is supposed to justify or redeem its tribulations, it is difficult to see why this future life should not be as puzzling as our present one. If, on the other hand, the future life is discontinuous with our present one, how can it have anything to say to the bewilderment we may feel faced with life's limits? As we have seen, however, there are logical difficulties prior to these. They concern the super-explanations of the details of human tribulation that we discussed in Part I.

It will be noted that there is a similarity between theodicies and secular, rationalistic responses to human suffering. Both think that the limits of human existence call out for *explanation*. Of course, it is the secularist's view that the religious quest for explanation ends in ridicule. We saw this in Tennessen's analysis of the Book of Job. This view seems to be confirmed when he describes the inanity of the creator as he surveys his work: '*Do you know what is my most outstanding work? No, it is not the human spirit with its sickly sense of justice, as you believe, you fool. No, my dear boy, it's the hippopotamus!*'[7] At this point, the reader would have expected Tennessen to deny the existence of God and to turn to the secular alternatives. Or perhaps one might expect him to say, with those whom life does not bewilder, 'Strange? No, that's exactly how life is, full of ups and downs. We must get on with what we can do something about, and come to terms with those things which cannot be changed.' I am not saying that such reactions are to be despised. I see nothing philosophically suspect in them. Sometimes, they act as timely interventions to put a stop to romantic indulgences in angst.

Yet, this is not how Tennessen reacts. For him, too, human life is strange, baffling, bewildering. He sees theodicies as having the audacity to try to impose a false order on life's contingencies. But he does *not* conclude that he must seek an order of a different kind to explain those contingencies. More surprisingly, he does not conclude that there is no God. Towards the end of his paper, he suddenly asks the following question:

But this god in the Book of Job, does *he* concern us? Is the whole of it any more than a poetic game with an alien and outdated concept of the divine? Do we *know* this god?[8]

He replies:

> Yes, we know him from the history of religion; he is the god of the Old Testament, 'the Lord of Hosts' or, as we might put it, the Lord of Armies: the jealous Jehovah.[9]

If that were all, Tennessen would simply be making a descriptive, historical remark. It would be quite consistent, having made it, if he were to say that we have outgrown it. But Tennessen is not simply speaking of history. For this reason he pursues his questions further:

> But does he live only in the history of religion? No, he also lords it over our experience, today as many millenniae ago. He represents a familiar biological and social milieu: the blind forces of nature, completely indifferent to the human need for order and meaning and justice . . . the unpredictable visitations by disease and death, the transitoriness of fame, the treason by friends and kin. He is the god of machines and power, of despotism and conquest, of pieces of brass and armoured plates. There are other men than Job who counter him with weapons of the spirit. Some of them are being trampled down in heroic martyrdom. Others recognize the limits of martyrdom, then yield on the surface, but hide the despair in their hearts.[10]

So we find Tennessen recognizing the vicissitudes of human life. He is too much of a humanist and a poet to want to gloss over them or to tidy them up. More importantly, Tennessen is admitting that these vicissitudes are beyond human understanding. Up to this point, Tennessen has criticized theodicies because they violate the claims of justice. He had said, 'The human demand for order and reason is leaping towards the heavens like a flame.'[11] But now, it seems, that same flame is leaping towards the limits of human existence itself, limits which are 'completely indifferent to the human need for order and meaning and justice'. *The important conclusion that follows is that, whether one is reacting to the vicissitudes of human life religiously or non-religiously, one is reacting to something that is beyond human understanding.*

The great divide in contemporary philosophy of religion is between those who accept and those who reject this conclusion. It has certainly been rejected by religious and secular apologists alike. When a sense of the limits of human existence has led to bewilderment and to the natural cry, 'Why is this happening to me?', 'Why are things like this?', it is essential to note that these questions are asked, not for want of explanations, but *after* explanations have provided all they can offer. The questions seem to seek for something that explanations cannot give. This is what theodicies and secular attempts at explanation fail to realize.

The god who lords it over us, for Tennessen, is not the God of theodicies. *Nothing* could be that. The god Tennessen believes in is a god of blind caprice. The only decent response to such a god, according to Tennessen, is one of rebellion. This is not a god to be worshipped. Tennessen would agree with Camus's Dr. Rieux when he asks, '. . . since the order of the world is shaped by death, mightn't it be better for God if we refuse to believe in Him and struggle with all our might against death, without raising our eyes toward the heaven where He sits in silence'.[12] For Tennessen and Camus, better silence than theodicies.

## 3. Beyond Caprice?

After his reflections on the Book of Job, Tennessen does not deny the reality of God. But his God, against whom he rebels, is a God of blind caprice. When I ask whether there is anything 'beyond caprice', it may be thought that I am asking a theological question, as though I were engaged in a theological prescriptive discussion about the kind of God we *ought* to worship. That is not the point of my investigation. It may seem otherwise, given the critical character of the discussion in Part I. Surely, it will be claimed, I was rejecting a conception of God there, namely, the God of the theodicists. True enough, but that rejection was of certain *philosophical* construals of religious belief which, I argue, are confused. It is not for me to judge the extent to which those construals reflect the lived religion of their authors, but, clearly, confusion in philosophy can often lead to confusion in our lives about the matters under discussion. Philosophy must be committed to exposing confusion whenever it finds it. But that is very different from using philosophy as an arbiter between different conceptions of God or different theological views concerning the same God, which are *not* confused. I see nothing confused in Tennessen's God of blind caprice. There are times when I find it all too easy to believe in such a God, but that is a personal matter. To believe in Tennessen's God is to embrace that whole way of looking at the world. To say that his God exists would be to confess that belief in him.

Part of the misunderstanding here may be due to what one understands by philosophy's investigation of *the reality* of religious belief. This is not the same as asking, 'Is this really God?' The latter question is like asking, 'Art thou God?' It is a question which belongs to a *religious* search, and its answer, if positive, would be a confession of faith. Philosophy cannot *settle* that question, although it may influence it for good or ill in various ways. But when philosophy investigates the reality of a religious belief, it is an investigation of its *sense*, of its conceptual character.

This would apply to worship of a God of caprice. Philosophy would be interested in the kind of belief it is, an interest that would be part of its engagement with the central question of what it is to say something. It would be interested in what 'saying something' comes to in this context. Some analytic philosophers of religion, along with their counterparts in Process thought, see it as part of their task to arrive at an *adequate* conception of God. This seems to me to be primarily a *theological* enterprise, despite the fact that philosophy may be used to assist it. The confusion comes from thinking that the theological judgement can be underwritten by philosophy. It is one thing to say that philosophy may find certain confusions in a religion (although there is always the danger of misunderstanding), and quite another to say that after confusions have been avoided, only one, or relatively few, religious possibilities will remain.

Certain philosophers may want to say that there is something logically odd in the worship of a God of caprice or in the worship of the terrible. Perhaps they can only see perversion there, or an attempt to appease, or to avoid the contingencies of human life. This is one of the reasons Wittgenstein has for criticizing Frazer's account of primitive rituals in his *The Golden Bough*. He makes them sound like the failed attempts of a primitive science. Yet, as Wittgenstein points out, the very language Frazer uses is not the language of reporting such failures: Instead of trying to *explain* the practice in this way, he should not try to get behind it, but let it speak for itself. Wittgenstein writes:

> I think one reason why the attempt to find an explanation is wrong is that we have only to put together in the right way what we *know*, without adding anything, and the satisfaction we are trying to get from the explanation comes of itself.
>
> And here the explanation is not what satisfies us anyway. When Frazer begins by telling the story of the King of the Wood at Nemi, he does this in a tone which shows that something strange and terrible is happening here. And that is the answer to the question 'why is this happening?': Because it is terrible. In other words, what strikes us in this course of events as terrible, impressive, horrible, tragic, etc., anything but trivial and insignificant, *that* is what gave birth to them.
>
> We can only *describe* and say, human life is like that.[13]

In order to see what is in the ritual, one has to put aside one's own religious or theological viewpoint, if one wants to see how the ritual is an expression of what goes deep with those who participate in it. Wittgenstein says of Frazer:

> When he explains to us, for example, that the king must be killed in his prime because, according to the notions of the savages, his soul would not be kept fresh otherwise, we can only say: where that practice and these views go together, the practice does not spring from the view, but both of them are there.[14]

Rhees comments:

> The idea doesn't arise from the practice or vice versa. They are
> both possessed by these people – it is natural to think of them
> together like that. If you ask: Why this ritual? Why should the
> priest devote his whole life to this role knowing he is to be
> sacrificed? Or: What are they trying to achieve by it? Why
> should they be striving to achieve anything? Various things
> happen round about or in the lives of these people in primitive
> societies, which impress them, and are very different from
> urban or industrial societies. Death is one of them. If you ask:
> Why should it? – that's your privilege. It may not impress us –
> Dr. Bernhard will see to it. But it *did* impress them.[15]

Where does Tennessen stand on these issues? As we have seen,
he has little time for the God of theodicies. On the other hand, he
has a sense of the radical contingency of human life, which
enables him to have some appreciation of how human beings
might feel they were in the hands of the gods. Given his conception of a god of caprice, however, his reaction to it, unlike that of
the primitives, is one of disdain and rebellion. That, one might
say, is *his* privilege. But he does not let matters rest there. He
presents a wider philosophical thesis in which he wants to argue
that there *can* be no alternative to the conception of God against
which he rebels. His choice is exclusive: either the confused God
of theodicies or the God of caprice.

Tennessen takes his conclusion to be governed by 'the human
demand for order and reason'. As such, he thinks that one cannot simply *begin* with a notion of God. One must show how one
arrives at it *on the basis of agreed canons of reason*. He writes:

> The conception of the deity is not to be derived from 'the given
> God'. But that God which we can accept must flow from the
> norms of the deity, with our image of God as an optimum . . .
> We also demand that God shall represent the highest wisdom,
> shall inspire creation with order and meaning.[16]

According to Tennessen, God must be judged by *pre-existing standards* as the highest exemplification of them. These standards are our moral, human standards. Otherwise, as we have seen, 'God may be as "just" as he pleases, in his own language.'[17] This point of view echoes the terms of reference of the dispute between Cleanthes and Philo in Hume's *Dialogues*, namely, that an argument for God's existence *must* be an a posteriori argument. Cleanthes imagines a person coming into the world with an *antecedent* conception of God's goodness and benevolence. Philo argues:

> Supposing now, that this person were brought into the world, still assured, that it was the workmanship of such a sublime and benevolent Being; he might, perhaps, be surprised at the disappointment; but would never retract his former belief.[18]

This admission does not amount to much, since the person Philo portrays is of limited intelligence, unacquainted with the world, ready to resort to the appeal to ignorance we have already encountered, when confronted by the gap between the world and what he had expected of a God described as good, benevolent and all-powerful. In short, the antecedent conception of God is *the same* conception as the one hoped for as the result of a posteriori argument. That is why Philo does not dwell on this case, because he quickly points out that we are not in the position of such a creature. We are *in* the world. We are not: 'antecedently convinced of a supreme intelligence, benevolent, and powerful, but [are] left to gather such a belief from the appearances of things; this entirely alters the case, nor will [we] ever find any reason for such a conclusion'.[19]

Interestingly, we find Hick, as opposed to Swinburne, admitting the inefficacy of a posteriori arguments. He writes:

> Can a world in which sadistic cruelty often has its way, in which selfish lovelessness is so rife, in which there are debilitating diseases, crippling accidents, bodily and mental decay, insanity, and all manner of natural disasters, be regarded as the expression of infinite creative goodness? Certainly all this

could never by itself lead anyone to believe in the existence of a limitlessly powerful God. And yet even in such a world, innumerable men and women have believed and do believe in the reality of an infinite creative goodness, which they call God. The theodicy project starts at this point – with an already operating belief in God, embodied in human living.[20]

Hick wants to begin where Philo and Tennessen say we should *not* begin, namely, 'with an already operating belief in God'. We have already had reason to question, however, whether that operating belief is captured by a theodicy. We have seen the results of thinking that, 'The theodicy project is thus an exercise in metaphysical thinking, in the sense that it consists in the formation and criticism of large-scale hypotheses concerning the nature and process of the universe.'[21] Perhaps Philo and Tennessen think that if we say that we must begin, philosophically, with 'an already operating belief in God', calling it the *received* or *given* conception, this means an advocacy of receiving what is given, religiously. As I have said, this is not so. The 'operating belief' is 'given' only in the sense that this is where we should begin our conceptual investigations. It is not a belief 'built up' out of standards prior to it. It is offered as a system of reference in itself, one that is not a hypothesis about the world, but an element, a light, that is constitutive of a vision of the world. It offers a spirit in which to see the world, and believers call that spirit, God.

This raises the question of the relation of the Spirit to the world. Is it self-authenticating, not needing any such relation to be understood? The following remarks by Simone Weil show us what would be wrong with that view:

> The Gospel contains a conception of human life, not a theology.
>
> If I light an electric torch at night out of doors I don't judge its power by looking at the bulb, but by seeing how many objects it lights up.
>
> The brightness of a source of light is appreciated by the illumination it projects upon non-luminous objects.

The value of a religious or, more generally, a spiritual way of life is appreciated by the amount of illumination thrown upon the things of this world.

Earthly things are the criterion of spiritual things.[22]

This does not mean that the earthly criterion is *prior* to 'the spiritual' (Philo and Tennessen's contention), but that 'the earthly' and 'the spiritual' go together as 'belief' and 'practice' do in the slaying of the King of the Forest at Nemi.[23] The *philosophical* task is to examine this notion of 'illumination'. In doing so, it will be examining what is meant by divine reality at the same time.

What stands in the way of Tennessen's appreciation of these conclusions? He does not dispute that we must look to our language to find out what is meant by 'the ways of God', but he simply answers that *human language only speaks of human standards*. Evidently, that is not so, since *already operative* in that language is talk of the ways of God. Nothing Tennessen has said shows why the philosopher cannot explore the meaning of this talk. The exploration will not be successful, however, if *prior* to looking at the use of language in question, we come to it with our minds already made up about what it *must* mean. Tennessen comes to that language armed with conceptions of 'the norms of the deity', and an 'image of God as an optimum'. Inevitably, it fails the test of answerability to those conceptions. God fails, however, given Tennessen's preconceptions about what religious language must mean. To free himself from these preconceptions, Tennessen must be prepared to do something he warns us against, namely, to find a concept of God in 'the given God'.

Yet, were Tennessen to look in this direction, he would find that many believers would agree with the criticisms of theodicies advanced by Camus and himself. In fact, many are horrified by them. So whatever they mean by religion *cannot* be what theodicies offer. Tennessen would also find such people insisting that religion should not falsify what we know about our world, a fault exposed again and again in our discussions of theodicies in Part I of this work. Here are some examples.

Flannery O'Connor, a devout Catholic, insists that we must not 'reflect God with what amounts to a practical untruth'.[24] She insists that if someone wants to show how 'the natural world contains the supernatural . . . this doesn't mean that his obligation to portray the natural is less; it means it is greater'.[25] O'Connor is speaking of Catholic novelists, but the same can be said of a philosopher who wants to elucidate concept-formation where belief in the supernatural is concerned:

> if he is going to show the supernatural taking place, he has nowhere to do it except on the literal level of natural events, and . . . if he doesn't make these natural things believable in themselves, he can't make them believable in any of their spiritual extensions.[26]

In the task of giving perspicuous representations of these spiritual extensions, O'Connor refers to Conrad's conviction that he had to do the highest possible justice to the visible world because it suggested an invisible one,[27] and to Baron von Hügel's insistence that the apologist for religion should not try 'to tidy up reality'.[28] This last reminds one of Wittgenstein's insistence to philosophers that 'what's ragged should be left ragged'.[29] I hope to have been faithful to these injunctions in Part I of the book.

Tennessen's complaint, one I agree with, is that theodicies do not succeed in making the natural believable, or in doing justice to the natural world; they do try to tidy up the world and refuse to leave the ragged ragged.

In the second part of the book my aim is to show a conception of human life found in Christianity, but not only there, that avoids the pitfalls of theodicy, but, at the same time, shows the possibility of a response to the contingencies of life that is other than celebration of the terrible, or a rebellious response to a God of caprice. It will involve showing how, from the very contingencies Tennessen emphasizes, concept-formation involving belief in a God of grace is possible. But no spiritual extension from the facts Tennessen mentions can be believable, unless the believability of the facts themselves is retained.

## Notes

1. I have examined these traditions of thought in *Religion and the Hermeneutics of Contemplation*, Cambridge: Cambridge University Press 2001.
2. John K. Roth, 'Rejoinder' in Stephen T. Davis (ed.), *Encountering Evil*, Louisville: Westminster John Knox Press 2001, p. 34.
3. Lucretius, *De Rerum Natura*, Bk VI, London: The Loeb Classical Library, pp. 471–3.
4. Flannery O'Connor, 'Some Aspects of the Grotesque in Southern Fiction' in O'Connor, *Mystery and Manners: Occasional Prose*, selected and edited by Sally and Robert Fitzgerald, New York: Farrar, Strauss and Giroux 1974, p. 41.
5. Rush Rhees, 'Science and Questioning' in Rhees, *Without Answers*, ed. D. Z. Phillips, London: Routledge and Kegan Paul 1970, p. 16.
6. Rhees, 'Science and Questioning', pp. 16–17.
7. Herman Tennessen, 'A Masterpiece of Existential Blasphemy: the Book of Job', *The Human World*, No. 13, November 1973, p. 8.
8. Tennessen, 'Masterpiece', p. 10.
9. Tennessen, 'Masterpiece', p. 10.
10. Tennessen, 'Masterpiece', p. 10.
11. Tennessen, 'Masterpiece', p. 5.
12. Albert Camus, *The Plague*, London: Penguin 1960, pp. 107–8.
13. Ludwig Wittgenstein, 'Remarks on Frazer's *Golden Bough*', *The Human World*, No. 3, May 1971, p. 30. For an alternative translation, see Ludwig Wittgenstein, *Philosophical Occasions*, ed. James Klagge and Alfred Nordmann, Indianapolis: Hackett 1993.
14. Wittgenstein, 'Remarks on Frazer's *Golden Bough*', p. 29.
15. Rush Rhees, *Wittgenstein's 'On Certainty'*, ed. D. Z. Phillips, Oxford: Blackwell 2003, p. 41.
16. Tennessen, 'Masterpiece', p. 7.
17. Tennessen, 'Masterpiece', p. 5.
18. David Hume, *Dialogues Concerning Natural Religion*, ed. N. Kemp Smith, Indiana: Bobbs-Merrill 1947, Part XI, p. 204.
19. Hume, *Natural Religion*, p. 204.
20. John Hick, 'An Irenaean Theodicy' in Davis, *Encountering Evil*, p. 38.
21. Hick, 'An Irenaean Theodicy', p. 38.
22. Simone Weil, *First and Last Notebooks*, Oxford: Oxford University Press 1970, p. 147.
23. Cf. pp. 136–7 of the present chapter.
24. Flannery O'Connor, 'Catholic Novelists and Their Readers', in *Mystery and Manners*, p. 174.
25. O'Connor, 'Catholic Novelists', p. 175.
26. O'Connor, 'Catholic Novelists', p. 176.

Goodbye God? 143

27  O'Connor, 'Catholic Novelists', p. 80.

28  O'Connor, 'Catholic Novelists', p. 177.

29  Wittgenstein, *Culture and Value*, Oxford: Blackwell 1980, p. 45.

# Part Two

# A Neglected Inheritance

# 7

# God, Contracts and Covenants

## 1. Covenant as Contract

God's covenant with his people is spoken of, sometimes, as though it were a contract. If people obey his will, God will protect them. If they disobey, harm of some kind will befall them. Understood thus, the covenant is thought of as a system of rewards and punishments. How can the sufferings of human beings be understood within these parameters? Many have concluded that they cannot. This delineation of the relationship between God and human beings is no longer tenable. Some say that a new conception of God's covenant is needed, but there is disagreement about its nature.

As long as the covenant between God and his people is understood in contractual terms, deeper conceptual issues involved in doing so are being evaded. In order to treat the covenant as a contract, a system of rewards and punishments, there must be an intelligible correlation between sin and suffering. As we saw in the Interlude, the Book of Job is an exposure of the lack of any such correlation. In trying to establish one between Job's sins and his sufferings, a God of a certain kind is ridiculed to death.

If, in terms of a contractual covenant, God is supposed to *protect* his people, what are we to say in face of human suffering? Are we to say that it is a *breach of contract* on God's part? That seems inadequate to the point of absurdity. It would be like saying that a child who says that 2 + 2 = 9000 has made a mistake. That is too big for a blunder! The child has not made a mistake *in* counting. It is still struggling to grasp what counting is. To say that the evils are a breach of contract is to betray a failure to grasp the key notions that enter into the alleged making of a contract; concepts such as 'promise', 'protection', 'fault' and 'desert'. They cannot be given an intelligible application. That is why human suffering is too big to be God's mistake, too horrendous to be his breach of contract.

If talk of a breach of contract were appropriate, it would also be appropriate to speak of 'excuse', 'mitigation' and 'compensation'. Here, too, we cannot find an application for these concepts. A breach of contract has its sense within a contractual relation. The breach does not undermine that relation, conceptually, since it is understood in terms of it. Horrendous evils cannot be understood in these terms, any more than Job's tribulations can. Confronted by them, the language of covenant, conceived as contract, is in complete disarray.

In the Interlude, we saw that this outcome faces us with a choice in reflecting on the notion of a divine covenant. If we retain the concept of the covenant as a contract, God emerges, not as someone who stands in breach of it, but as a monster who is beyond its reach. On the other hand, the alternative is to explore whether there is a concept of a covenant that is not to be understood in contractual terms.

## 2. *God as an Agent Among Agents*

If God is to be thought of as party to a contract, he must also be thought of as an agent among agents, standing in reciprocal relations of rights and obligations to the other parties to the contract. But God does not participate in a form of life in the way he must, if talk of him as an agent among agents is to be intelligible.

R. F. Holland has expressed the point well:

It makes sense for *us* to have or fail to have moral reasons for our doings and refrainings because as human beings we are members of a moral community. We have been born and brought up into a shared form of life in which there are, as there would be in any other form of human life, customs and traditions; ideas, more than one set of them perhaps, about what it is for instance to keep or break faith with another, what ways of behaving incur ignominy, what it is to treat someone well or badly, what justice and injustice are . . . But God is not a member of a moral community or of any community . . . To credit the one true God with having a moral reason for doing anything is to conceive Him . . . as a one among many . . . subjectable to moral judgement; and within a moral community of course it would make perfectly good sense for the one by whom, or let us say the chief one by whom we are judged, to be submitted to our moral judgement.[1]

This judgement and counter-judgement is exactly what we have seen in the reasonings that constitute theodicies: 'That looks pretty rough, why did God allow that?' – 'Well, he did it for such-and-such reasons.' – 'Alright, but did he have to go to such lengths?' – 'I understand your concern, but he wanted to achieve these ends, and unfortunately, there's no other way to get there.' And so on. God is part of a community of criticism and counter-criticism. It is almost as though an end-of-term report were being compiled on God's performance. Some say that God has definitely failed the test; some say that he has done very well, exactly what one would expect of a being of high moral calibre; some *believe* he has done well, but without understanding how just now, and look forward to eschatological clarification; some say that he could do better; and some say that he does what he can in the circumstances. As Holland says:

There is a tone of voice which often goes along with this. Listen to Professor Swinburne: 'For myself I can say that I would not be too happy to worship a creator who expected too little of his creatures' (*Reason and Religion*, ed. S. C. Brown, Cornell University Press 1977, pp.101–2). It seems to me that Swinburne there is invoking a moral fairy and that the creator he *would* be happy to worship would be another fairy out of the same pack – one who would set a more commendable standard.[2]

Where are we to find the standards that would make us happy were God to live up to them? As we have seen, philosophers claim that they are found in the morally sufficient reasons that God can produce for allowing evils, however horrendous, to exist. As we have also seen, it is the availability of these reasons, or their possible availability, that, according to philosophers, makes it possible for believers to acknowledge evil and still believe in an omnipotent, perfectly good God, without inconsistency. But these reasons are operative within a moral community. Since God is not a member of such a community, such reasons cannot be ascribed to him. Thus, Holland is able to conclude with respect to a reason of this kind:

> So in arguing that God cannot have one I have been offering to any theologian who, like Plantinga, has drawn sustenance from Pike's argument a proof that God does not exist. Other theologians need not be downhearted: it is only God's Pikean or Plantingarian existence I am disproving.[3]

As in the case of the contractual concept of the covenant, our conclusions leave us with a choice. On the one hand, we can simply be content with those who say God has failed the test. On the other hand, we can give up the notion of God as an agent among agents. We would be giving it up in the same way as we gave up the notion of 'covenant' as 'contract', since the test God fails is not one of competence, but of intelligibility. It simply makes no sense to think of God as an agent among agents. Rowan Williams has shown that the reasons why this is so lie deep in orthodox belief.

> Plenty of theologians and philosophers have pointed out that, if God is conceived as acting in a punctiliar way, the divine action is determined by something other than itself; likewise if God is conceived as 'reacting' to anything. If either of these conceptualities gets a foothold in our thinking about God, we ascribe to God a context for God's action: God is (like us) an agent in an environment, who must 'negotiate' purposes and desires in relation to other agencies and presences. But God is

not an item in any environment, and God's action has been held, in orthodox Christian thought, to be identical with God's being – that is, what God does is nothing other than God's being actively real.[4]

More needs to be said on the sense in which love and goodness, for example, can be identified with God.[5] For now, however, it can simply be noted that if divine action is not determined by anything other than itself, love and goodness cannot, and need not, be subject to morally sufficient reasons that explain their presence on some occasions and their absence on others. For similar reasons, we saw, in Chapter 2, section 1, that God's will cannot be treated as sheer power, disposed to be loving or good if it wants to be so. Rather, we saw that God's nature (his love and goodness) is the grammar of God's will. Once again, God's activity and being are one.

## 3. *God as Pure Consciousness*

If we should be prepared to say a conceptual farewell to the idea of a covenant as a contract, and to the idea of God as an agent among agents, we must still account for the persistence of an anthropomorphic conception of God in discussions of the problem of evil. The two concepts I have said we should reject play a part in forming such a conception. This being so, the logic of divine agency does not differ, conceptually, from the logic of human agency. God simply becomes the invisible man of theology. In order to do so, however, he must retain what is thought to be essential to personal agency. That essence is said to be consciousness.

The only difference between God and man is that, whereas man is an embodied consciousness, God is a disembodied consciousness. Swinburne writes, 'I take the proposition "God exists" . . . to be logically equivalent to "there exists a person without a body (i.e. a spirit) who is eternal, is perfectly free, omnipotent, omniscient, perfectly good, and the creator of all things".'[6] Hick makes the distinction central in determining whether philosophers give a satisfactory account of the objective reality of God, and berates them for not giving his question a direct answer. He asks philosophers whether they admit that, 'in addition to all the many human consciousnesses there is another consciousness which is God'.[7] Davis, too, thinks this is an important question. He writes, 'Phillips knows good and well what Hick is driving at – as I do and as everybody else does – and . . . Hick's question deserves a straight answer.'[8]

I do not think everyone knows what Hick is driving at, if that means that what he is saying has a *sense* which everyone appreciates. I do not think Davis knows what Hick is driving at. Indeed, I do not think Hick knows. I certainly do not know. By this I mean that no coherent account can be given of what Hick thinks he is saying. Hick is obviously exasperated by my refusal to reply in his terms. But I do not think anyone can, though they may think otherwise. The reason why he cannot be given a straight answer is because he hasn't asked a straight question. Unless this possibility is at least recognized, the consequence, as Hartshorne says, is that '[c]onfusion in the posing of a question generates confusion in the answering of it'.[9] That is why I do not deny what Hick says. It is not intelligible enough to deny. The notion of consciousness being invoked is a philosophical chimera. If this is so, it cannot be attributed, meaningfully, to either human beings or God.

If consciousness is the essence of a person, one would expect it, at the very least, to be the guarantor of that person's identity. But consciousness cannot tell me who I am. How is it supposed to do this? Presumably, by telling me that I am *this* consciousness as distinct from any other. But, again, how is this to be accomplished? Even the advocates of this way of thinking admit that it cannot be done by my picking out one consciousness, namely, mine, from a number of consciousnesses. For, according to the tradition being examined, although Hick speaks of human consciousness in the plural, every human being is only acquainted with one, namely, his own. But this brings us back to where we began: how do I know that this consciousness, the only one I know, is *mine*?

It may seem that the obvious way out of this difficulty is to say that the only consciousness of which I am aware tells me immediately that it is *mine*. I can say, 'I am *this*.' The demonstrative is a self-authenticating reference. But as long as we are talking about self-identity, the logical problem remains unresolved. I am 'this' as opposed to 'that'. Yet identity requires such a contrast, in order that there is an independent standard by means of which one can check whether the identity is correct.

We must ask, however, whether the consciousness being referred to is a matter of my identity at all. It is not to be identified with D. Z. Phillips, since it is meant to be consciousness of the world about me. I am said to be conscious of talking to people; of being talked to by them; of working alone and with others; of buying and selling; of eating and drinking; of reading and hearing of events in different parts of the world; and so on. While it is unobjectionable to say, on appropriate occasions that I am conscious of these things occurring, it would be absurd to say that they occur in my consciousness. Furthermore, in the things I am conscious of, I, as D. Z. Phillips, have nothing of the special status consciousness was supposed to bestow on me. I am not the subject or focal point of the things I am conscious of. It is those things themselves that hold centre stage. That is why it has been said that, under analysis, the claim for the primacy of consciousness collapses into ordinary realism.

When we turn our attention to the context of ordinary realism, with respect to ourselves, it turns out to be our being in the world. What tempts us to speak of the primacy of consciousness in this context? Part of the answer lies in the distinction between first-person and third-person usage of psychological concepts. For example, while I observe your anger or sadness, I do not observe my own anger or sadness in order to know that I am angry or sad. I am simply angry or sad. To ask how I know I am would be absurd. If someone asks, 'Are you angry?' we don't reply, 'Let me check to find out.' The immediacy of our acquaintance with our own anger or sadness can easily lead us to think of consciousness as the primary realm of experience.

The grammatical differences between first-person and third-person uses of psychological concepts should not be denied, but what they may hide is that they exist in our life with those concepts, a life that embraces *both* contexts. I do not learn what anger or sadness is from my own case alone. I grasp the concepts in a form of life in which I am constantly alternating between ascribing these states to others and hearing them ascribed to me; between observing anger and sadness in others, and expressing them in my own speech or behaviour. What is more, despite the important grammatical differences noted between uses of psychological concepts, in many situations things are more complicated. Expressions of anger by a person may not always be accepted by his listeners, since, in the form of life they share with him, there is room for notions such as feigned anger or sadness, and exaggeration or self-deception regarding them.

It can be seen that what is fundamental in our being in the world, is not something called the primacy of consciousness, but the form of life in which we engage in the complex ways I have indicated. As we saw in Chapter 2, section 2, if we sever consciousness, as the realm of thought, from our active engagement in forms of life, it is not as though 'consciousness' and 'thought' would remain intelligible, though isolated. The notions would become quite vacuous.

If a person says, 'I'm leaving now', but makes no effort to do so, in the absence of any excuse or explanation, his thought does not retain its sense. If a person behaved generally in that way, we wouldn't know what to make of him. He could not say, 'I'm simply someone who has these thoughts, but never acts.' The incoherence would be in describing him as thinking at all. Certain examples may tempt us to resist this conclusion. A person may harbour thoughts of a love that he never expresses to anyone. But his thoughts are in the language of love, a language influenced by deeds of love; thwarted love; deep and shallow expressions of love; traditions of love, spoken of in literature and expressed in music and dance. The latter may both reflect and contribute to possibilities of love among a people. Undeclared love is logically parasitic on these contexts. It does not owe its character to the primacy of consciousness.

What of my personal identity as D. Z. Phillips? That does not emanate from a primary consciousness from which I view the world. I am in the world and have a biography. I was born of particular parents in a particular place, grew up in a certain way with innumerable acquaintances of various kinds, was influenced by a number of factors, became a husband, a father and grandfather, engaged in philosophy, held a host of beliefs and opinions, and so on. I am who I am in a human neighbourhood.

If my essence were something called consciousness, it should be possible to imagine it occupying an entirely different body, say, that of a crocodile. The crocodile, to convince the sceptics might say, 'I am D. Z. Phillips.' What more could they want – a direct communication from consciousness? But we could make nothing of this eerie phenomenon, not even if the crocodile added, 'I've just finished a book on the problem of evil.' This is not because the consciousness of the crocodile is out of reach, but because the crocodile does not participate in the form of life in which the words would have purchase. The crocodile is not saying anything. The crocodile cannot be D. Z. Phillips because the latter has a biography, including the things I have mentioned, that it would make no sense to attribute to a crocodile. And that is what I do have – a biography, not a consciousness.[10]

It may seem odd that in a section of this chapter called 'God as Pure Consciousness', there has been hardly any mention of God. But that is no accident. Early in the section, I said of the notion of consciousness, as employed in the philosophical ways I am criticizing, that it is a philosophical chimera. If that is so, it cannot be ascribed to God or man. That is why the section has been devoted to exposing that chimera.

Only because it is thought possible to isolate something called 'consciousness' from the surroundings of human life, can it be thought possible to define God as 'pure consciousness'. Human beings, it is thought, have a consciousness that only happens to be embodied. There is no difficulty, therefore, in thinking of God as a disembodied consciousness. What we have seen, however, is that if we take away the involvement of people in their human neighbourhoods, what we are left with is not consciousness, but vacuity. Not even God can be a pure consciousness, for there is nothing for God to be. As with the notions of 'covenant' or 'contract', and God as an agent among agents, it is time to bid a conceptual farewell to the notion of God as pure consciousness.

## 4. A Purifying Atheism

Looking back at the cumulative effect of the arguments of Part I, concerning our problematic inheritance with respect to the problem of evil, the comic and satirical challenges of the Interlude, and now the three concepts, in the previous sections of the present chapter, to which I argue we should bid a conceptual farewell, the overwhelming conclusion being drawn is clearly one concerning *what God cannot be*.

What are the likely reactions to this conclusion? No doubt there will be enormous resistance from within the philosophical traditions I have criticized, although one hopes that a strategy of silence in face of challenge will give way to creative debate. This reaction is to be expected, since the language of theodicy constitutes, for many, the parameters within which the problem of evil is discussed, without any questioning of its appropriateness. The suggestion that that language is itself suspect, and that it places 'God' in wrong conceptual categories, is not one one would expect to be readily embraced, since it does not constitute a modification in a certain way of thinking, but its abandonment.

Consider, for example, the centrality of the notion of 'spirit' in Christianity.[11] We are told that God is Spirit (not *a* spirit), and that those who worship him must do so in spirit and in truth – otherwise, presumably, it simply is not worship at all. How is the term 'Spirit' to be understood? Plantinga writes, 'To accept Christian belief, I say, is to believe that there is an all-powerful, all-knowing, wholly good person (a person without a body) who has created us and our world . . .'[12] I have argued that this conception of a person without a body is meaningless. If we try to employ it in the central context of the Christian employment of 'Spirit', we have, 'God is a person without a body, and those who worship him must . . .' How would one go on from there? This question is not meant facetiously. It is meant to indicate a crisis in grammatical appreciation of the kind O. K. Bouwsma pointed out in his writings, again and again. For example, he considers the deep philosophical assumption that when we refer to God in sentences which have an indicative form, we must be giving descriptive information about their object, namely, God. He considers the religious use of sentences such as 'Great is Jehovah and greatly to be praised' (Psalm 48.1); 'Jehovah reigneth; let the people tremble. He sitteth above the cherubim; Let the earth be moved. Jehovah is great in Zion' (Psalm 99.1–2); 'Bless Jehovah, O my soul. O Jehovah, my God, though art very great' (Psalm 104.1); 'Great is Jehovah and greatly to be praised. And his greatness is unsearchable' (Psalm 145.3). Bouwsma emphasizes that 'great', in these sentences is being used as a superlative, as is the word 'high' in 'It is a good thing to give thanks unto the Lord and to sing praises unto thy name, O most high' (Psalm 92.1). Though the sentences from the psalms have the form of indicatives, that is their surface grammar, their actual application (their depth grammar) is as imperatives of praise as in 'O let the nations be glad and sing for joy' (Psalm 67.6) and 'Let the Lord be magnified' (Psalm 35.2). Bouwsma then makes the following grammatical observations:

> The earlier set of sentences have the form of indicatives – 'Great is Jehovah', etc. When removed from their surroundings and cooled for purposes of proof, they may be mistaken for sentences about God, as though they furnished information or descriptions. But they are no more statements or descriptions than the sentences just quoted. Those by their imperative form prevent at least that misunderstanding. The sentence, 'Great is our God above all other gods' is not meant to be mistaken for such a sentence as, 'High is the Empire State Building above all buildings in New York'. Or is it? I'm afraid so.[13]

Outside the tradition I am criticizing, there will be philosophers who will react to these conclusions with charges of reductionism or mystification. For them, their criticisms of religion are as dependent on our problematic inheritance, as are the theodicists' defence of it. Indeed, critics and defenders of that tradition may regard any alternative to it as atheism, and, of course, insofar as that alternative argues for the unintelligibility of certain conceptions of God, it *is* a form of atheism. But it is a purifying atheism.

How is the term 'purifying atheism' being used here? It can be used in a number of ways. It can be used by those who welcome my conclusions as a release from a religion that confused them. 'So there's no one there! No policeman in the sky looking out for me. The bogey man won't get me after all.' The release purifies, in that it rescues people from low fears. Those rescued may not be interested in any possible religious alternative. 'As long as the sky is open, the fear unreal, everything is permitted!' If *that* is what happens, the 'liberated' one may be plunged into 'a low' of an equal, if not greater, gravity.

Others may see the purifying atheism as a prelude to turning in a different religious direction, or as the necessity to appreciate a different religious direction already recognized. Some commentators on my work see me as engaged in this religious advocacy. Their reaction is understandable, because I am philosophically interested in the directions some may advocate. Nevertheless, it misconstrues the central character of my philosophical discussions. If my conclusions can be called a purifying atheism, this is not because their aim is to advocate a worthy conception of the divine. If I have provided a proof of the non-existence of a certain kind of God, it is a *conceptual* proof. It shows that certain ways of talking, which seemed to make sense, in fact have no application: talk of God's covenant with his people in terms of a contract; talk of God as an agent among agents; and talk of God as pure consciousness. Atheism with respect to a God, understood in these terms, is conceptually purifying. It is a prerequisite for appreciating other religious possibilities, other forms of religious belief. Whether the reader is attracted or repelled by these religious beliefs is not the philosopher's concern. His concern is with doing conceptual justice to them and to the kind of illumination they purport to offer. In doing so, so far as contemporary philosophy of religion is concerned, he will be giving attention to a neglected inheritance.

In the Interlude, we noted one great divide that separates our problematic inheritance, with respect to the problem of evil, from the inheritance that has been neglected. This has to do with those who assert, and those who deny, that the limits of human existence admit of further explanations. It is important to emphasize the difference between talk of *the limits* of human existence, in this context, and talk of its *limitations*. The latter notion, as we have seen, looms large in our problematic inheritance. It has to do with what is said to be our failure, as finite creatures, to penetrate the ways of God. There is something to understand there, but we'll only know what it is in the *eschaton*. But to recognize *the limits* of human existence, is to recognize that there is nothing to be put right by any understanding of that kind. There may be protest or praise, but that is a different matter. Responses to the limits of human existence need not be explanations of them. Regarding God as the maker of contracts with us, acting alongside us as an agent among agents, is one way of trying to explain life seen as a limitation. Responding to the limits of human existence religiously may, however, express belief in a divine covenant of a very different kind.

### 5. An Eternal Covenant?

We began the chapter with a discussion of 'covenant' as 'contract'. A covenant so conceived takes the form of a *temporal* covenant. It says that if the people do *x*, God will do *y*. Such a covenant can easily be broken. All it takes is for the people to do *x*, and God not to do *y*. As we saw, many see horrendous evils as a horrendous breaking of the contract between God and his people. For example, it makes no sense to speak of the Jewish people as deserving the Holocaust, so God should have protected them from it. He did not. Result: end of contract. But there is an added complication. A covenant with God is meant to be an *eternal* covenant. But how can it be so, if one can cite temporal events that would show the covenant to have been broken? The trouble, as we shall see, comes from regarding an eternal covenant as a *long-term* temporal contract. The problem lies, however, not in the length of a contract, but in thinking of a covenant in this way.

The main problem can be stated as follows: how can there be an eternal covenant that is not, at the same time, subject to being overturned by temporal events? In other words, aren't all covenants temporal? Does the notion of an eternal covenant even make sense? For many theologians, the question takes the following form: how can there be an *eternal* covenant with a God who is also the God of history? If God is the God of history, must not any covenant with him be subject to the events of history; in other words, must it not be a *temporal* covenant? How can faith be insulated from history? Is it not a mistake to try to so insulate it? But if one says that God *is* involved in history, can a covenantal relation be anything other than a temporal one?

On the other hand, once we say that the covenant is temporal, one can specify the historical events that would break it. There is no more guarantee that our specific hopes will be realized, than there is that another Holocaust will not occur. Any idea that another one *could not* occur would repeat the original mistake of thinking that the Holocaust *could not* occur in modern Europe. This is a point made strikingly by Camus in *The Plague*. The two doctors, Castel and Rieux, discuss the early symptoms of the plague.

'And then, as one of my colleagues said, "It's unthinkable. Everyone knows it's ceased to appear in Western Europe". Yes, everyone knew that – except the dead men. Come now, Rieux, you know as well as I do what it is . . .'

'Yes, Castel,' he replied, 'It's hardly credible. But everything points to its being plague' . . .

'You know,' the old doctor said, 'what they're going to tell us? That it vanished from temperate countries long ago.'

'Vanished? What does that word really mean?'

When the plague is over, Camus, of course, does not condemn the rejoicing that occasions, but he also emphasizes a lesson that needs to be learned at such a moment.

And indeed, as he listened to the cries of joy rising from the town, Rieux remembered that such joy is always imperilled. He knew what the jubilant crowds did not know but could have learned from books: that the plague bacillus never dies or disappears for good; that it can lie dormant for years and years in furniture and linen-chests; that it bides its time in bedrooms, cellars, trunks, and bookshelves; and that perhaps the day would come when, for the bane and enlightening of men, it roused its rats again and sent them forth to die in a happy city.[14]

Notice, when that day comes, when the rats are roused again, it is for the bane and *enlightening* of men. Its bane is obvious, but what is the enlightenment? Is it not the enlightenment of those who thought, foolishly, that we are beyond horrendous evils, that they cannot happen, or, after they happen, that they cannot happen again? In a world of such contingencies, can any sense be given to the idea of an eternal covenant with God? Is it not better to say that all covenants are temporal, since it is all too clear what events would overthrow them?

John Roth argues that it is crucial to learn from the Holocaust, 'to resist the world's horror with undeceived lucidity',[15] and to accept our responsibility for what happens around us. Who would want to argue against the importance of what he says? But could an eternal covenant be thought of in these terms, one with which there would be no shadow of turning? What if we do not remember, or feel responsible? In that event, does Hitler win a posthumous victory? Does Hitler defeat God?

Many will say, from a religious perspective, that, no matter what happens, it is important not to lose hope. How is this to be understood? Is it saying, 'Live *in* hope, no matter what happens, though, of course, one hopes that certain things will happen'. If so, this is akin to the notion of an eternal covenant, whereas, if the hope is deluded, if those things do not, in fact, happen, it seems to belong to the concept of a temporal covenant. This is because the emphasis, religiously speaking, seems to be upside down. The point of loving God is not that hope should not perish or that the world should be a meaningful place. The point of loving God is not even to be found in the persistence of belief in him on earth. In an eternal covenant God is the only point of loving God. Other outcomes, however desirable, are, thereafter, in God's hands.

An eternal covenant cannot be understood as a contract. It is not a matter of thinking of God as an agent among agents who says, 'If you do *x*, I'll do *y*.' An eternal covenant offers *a conception of human life*, such that *anything* that may happen within it is understood in a certain way. *What happens in history will be the occasion for such an understanding, but not the criterion for it*. In this way, what happens in history can still be of eternal significance.

The distinction between temporal and eternal covenants may appear in religions of radically different kinds. Contrast, for example, a covenant with a warrior God who promises to grant victory in battle, and a covenant with such a God where victory or defeat are understood in terms of the values of the warrior religion. To die well would be as important as living well.

When a contractual covenant is broken, this occurs within a wider context of contractual arrangements which retains its intelligibility. When one loses hold of an eternal covenant, on the other hand, one loses hold of a whole conception of the world.

In Judaism and Christianity, covenants are said to be between a Creator and the creatures he has created. Can such a covenant be understood to be eternal? Or better: how *is* it understood to be a covenant of that kind? The first step towards an answer is to give up the notion of creation as an act of power.

## Notes

1 R. F. Holland, 'On the Form of "The Problem of Evil"' in *Against Empiricism*, Oxford: Blackwell 1980, pp. 237–8.
2 Holland, 'On the Form of "The Problem of Evil"', pp. 238–9.
3 Holland, 'On the Form of "The Problem of Evil"', p. 239.
4 Rowan Williams, 'Redeeming Sorrows' in *Religion and Morality*, ed. D. Z. Phillips, Basingstoke: Macmillan 1996, p. 143.
5 See Chapter 8, section 4.

6 Richard Swinburne, *The Existence of God*, Oxford: Clarendon Press 1979, p. 8.

7 John Hick, 'Remarks' in Stuart Brown (ed.), *Reason and Religion*, Ithaca: Cornell University Press 1977, p. 122.

8 Stephen T. Davis, 'Critique of D. Z. Phillips' in Stephen T. Davis (ed.), *Encountering Evil*, Louisville: Westminster John Knox Press 2001, p. 168.

9 Charles Hartshorne, 'A New Look at the Problem of Evil' in F. C. Dommeyer (ed.), *Current Philosophical Issues: Essays in Honour of Curt John Ducasse*, Illinois: Charles C. Thomas 1966, p. 202.

10 The issues in this section have been explored in 'The Dislocated Soul and Immortality' and 'The World and "I"' in my *Recovering Religious Concepts*, Basingstoke: Macmillan and New York: St. Martin's Press 2000.

I am mindful of the fact that there have been and are religions in which notions of reincarnation involve assertions about previous or future lives of human beings as animals. I am not denying such beliefs. I do not think they rely, however, on the confusions I am discussing, but I cannot pursue these issues further here.

11 Despite its religious centrality, the notion of 'spirit' is neglected in contemporary philosophy of religion. As a step towards rectifying this situation, see D. Z. Phillips and Mario von der Ruhr (eds), *Language and Spirit*, Basingstoke: Palgrave, 2004.

12 Alvin Plantinga, *Warranted Christian Belief*, Oxford: Oxford University Press 2000, p. 3. For an impressive critique of the notion of God as 'a person without a body', and a comparison of it with biblical language concerning the spirit of God as 'breath', or 'wind', see Patrick Sherry, 'Are Spirits Bodiless Persons?', *Neue Zeitschrift für Systematische Theologie und Religionsphilosophie*, Vol. 24, No. 1 and 'Is a Spirit a Person Without a Body? in Phillips and von der Ruhr, *Language and Spirit*. For an argument which states that dominant tendencies of thought in contemporary philosophy of religion would be quite foreign to classical theist writers, patristic writers and the giants of the Middle Ages, see Brian Davies O.P., 'Letter from America', *New Blackfriars*, July/August 2003.

13 O. K. Bouwsma, 'Anselm's Argument' in *Without Proof or Evidence*, Lincoln and London: University of Nebraska Press 1984, p. 47.

14 Albert Camus, *The Plague*, London: Penguin 1965, p. 278.

15 John K. Roth, 'On Losing Trust in the World' in John K. Roth and Michael Berenbaum (eds), *Holocaust: Religious and Philosophical Implications*, New York: Paragon House 1989, p. 251.

# 8

# God's Absence and Presence

## 1. Is 'God' Epistemically Distant?

All theistic religions have spoken of the distance that separates God from human beings. That notion of 'distance' may puzzle us. How is it to be understood? If the distance involved is said to be infinite, it may seem futile to think that human beings can ever make contact with him. If God is said to be far off, we may begin to wonder *how* far off that is. Yet, clearly, the distance between God and human beings cannot be understood in spatial terms. R. W. Hepburn gave an early expression of the difficulty one gets into if one tries to think so.

> [C]ompare these sentences – 'Outside my room a sparrow is chirping', 'Outside the city the speed limit ends', 'Outside the earth's atmosphere meteors do not burn out', and finally 'God is outside the universe, outside space and time'. What of this last statement? The word 'outside' gets its central meaning from relating item to item *within* the universe. It . . . is being stretched to breaking-point in being applied to the whole universe as related to some being that is not-the-universe: its sense is being extended to the point where we may easily come to speak nonsense without noticing it[1]

One could add to these objections one that goes deeper, namely, that since the world, everything there is, does not have the unity of a thing, it cannot be regarded as a bounded big thing that one could get outside of. A false picture leads us into confusion in searching for such a use of 'outside'. Yet, in the metaphysics of many philosophers of religion, that is where God is said to dwell.

Notice, however, that Hepburn speaks of language being stretched to breaking point in religion, so that believers can come to talk nonsense without realizing it. He speaks as though language has limits that religion transgresses. But the logic of our language does not consist of a set of limits that predetermines the application of concepts, but is found in the application of those concepts. This applies to religious language as much as to any other. It will apply to the application of the notion of distance, when it is said that God is at a great distance from human beings. Thus, seeing that God is not spatially distant from human beings may be part of the purifying atheism we discussed in section 4 of the previous chapter. It clears the ground for the recognition of the conceptual location of the religious use of 'distance'.

John Hick agrees that God cannot be said to be spatially distant from human beings, if only because God is said to be omnipresent. But, then, he proceeds to make an alternative suggestion.

> The distance must be epistemic, a distance in the cognitive dimension. And the Irenaean hypothesis is that this 'distance' consists, in the case of humans, in their existence within and as part of a world that functions as an autonomous system and from within which God is not overwhelmingly evident.[2]

If what I have said about logic and language is correct, the concept of God's distance from human beings *is not itself* epistemically distant from us. Like all concepts which have an application, it lies open to view. Clarifying its meaning does not decrease, or negate, God's distance from human beings. On the contrary, it clarifies the place that belief has in religion. Obviously, this is a matter of some consequence for the philosophy of religion.

Hick tells us that to say God is distant is to say that we live in a world where God is not overwhelmingly obvious. Suppose we ask, To whom? Are there still people like the Psalmist who says, 'God is our refuge and strength, a very present help in trouble' (Psalm 46.1). No sign of epistemic distance there. For the Psalmist, God's presence seems overwhelmingly evident. Has he made a mistake? He doesn't seem to think so. 'Therefore will we not fear, though the earth be removed, and though the mountains be carried into the midst of the sea' (Psalm 46.2). Do we philosophers know better? But there are other moments when the Psalmist asks, 'Why standest thou afar off. O Lord? why hidest thou thyself in times of trouble?' (Psalm 10.1). Here, God is distant precisely when the Psalmist's relation with him becomes problematic in time of trouble. Is it not clear that the distance between God and human beings is *not epistemic but spiritual*? The spiritual relation to God waxes and wanes as testified by the experience of the Psalmist. But 'distance' is used in a number of ways. Even when God is said to be overwhelmingly present, there is still a sense in which there is a distance between human beings and God. They cannot possess God's spirit fully. Thus, in section 4 of the previous chapter, we saw O. K. Bouwsma also quoting the Psalmist as saying, 'Great is Jehovah and greatly to be praised. And his greatness is unsearchable' (Psalm 145.3). Bouwsma is not presenting us with a report of epistemic distance, a failure to praise because of trouble in the cognitive dimension. Praising is exactly what the Psalmist is doing, but, before God, our praise is never adequate. We cannot overpraise him, as we could a human being. Neither can we say, 'Well, that's over. That's praise enough for one day'!

We have found out the *kind* of distance there is said to be between God and human beings by looking at the applications of the word 'distance' in religious language. Hick is unhappy with this procedure, but his description of it shows that he does not understand what it involves. This has been a problem in our philosophical relationship for over 25 years. Hick says that if he is wrong about my position, this has never been made clear to him by myself or others who agree with me, but he cannot mean that it is for want of trying. What is the nature of the problem? As we shall see, tackling it is a necessary prelude to an appreciation of the sense in which God can be said to be absent and present.

As we saw in section 3 of the previous chapter, Hick is puzzled as to why philosophers, such as myself, won't give straight answers to his questions. I am puzzled as to why he does not realize, by now, that it is because they do not think he is asking straight questions. Hick may not agree, of course, but that is another matter. His critics are saying that his confusions are shown *in* the questions he asks. They have tried to show why on many occasions. It is not enough for Hick simply to say that they haven't convinced him. What he must do, but doesn't, is to show why the accusations of incoherence are misplaced. The confusions of which he is accused emerge, once again, in his latest expression of dissatisfaction with what he thinks I am saying. Hick thinks that what I am saying is intelligible, but false, whereas what Hick attributes to me is, in fact, incoherent. That is why it has to be given a therapeutic, rather than straight answer. The confusion emerges right at the outset. Hick writes:

> I understand Phillips as saying, or rather implying, that the concept, or idea, or picture of an objectively real God is a very powerful concept which, although uninstantiated, is nevertheless central to a whole coherent way of thinking, imagining, and living, which is the religious form of life.[3]

What I am actually saying is quite different. If, as Hick says, I think a religious form of life is coherent, then obviously, it is to that form of life that one would look for the meaning of its central concepts. Where else would one look? As a result of looking to religion, I conclude, according to Hick, and to use Hick's language, that the concept of an objectively real God has no instantiation. This, in ordinary use, means that I conclude that there is no God. So I seem to be saying that if we examine the concept of God, we'll see that there is no God. I might hold this view if I thought the alleged concept was confused, but Hick, as we have seen, allows that I find it to be coherent. So I am supposed to be saying that a coherent application of the concept of God shows that there is no objectively real God. Of course, I am saying no such thing. What I *am* saying is that it is by looking at the application of religious concepts that we find out what it *means* to speak of an objectively real God who is at a distance from human beings. We find out, for example, as Hick does, that the distance is not understood in spatial terms.

Instead of looking to the relevant conceptual context, Hick seems to know what is meant by the 'instantiation' of what a concept shows us, *without looking anywhere*. As we saw in the previous chapter, the trouble with his notion of God as 'an additional consciousness to all human consciousnesses', is precisely that it has not been given, or been shown to have, any coherent application.

The second claim Hick makes about my position reads as follows:

> He and his followers customarily say that the question whether God exists independently of our believing that God exists is a wrong question.[4]

So far from saying that this is a wrong question, I and others recognize that the independence of the reality of God from what a believer believes plays a central role in religious belief, and does so for a number of reasons. Without the distinction, there would be no worry about idolatry, no concern over whether one was really worshipping God, since believing would guarantee the reality of what is believed in. For example, the dispute between Job and his Comforters is precisely over whether he, or they, are turning to a false god in face of evil. When Job repents in sackcloth and ashes, it is because he has been tempted to *depart* from God in his beliefs. But, if, as Hick thinks, I am saying that God is not independent of belief, how could any such departure be logically possible? Again, think of someone who regrets coming to God late in life, because he had believed in false gods. If the reality of God only comes into existence with a person's belief, what would there be to regret?

Hick's second claim implies a third, namely, that if I deny that God exists independently of someone believing that he does, I must locate God's reality in the mind of the believer. If God is not outside it, he must be inside it – that's how the argument seems to go. Do I hold this position? No I do not, and it would be a very odd position to hold.

Religions will have, within them, distinctions between 'what is real' and 'what is in the mind'. Suppose someone gives up a faith of the following kind and tells of it thus: 'I was so afraid of a bogey man. A kind of policeman in the sky. I was always thinking, Watch out, he'll get you in the end. Then one day I suddenly realized that the sky was open. There was no one there. It had all been in my mind, a stupid, shallow imagination.' A friend might respond, 'Yes it was.' The master of novices might tell a young novice who claims to have had an early experience of mystical union, 'Beware of vain imaginings. It's all in your mind.' What would it mean to say of *all* forms of religious belief that they are in the mind? Freud made such a claim, but Hick can't be imputing any such reductionism to me since, again, he allows that I recognize the coherence of religious belief. Therefore, if I were to say that any religious belief, and the reality of the God believed in, are only in the mind of the believer, that would make it impossible for me to recognize, as I do, religious distinctions between genuine beliefs and those which are all in the mind.

Hick's fifth description of my position is the most curious of all. He writes:

God exists only as a factor in our religious language.[5]

The phrase 'a factor in our language' is a curious one, and it is rather difficult to find an application for it. I suppose we can just about imagine someone responding to a person known for rhetorical protestations of love, 'Did you mean that, or am I just a factor in your language?', although the response would not win any marks for style. 'Do I impact on your life, or only impact on your language?' would be worse! Not even Hick would want to impute any such thesis to me. 'God is just a fancy word!' But, then, he may think I mean, 'God is just a powerful word.' Am I saying that believers are only answerable to their words? Obviously not. They are answerable to God.

The context that comes naturally to mind if I hear the phrase 'a factor in language', is one in which one would be referring to some technical aspect of a language's syntax or grammar. Is Hick seriously suggesting that God's existence is being construed by me as the existence of one of these technical features? The reader may find it odd that I should attribute such a bizarre hypothesis to Hick. In one sense, I agree. The point of doing so is to illustrate how difficult it is to find any application for his descriptions of my position, and, hence, to find any sense in them.

The core of Hick's difficulties comes from an assumption that underlies most of what Hick is saying, namely, that *if I refer to something in the language we speak, language itself must be the object of the reference.* This enters into the fifth description Hick offers of my position, the one, I suspect, he regards as most important.

> I take him to imply that this concept of God does not answer to any reality beyond human language and human forms of life. One can further clarify this reading of Phillips by noting its implication that before there were any humans there was no God, for God exists only as a factor in our religious language and behaviour.[6]

Let us take this matter slowly. Suppose that Hick makes the assertion, 'There are seven sheep in that field.' In order to make this assertion, he must participate in a form of life in which he learned how to count, learned what sheep and fields are, how to refer to them, and so on. The language he speaks gives *sense* to his assertion. But when he makes the assertion, he is not saying anything about language. He is saying that there are seven sheep in a field. Notice that even in this example, different kinds of discourse cross over. 'Reference' in mathematics is not the same as 'reference' in language concerning physical objects. Numerals are not objects. Nevertheless, mathematics makes possible the discernment of certain facts, as when we ask, 'How *many* sheep are in that field?' or 'How *many* mountains are in that range?' The sense of the concepts, in the latter question, are such that we understand what is meant by saying that the seven mountains in the range existed before human beings, as did the earth itself.

Because the *sense* of the above assertions is to be found in language, Hick would not be even tempted to say that in saying, 'There are seven sheep in that field', I am saying, 'There are factors in our language in the field'! Why should he be tempted to say something like this of my account of the logical parallel in religion?

In order to say that God is our creator, who existed before the mountains were brought forth, or the earth was made, we would have to participate in the religious form in which this confession has its sense. But in making the confession, we would not be saying anything about language. We would not be saying that 'a factor in our language' existed before the mountains were brought forth. We would be confessing God as our creator.

So the crucial question which separates Hick and myself is *not* that he asserts, and I deny, the existence of a creator before the mountains were brought forth, etc. (which is how Hick puts the matter), but the question of *what saying that amounts to*. After all, the sense of these words is not simply *given*. God is said to be beyond space and time. That is why Hick denies that God is spatially distant from us. But why does he ignore the fact that God cannot be temporally distant either in that case? The 'before', in 'before the mountains were brought forth', cannot be a temporal 'before', as it is the case when we say that the mountains existed before human beings.

Of course, this leaves us with the task of elucidating what we *do* mean by God's independent existence, by saying that he is our creator, who existed before the earth was formed, etc. Where are we to look to see what these beliefs amount to? Where else but in the direction which Hick resists, to the language and forms of life in which the belief has its sense? This is not to deny God's independent existence. It is precisely to see what talk of 'independent existence' comes to in these religious beliefs.

I do not know whether, at the end of this section, Hick will find things any clearer than he did before. Hick's difficulties go back at least to 1972, difficulties which he expressed at the Royal Institute Conference at Lancaster, at which he chaired my Problem of Evil symposium with Swinburne. On that occasion, too, Peter Winch responded to remarks made in discussion by Hick, which were essentially the same as those I have been discussing. So perhaps I am over-optimistic in my hope for progress.

Winch makes the response to Hick's core confused assumption as follows:

> I am *not* saying the 'existence' of what is spoken of simply con-
> sists in the fact that people talk in a certain way; I am saying
> that what the 'existence' of whatever it is amounts to is
> expressed (shows itself) in the way people apply the language
> they speak.[7]

Winch adds in a footnote: 'Most of the qualifications in this paragraph are designed to meet comments made by John Hick in discussion at Lancaster.'[8]

Of course, the hard work now lies before us. I have suggested, at the outset, that the distance between God and human beings expressed in religion is said to be a *spiritual* distance. If that is so, could it be that it is to spiritual contexts one should look to see what is meant by belief in a God who exists *outside* the world?

## 2. *Outside the World*

I began the previous section by referring to the fact that the belief in a divine order, which is *other than* the world, is a widespread phenomenon in religion, although the forms taken by the belief may vary enormously. We saw that *the sense* of this 'other than' may puzzle us. We concluded that it cannot be understood in spatial or temporal terms, and that to see what it amounts to we must look to the religious context in which it has its sense. Yet, it is not easy to dispel a scepticism, which says that the dwelling place of God, or the gods, outside the world, is no place at all. Peter Winch illuminates this fact by comparing it with a scepticism about certain geometrical concepts.[9]

We are told, in geometry, that parallel lines meet at infinity. If we leave the geometry out of account, the claim may puzzle us. If the lines are parallel, how *can* they meet? We have an image of two lines meeting or crossing each other physically, and are led to say, not only that parallel lines do not meet, but that they *can-not* meet. A false picture holds us captive. And if we are told that the place where the parallel lines meet is infinity, we are likely to conclude that that is no place at all. Perhaps we will say, even, when we hear geometricians speak in this way, that language is being stretched to breaking point, and that geometricians are talking nonsense without realizing it.

Those who accuse religious believers of talking nonsense when they speak of a place outside the world, where God, or the gods, dwell, will hardly embrace the above conclusions about geometry. Why not? They will point out that the notion of parallel lines meeting at infinity has an application in geometry, the fruitfulness of which is seen in the proofs and constructions it illuminates.

By the same token, however, the idea of God, or gods, outside the world, has an application in religion. If we leave religion out of consideration, then, as in the case of geometry, we will conclude that the place 'outside the world', because of difficulties of the kind discussed in the previous section, is no place at all. It is not that the place is unoccupied by God or the gods, but that there is no place to be occupied.

Alternatively, in a search for a place outside the world, we can go in radically wrong directions. We may start postulating some other realm, with laws of its own, or wait on the latest findings of the Society for Psychical Research. We are back with Hick's notion of epistemic distance, a problem in the cognitive dimension. But, as in the case of geometry, the belief in a divine reality outside the world has an application in religion. That application is not epistemically distant. It awaits conceptual elucidation for those puzzled by it. We are not in the game of framing hypotheses about unknown realms.

Critics will say that this conclusion is too hasty. Unlike the case of geometry, why do we have to allow that there *is* an intelligible relation between our world and a divine order said to be *outside* it? Even if we grant that the relation is to be understood in spiritual terms, what can *that* mean? In the course of our deliberations we have accumulated a body of evidence which would lead to the answer, 'Not much'.

In Chapter 6, section 1, we discussed Lucretius' challenge to relate human misdemeanours and the occurrence of thunderbolts, via the notions of punishment and desert, to an order of the gods outside the human order. His aim was to expose absurd-ity, and he succeeded. In the Interlude, we saw also how a simi-lar attempt by Job's Comforters to understand his sufferings in these terms led to the same result. In the previous chapter, we saw the impossibility of relating the human order to the divine order in terms of a contract to which God is party, as a moral agent, like ourselves. These considerations form a cumulatively strong range of difficulties.

On the other hand, at the end of the previous chapter, we con-trasted the notion of a temporal, contractual conception of a covenant, with the conception of an eternal covenant. I empha-sized that, in the latter conception, one is given *a whole concep-tion of human life* in terms of which *anything* which occurs is to be understood. Such conceptions have often been in opposition to the conceptions of the divine that have occasioned our diffi-culties. In reminding you of some of them, I am using examples I have used before.[10] I do so, not only because I cannot think of better ones, but because of the historical and cultural importance of the examples themselves. They also show that notions akin to eternal covenants are not confined to Judaeo-Christian tradi-tions.

Let us begin with Horace's response to Lucretius. The latter's scepticism can be summed up in a simple challenge: Show me Jupiter thundering from a clear sky. Why does he need to hide in clouds to deliver his thunderbolts? Horace admits that he too had thought of religion as irrelevant, in this way, but now had reason to reconsider the whole matter. This comes about by his recognition that the very *lack* of correlation between thunder-bolts and moral desert, which Lucretius used to demonstrate the irrelevance of religion, can itself be seen as a divine order that illu-minates human life. The contingencies over which we have no control are seen as 'the way of the gods', which teaches us that we are not masters of our fate. The ways of the gods warn us against self-sufficiency. To forget the gods was the sin of *hubris*. Horace illustrates this by showing how the notion of 'Jupiter thundering from a clear sky' can have a spiritual application.

For though it is the clouds that Jove is wont to cleave with his flashing bolts, this time he drove his thundering steeds and flying car through a sky serene – his steeds and car, whereby the lifeless earth and wandering streams were shaken . . . Power the god does have. He can interchange the lowest and the highest; the mighty he abases and exalts the lowly. From one man Fortune with shrill whirring of her wings swiftly snatches away the crown; on another she delights to place it.[11]

The king was guilty of hubris. He had forgotten his dependence on the gods. He had forgotten Fortune. Then, 'out of the blue', as we say, his crown is given to another – Jupiter thundered from a clear sky.

Could not the same be said of another king, Oedipus, who thought that he *could not* be the one who was cursed by the gods; the one who had murdered his father, and married his mother? He thought he was in control of his destiny. And all the time, the Chorus is reminding us of his foolishness. He has to face up to his dependence – Jupiter thundered from a clear sky!

A philosopher may ask, Why speak of the gods at all? Why not say in face of the contingencies of human life, as Euripides did, that 'it is simply a banal truth that human affairs are likely to prove unpredictably ruinous'?[12] My answer is that there is no necessity to speak of the gods, and I am not advocating doing so. Certainly, it is not as though the contingencies of life *force* one to speak of the gods. Philosophically, what we need to ask is not *why* people spoke of the gods, but to recognize that they *did*. As philosophers, we have an obligation to do conceptual justice to what they say, to see the kind of illumination it offers, no matter whether we can appropriate it personally or not. Talk of the gods is no more underwritten by philosophy than are the views of Euripides.

Bernard Williams's views are nearer to those of Euripides. I summarized them as follows. In relation to us, as moderns:

there is no vantage point outside the world or history which guarantees or underwrites our activities. We must accept responsibility for our mistakes, no matter how horrendous or far-reaching they may be. We are free of thinking that there is a redeeming pattern in reason or history.[13]

Enough has been said, in the course of this book, in criticism of theodicies, to show that Williams's criticisms will find their target in many of the arguments of religious apologists. Williams does not recognize, however, as Horace does, that certain religious beliefs are formed, not by ignoring, but in response to the very contingencies Williams wants to emphasize. Instead, Williams goes on to say that the *only* choice facing us, as moderns, is that of living our imperfect, fallible and incomplete lives with as few lies as possible, with our feet on the ground.[14] That is an unearned generalization. Further, it is advocacy masquerading as philosophy.

Williams cannot say, in the name of philosophy, that we do not need religious responses to the contingencies of life. But I do not respond by saying that we *do*. Instead, I am arguing that philosophy has the contemplative task to do justice to different responses to the contingencies of life. Williams would have to recognize that religion, too, has responses to the fallibility and incompleteness of human life, without falsifying them, or tidying them up. Horace and the example of Oedipus show this, but there are parallels in Christianity. Peter boasted that whoever would let Jesus down, it would not be him. He denied a reliance on grace in making his promise. As we know, all it took was an accusation that he was with Jesus for him to deny him. But he was so sure of himself. Jupiter thundered from a clear sky!

In very different reactions to the contingencies of life, they can be seen as terrible. A sense of the terrible may be expressed in rituals, rituals in which the participants wonder at the terrible; the terrible seen as sacramental.

In the diverse examples we have mentioned, we have seen how the divine order is conceived as *other than* this world. It acts as a mirror in which life is illuminated, by being seen under certain aspects. What I go on to discuss is only *one* notion of divine order in relation to the evils of the world. Yet, as far as contemporary philosophy of religion is concerned, it is a tradition that has been neglected.

## 3. Creation, Power and Freedom

One central belief, in terms of which evils are to be understood, is that human beings are the creatures of a Creator-God. But how is the relation between the Creator and his creatures to be understood?

Many thinkers who have reflected on the Holocaust have commented on the disgraceful silence of those who knew what was going on, but, for reasons of policy or prudence, kept silent. But the silence that puzzled them most is what they have called the silence of God. In contrast to this silence, what was God expected to do?

Part of the story of creation is the gift of freedom that God gives to human beings. But, as we have seen, some philosophers treat 'the gift' in a curious way. It becomes part of the instrumentalism and consequentialism endemic in theodicies. In Chapter 4, in the discussion of the free-will defence, we saw how free will is regarded as a good in itself, and as the greatest good of all which human beings possess. As a result, any bad choices made by them, no matter what their consequences, are justified by the greater good of the free will that makes it possible for us to have choices at all. In this way, even the Holocaust can be justified. One wonders what has happened to philosophy, if it can lead one to say that, horrendous though it was, the Holocaust is justified as the result of the greater good of the free will of those who perpetrated it.

I argued against the view of free will as a general good. True, life, as recognizably human life, would not be possible without free will, but it is a life in which freedom can involve anything, from magnanimous goods to horrendous evils. In other words, freedom has no strings attached to it that will show it to be an overall good. Creation, understood as involving the gift of freedom, is a creation that involves *risk*. This being so, the granting of human life is, at the same time, the granting of something which cannot be controlled to ensure that the result is good.

We are still faced, however, with the central issue of *how belief in God as Creator informs living human life in that freedom.*

Does the responsibility for history belong to man, but the responsibility for creation belong to God? Is the solution of the tensions between the plan of creation and the facts of history postponed to an eschatological resolution? But we are still left with our question: in what sense can belief in God as Creator be a very *present* help in time of trouble, without recourse to the view that, though things have gone wrong, they'll be fixed later? Solution by postponement raises the awkward question posed by Rowan Williams, 'Is the divine action in creating somehow deficient or incompetent?'[15]

There have been Christian theologians, too, who have emphasized that creation should not be understood in terms of power as depicted in theodicies. Swinburne refers to such theologians, but writes of them as follows:

> In our century many Christian theologians have talked in a vague way about the 'weakness' of God and seen this exemplified in the crucifixion of Christ. But I do not think that many of them have really meant to claim that God (either the Father or the Son, God incarnate) was too weak to prevent the crucifixion. Rather I suspect that talk about God being 'weak' was, for most of them, a somewhat misleading way of putting the point that God humbled himself in his incarnation in Christ and did not exercise the power he possessed.[16]

Swinburne's way of putting the matter suggests that God's essential nature is sheer power, but that, now and again, at rather crucial moments, he decides not to exercise it. Apart from the difficulties of ascribing 'all power' to God, which we have already discussed,[17] the 'humbling' seems to be a decision to do what he would not normally do. Orthodox Christian teaching, however, teaches that the 'humbling' teaches us something essential about God. That he took 'the form of a servant' is not meant to imply that normally his form is quite different. God does not go slumming in the Incarnation! Rather, it implies that if God wanted to reveal something essential about himself on earth, 'the form of a servant' was itself essential to his doing so. Put philosophically, 'the form of a servant' is a grammatical remark about God. It offers us a certain *conception* of God, and does not refer to an act in which, for particular reasons, he constrains his true nature.

Kierkegaard makes the point, beautifully, in a parable-like story of a king and a lowly maiden he wants to make his own. The maiden is of lowly birth, and the king is afraid that a display of his splendour and majesty will put her off. He considers turning her, by magic, into a princess, but pulls back from what would be an act of deception. It would also be a risky act, one that could end in disaster if the maiden discovered, somehow, that she had been tricked, and was not really a princess at all. The king decides to approach the maiden in the disguise of a lowly person, and, by so doing, slowly win her affection. Gradually, he could then reveal who he really was.

God, too, Kierkegaard argues, comes to earth in a lowly form, in an effort to make us his own. He enters the world as a beggar. But, Kierkegaard emphasizes, there is an essential difference between God and the king. Unlike the king, God does not come in disguise. When God comes as a beggar he reveals something essential about himself.[18] Think, too, of Michelangelo's painting of God creating Adam. The Creator is not dressed in pomp and splendour. He is naked. Wittgenstein said that religion could be taught by means of such pictures.[19] Here, too, one is offered a certain conception of God. One of the things it teaches us is not to think of creation as an act of controlling power. An explicit statement of this view is found in Simone Weil.

The act of creation is not an act of power. It is an abdication. Through this act a kingdom was established other than the kingdom of God. The reality of this world is constituted by the mechanism of matter and the autonomy of rational creatures. It is a kingdom from which God has withdrawn. God having renounced being its king, can enter it only as a beggar.

As for the cause of this abdication, Plato expressed it thus, 'He was good'.[20]

We will misunderstand what Simone Weil is saying if we read her remarks as implying that God renounces or abdicates from what he really is, namely, a king. Her remarks are grammatical. She is saying that creation should not be understood as the act of a powerful king. In this respect, her remarks are very different from the thinking that governs theodicies. Simone Weil recognizes the world as a place where human beings are free, where anything may happen to them. In *that* sense, God is absent from the world. He is not an agent among agents, competing alongside human beings. In theodicies, by contrast, he is. Everything we do is related to his purpose in making the world as a moral obstacle course for our character development. In defences, the evils we suffer are related to an ultimate good that, in some unknown way, is going to redeem them. In the view we are considering, however, the world, and what happens in it, is genuinely independent of God. Yet, it is precisely through realizing the sense in which God is absent that believers may come to the *different* sense in which God is present. This is why Simone Weil says that God is present in the form of absence. All this seemingly paradoxical remark means is that recognizing the sense in which God is absent from the world is a conceptual precondition of recognizing the sense in which God is present in it. It is one of the lessons of the purifying atheism described in the previous chapter.

In theodicies, the tribulations people bear seem to be part of a lesson God wants to teach them. They are *something*, a something worthy of being instructed in this way. But if we take human freedom seriously, there is no *God-given* reason why things happen as they do. Of course, we have our ordinary explanations and reasons for why things are happening to us, but theodicies and defences look for a super-reason as to why this course of events is happening at all. God's plan is that reason. For Simone Weil, there is no such reason. This is one of the ways, for her, in which we have to learn that God is absent from the world. Yet, it is through this very realization, she argues, that we can come to see how God can be present in our sufferings. She expresses the point, or, at least, part of the point, in her typically forthright manner:

> If I thought that God sent me suffering by an act of his will and for my good, I should think that I was something, and I should miss the chief use of suffering which is to teach me that I am nothing. It is therefore essential to avoid all such thoughts, but it is necessary to love God through the suffering.
>
> I must love being nothing. How horrible it would be if I were something! I must love my nothingness, love being a nothingness. I must love with that part of the soul which is on the other side of the curtain, for the part of my soul which is perceptible to consciousness cannot love nothingness. It has a horror if it. Though it may think it loves nothingness, what it really loves is something other than nothingness.[21]

Simone Weil's remarks may create as many problems as the insights they can occasion. The philosophers in the traditions I have been criticizing will want to ask: What does she mean when she says that we must love with that part of the soul 'which is on the other side of the curtain'? What does it mean to want to be nothing? What would it mean to regard others in this way? Are they and their sufferings to be regarded as nothing? What a horrible idea! These questions are based on a misunderstanding, but they do express difficulties that need to be addressed.

We can begin to address them by noting that in both Judaism and Christianity, the recognition that anything may happen to one is extremely important. It is found in Job's reaction to the first calamities which befall him, before the Comforters begin to reason with him.

> Then Job arose, and rent his mantle, and shaved his head, and fell down on the ground and worshipped.
>
> And said, Naked came I out of my mother's womb, and naked shall I return thither; the Lord gave, and the Lord hath taken away; blessed be the name of the Lord.

In all this Job sinned not, nor charged God foolishly (Job 1.20–22).

The conception can be found also in Matthew's Gospel, where the Father in heaven is said to make 'his sun to rise on the evil and on the good, and (to send) rain on the just and the unjust' (Matthew 5.45). It is also central to the sense in which Christ is said to be a sacrifice for us, for God is said to be 'He that spared not his own Son, but delivered him up for us all' (Romans 8.32).

What does it mean to acknowledge this conception as central? I can do so descriptively and (hopefully) imaginatively, as I refer to it now in writing this book. But this is not a religious acknowledgement. For it to be that, its centrality has to be recognized in a person's soul, a person must see it as food and feed on it. That is a difficult matter, because there is a deep tendency in us to resist what it says, namely, that we are not people to whom the cosmos owes anything. We refuse to believe that. We believe, rather, in a system of checks and balances that will make everything alright for us in the end. Simone Weil writes of the resistance to the Judaic and Christian emphasis as follows:

> The principal claim we think we have on the universe is that our personality should continue. This claim implies all the others. The instinct of self-preservation makes us feel this continuation to be a necessity, and we believe that a necessity is a right. We are like the beggar who said to Talleyrand: 'Sir, I must live', and to whom Talleyrand replied, 'I do not see the necessity for that'. Our personality is entirely dependent on external circumstances which have unlimited power to crush it. But we would rather die than admit this. From our point of view the equilibrium of the world is a combination of circumstances so ordered that our personality remains intact and seems to belong to us. All the circumstances of the past that have wounded our personality appear to us to be the disturbances of balance which should infallibly be made up for one day or another by phenomena having a contrary effect. We live on the expectation of these compensations. The near approach of

death is horrible chiefly because it forces the knowledge upon us that these compensations will never come.[22]

When Simone Weil was quoted as saying that the chief use of suffering is to teach us that we are nothing, and that it is necessary to love being nothing, we saw how easy it is to respond with horror to her remarks. Was she saying that those who suffer count for nothing, because they are nothing? We can now begin to see that that reading is misplaced. So far from dismissing those who suffer, she is talking of a religious response to their suffering.[23]

To recognize that one is nothing, is to recognize that one is not the centre of the universe. The 'I' is not sacrosanct, immune from harm. The world can reach out and touch it at any moment. Nor is the 'I' the possessor of a cosmic right that will guarantee that things go in its favour. That much is recognized in the examples of Fortune and 'the way of the gods' discussed earlier. I noted, however, that religious responses to the contingencies of life vary enormously, from a recognition of the sin of hubris, to seeing 'the terrible' as sacramental.

In Christianity, the dying to the 'I' is linked to seeing the 'I', life itself, as something undeserved, as a gift of grace. To believe in a Creator *is* to believe in the givenness of life as a grace. One might ask, as Hume was inclined to do, *why* one should react to the contingencies of life in that way. I do not think there is any answer to that. Certainly, it is a superstition to think people *had* to react in that way, or that there is something in the contingencies which *makes* one react so. Instead of asking whether one can, or should, react in that way, the philosophical response should be to note that people *do* respond in that way. If one were religious, one might say that to be able to see life as a grace is itself a grace.

Hume, commenting on similar reactions among primitive people, to whom he refers, with condescension, as 'the raw and ignorant multitude', writes:

A monstrous birth excites his curiosity and is deemed a prodigy. It alarms him from its novelty; and immediately set him a-trembling, and sacrificing, and praying. But an animal, complete in all its limbs and organs, is to him an ordinary spectacle, and produces no religious opinion or affection.[24]

Hume is blind to the possibility of 'the monstrous' occasioning, not curiosity or alarm, but a kind of awe. So far from having no bearing on normality, it highlights its precariousness. Compare treating madness as sacred, even feeling a reverence towards it. It is not difficult, in this context, to see how sanity can be seen as a gift or grace. In response to Hume, I wrote, 'In this way "the disordered sense" may well lead people to see with astonished eyes "the first obscure traces of divinity", but not with the "disordered eyes" Hume attributes to them.'[25]

Some may not respond in the religious ways I am noting. In fact, they may point to dangers involved in them. Is not everything said, so far, compatible with a dangerous fatalism or quietism? Suppose we recognize that the 'I' is not the centre of the universe, that anything may happen to us. What more do we need to say? Aren't we back with what Euripedes called the banal truth that life is full of contingencies? Moreover, we may move dangerously to a fatalism that gives up on things saying, 'Whatever happens was going to happen, so why bother?'

This reaction, however, leaves out one essential element in the religious response I am elucidating. It omits the essential fact that in recognizing that life itself is a gift, and that the ways things go in it are a grace, *the believer dies to the 'I'* that sees itself at the centre of the universe. In fatalism, there is acceptance of the inevitable, but no love of it. In the religious response I am talking of, there is a requirement to love the fact that God has given life with its contingencies to human beings. This love is gratitude for existence.

It may still not be clear how this avoids quietism. One may think like this: if the way life goes is itself a matter of grace, this will seem to apply as much to the evil in it as to the good. Is the evil, then, as much from God as the good? This is a real difficulty that needs to be faced, for if it is not, we'll find ourselves saying that the Holocaust and other horrendous evils are from a God who did not prevent them from occurring.

At this point, we need to recall the rejection of creation as an act of power and control. God is seen as over against the world that is not-God, including human life. As such, in the granting of radical freedom to 'the other', the essence of the Godhead is seen as a renunciation of possessiveness, a renunciation of the desire to control. Weil speaks of a divine self-emptying as God's essence. That is how creation can be seen as an expression of love. To believe that one is a created being, in the image of God, is to see oneself as the recipient of that grace and love. That is why such belief involves a self-emptying of the ego, of the 'I' that sees itself as the centre of the universe.

It would be absurd to suggest, of course, that dying to the 'I' is an all-or-nothing affair, since the 'I' that stands in the way of doing so involves all our relations to other people and to the world of nature. We can never be entirely free of the self that wants to possess the other or draw attention to itself. Pride and possessiveness go deep. To actually become 'nothing', in the religious sense, would be to have a perfect love of God, to become a perfect vehicle of grace – something no human being can achieve. On the other hand, we should now be able to see why belief in creation, seeing oneself as the recipient of grace, cannot lead to quietism, since it involves fighting against everything in the world, and in oneself, that regards other people, and that world, as creatures to be exploited, possessed and used for one's own selfish purposes. This use of others can range from the crudest to the most subtle forms of possession and control. They constitute a refusal to see the other as a child of God.

Given the belief I have described it is not only difficult to die to the 'I'. What does the belief say about the sufferings that befall us in one form or another? What does it mean to say that God is with the believer in those sufferings? If the believer is able to testify to that fact, it means that the things of God, gratitude for existence, have not become pointless despite the sufferings. In that sense, it seems, the believer has something that the world cannot touch, something that maintains believers in their sufferings.

It can be said that such a believer stands in a covenantal relation with God, but the covenant is an eternal, rather than a temporal, one. It does not depend on life's events taking one course rather than another, since it sustains the believer no matter what course it takes. This does not mean, of course, that the believer does not care about what happens, but that he has something in which he stands even in the dark days. In this way the eternal God and the God of history become one in his belief, because those feelings that are of eternal significance inform the facts of history without being subject to them; they are informed by an eternal significance which, it seems, the world cannot touch.

It has to be admitted, however, that the greatest difficulty has yet to be faced. There still seems to be a predictive element in the religious belief I have described. It seems to say that, no matter how great the darkness, faith will abide and sustain. But must we not be honest enough to admit that the world may stretch out its hand and touch the believer in such a way that even that possibility of faith is crushed? What then? When the darkness deepens, what if the One whom one thought changeth not, does not abide? The person is crushed by affliction. What then? Does it mean anything to say that God is still with the believer?

I have emphasized the importance of a religious reaction to suffering very different from those discussed in what I have called our problematic inheritance in relation to the problem of evil. The reaction I have outlined boldly is an important one, but one that has been neglected in philosophical discussions. I have not discussed the difficulties it has to face in any detail. This is a task that still faces me. In discussing such difficulties, however, I hope that further light will be thrown, at the same time, on the religious response itself.

## 4. God's Grammatical Predicates

Before ending the chapter, I want to give another throw of the dice to the objections many philosophers will make to what I have to say. I have talked of the way in which the contingencies of life can give rise to a notion of grace. I have also suggested that the acceptance of this grace in the soul involves a dying to the self. To see oneself as nothing, and grace as everything, is pure love of God. That is what loving God amounts to.

It is at this point that some of my philosophical critics say, 'Stop! Hold it right there. How did God get into the picture? How do we get from 'grace' to God? We have allowed you to get away with talking of creation, but in your account of concept-formation, all you have talked about is 'grace' and 'love'. You have linked these to seeing life as a gift. But what about the Giver of the gift? He seems to be left entirely out of the picture. But how can there be a gift if there is no Giver? How can there be grace if there is no one to exercise it, or to be gracious? How can love be shown to human beings if there is no one to do the loving? We can put our objections in this way: for all your talk, all you have given us is the predicates, but no God. But if the predicates have no subject to which they can be attributed, it does not even make sense to call them predicates. Talk of predicates becomes, as you yourself like to say, a vacuous form of language. They are lost predicates for want of a subject.

These objections have been put in many forms, and from more than one direction. They are connected with Hick's concerns discussed in the first section of the present chapter, but also with Swinburne's and Plantinga's conceptions of God as a person without a body. All three might say that my predicates must be attributed to some kind of divine consciousness. We have seen the difficulties this notion of consciousness involves.

What is important to recognize, however, is that the objections have to do with worries about 'reference' in what I say. In what sense are we referring to something when we speak of God? Aren't we referring to something real? Of course, I do not want to dispute the importance of these questions for religious belief. What I am saying is that, despite assurances that no one means to say that referring to God is like referring to a physical object, the language of physical objects has played an unacknowledged role in forming the convictions that God must have a reference of a similar kind. This is held to be important, because unless there is a divine referent who is *independent* of the predicates I have talked of, there is nothing to support them, and hence nothing to justify the role I am ascribing to them in religious belief.

For my part, there is a failure to take seriously enough the claim that God is a *spiritual* reality. When I speak of 'creating', 'grace' and 'love' as predicates, I mean that they are *grammatical predicates*; that is, they are not related contingently to 'God', but are instances of what the word 'God' *means*. The predicates are grammatical in that they show us *the kind* of reality we are talking about. I want to illustrate this, not for the first time, by turning to a passage of analysis, in this context, by Rush Rhees, if only because I have not always expressed its point as clearly as I should have, but more importantly, because it expresses points that need to be answered by philosophers who accuse me of talking of the divine predicates while ignoring the substantive needed to support them. This is often said by reference to an *ontological* dimension I am supposed to be ignoring. But doing philosophy by italics is not enough. By all means use the word 'ontology' if it is thought that I am referring to some ethereal nothing in talking of God, but, sooner or later, the grammar or logic of the referent needs to be analysed. That is what Rhees does in such an admirable way, and why his analysis should be of help at this point. He writes:

> If one lays emphasis . . . on the fact that 'God' is a substantive, and especially if one goes on . . . to say that it is a proper name, then the natural thing will be to assume that meaning the same by 'God' is something like meaning the same by 'the sun' or meaning the same by 'Churchill'. You might even want to use some such phrase as 'stands for' the same. But nothing of that sort will do here. Questions about 'meaning the same' in connexion with the names of physical objects are connected with the kind of criteria to which we may appeal in saying that this is the same object – 'that is the same planet as I saw in the south west last night', 'that is the same car that was standing here this morning'. Supposing someone said 'The word "God" stands for a different object now'. What could that mean? I know what it means to say that 'the Queen' stands for a

different person now, and I know what it means to say that St. Mary's Church now is not the St. Mary's Church that was here in So-and-So's day. I know the sort of thing that might be said if I were to question either of these statements. But *nothing* of that sort could be said in connexion with any question about the meaning of 'God'. Now this is not a trivial or inessential matter. It hangs together in very important ways with what I call the grammar of the word 'God'. And it is one reason why I do not think it is helpful just to say that the word is a substantive.[26]

As I have said, while denying that they refer to God in the way they refer to physical objects, philosophers are still influenced by the use of the substantive in the way Rhees suggests. Hence the suggestion that my talk of the divine predicates needs a substantive before they can mean anything. Rhees's further observations on the difference between referring to God and referring to a human being bring out what is wrong with this.

Winston Churchill may be Prime Minister and also a company director, but I might come to know him without knowing this. But I could not know God without knowing that he was the Creator and Father of all things. That would be like saying that I might come to know Churchill without knowing that he had face, hands, body, voice or any of the attributes of a human being.[27]

One can easily miss what Rhees is saying here, as I have on occasions. He is *not* saying that whereas in the case of Churchill, after mentioning the fact that he is a prime minister and a company director, there is a further 'it' to refer to, in the case of God, there is no further 'it' to refer to. If we put the matter in that way, it encourages the very misleading analogy that Rhees wants to rescue us from. It makes it look as though whereas the offices held by Churchill refer to the person who held them (the desirable substantive), the attributes predicated of God hang in the air, without any substantive to support them.[28] Whereas, with respect to my argument, what Rhees is saying is that 'creator', 'grace' and 'love' stand to God, as 'face', 'hands', 'body', stand to 'human being'. They indicate what we *mean* by 'God' and 'human being', respectively. That is why in *both* cases the predicates are grammatical. The point could be put by saying that, in certain contexts, 'creator', 'grace' and 'love' are *synonyms* for 'God'. If God is Spirit then he is the creator spirit, the spirit of grace and the spirit of love. Once again, this is the point of calling the predicates grammatical. John Cobb expresses the point well, when he says, 'Our thought of God is inseparable from our experience of grace and our gratitude for it. We cannot abstract from the grace we find in life and seek its external cause in an entity we then call "God".'[29]

At this point a further consideration must be introduced that has a bearing on the subsequent arguments in the book. The meaning of 'God' is contentious in a way in which the meaning of 'human being' is not. If someone said that we had met a human being with no hands, feet, face or body, we wouldn't know what he was talking about. To meet a human being is not to meet a consciousness (whatever that means). But there *are* disputes about God, theological differences, that may be unresolvable. Rhees writes:

> Within a single tradition like that of the Hebrew religion, it can be said that the author of the second half of Isaiah meant the same 'God' as the author (or authors) of Genesis did, and that St. Paul meant the same 'God' as both of them, because of the continuity of Hebrew worship and of the kind of worship that was, the importance of such conceptions as 'the God of our fathers', 'the God of Abraham, Isaac and Jacob', and so on. But for Paul the same God could be worshipped by gentiles who were not the seed of Abraham and Jacob. And if the gentiles worship the same god, then this must appear in what they say about God, in the way they worship and in what it means to them to be creatures and children of God. To ask, '*Do* they worship the same God or not?' is to ask about that.[30]

Rhees imagines a reaction that is reminiscent of Hick's reaction to my work discussed in section 1.

> I said that children learn a theology when they learn how the word 'God' is used – perhaps that he is the 'Lord God of Israel', that he is the 'Creator of Heaven and Earth' and so on – and this may seem to be making theology superficial. Just learning the sorts of things it is correct to say – is that theology? Well, I do not see how theology can be anything else. If I tried to say in any 'material' sense what God is or what Creation is . . . that would suggest a kind of investigation to *find out* what God is, and that is absurd. All that theology can do is to try to indicate, perhaps even with some sort of formal proof, what it is correct to say, what is the correct way of speaking about God. The question of 'what God is' could only be answered through 'coming to know God' in worship and in religious life. 'To know God is to worship him.'[31]

So far from being a trivial question, how we should speak of God is an onerous question for theology to struggle with, not least in face of the evils human beings suffer in their lives. In the course of the present chapter I have endeavoured to elucidate one response to evil which is age-old, but not everyone shares it or will even want to have anything to do with it. Nevertheless, it is that response that I want to continue to explore, bringing out its conceptual character through a discussion of difficulties that it certainly has to face.

## Notes

1 R. W. Hepburn, *Christianity and Paradox*, London: Watts 1958, p. 5.
2 John Hick, 'An Irenaean Theodicy' in Stephen T. Davis (ed.), *Encountering Evil*, Louisville: Westminster John Knox Press 2001, p. 42.
3 Hick, 'Critique of D. Z. Phillips' in Davis, *Encountering Evil*, p. 162.
4 Hick, 'Critique of D. Z. Phillips', p. 162.
5 Hick, 'Critique of D. Z. Phillips', p. 162.

6 Hick, 'Critique of D. Z. Phillips', p. 162.

7 Peter Winch, 'Meaning and Religious Language' in Stuart Brown (ed.), *Reason and Religion*, Ithaca: Cornell University Press 1977, p. 200.

8 Winch, 'Meaning and Religious Language', p. 200.

9 Peter Winch, 'What Has Philosophy To Say To Religion', ed. D. Z. Phillips, *Faith and Philosophy*, Oct. 2001.

10 See *From Fantasy to Faith*, Basingstoke: Macmillan 1991 and *Religion and the Hermeneutics of Contemplation*, Cambridge: Cambridge University Press 2001, particularly Chapter 2: 'Bernard Williams on the gods and us'.

11 Horace, *Odes*, Bk 1, Ode XXIV: 'The Poet's Conversion' in *The Odes and Epodes*, trans. C. E. Bennett, London: The Loeb Classical Library 1919, p. 91.

12 See Bernard Williams, *Shame and Necessity*, Berkeley: University of California Press 1993, p. 151.

13 *Religion and the Hermeneutics of Contemplation*, p. 39.

14 See B. Williams, *Shame and Necessity*, p. 164 f.

15 Rowan Williams, 'Redeeming Sorrows' in D. Z. Phillips (ed.), *Religion and Morality*, Basingstoke: Macmillan 1996, p. 142.

16 Richard Swinburne, *Providence and the Problem of Evil*, Oxford: Clarendon Press 1998, p. 30.

17 See Chapter 2, section 1.

18 Søren Kierkegaard, *Philosophical Fragments*, Princeton: Princeton University Press 1946, p. 19f.

19 Ludwig Wittgenstein, *Lectures and Conversations on Aesthetics, Psychology and Religious Belief*, Oxford: Blackwell 1966, p. 63.

20 Simone Weil, 'Are We Struggling for Justice?', trans. Marina Barabas, *Philosophical Investigations*, Vol. 10, No. 1 (January 1987), p. 3.

21 Simone Weil, *Gravity and Grace*, London: Routledge and Kegan Paul 1952, p. 101.

22 Simone Weil, 'Concerning the Our Father' in *Waiting for God*, New York: Putnam's Sons 1951, pp. 223–4.

23 Weil was, in fact, prone to deny this emphasis in Judaism, but I am insisting that it is there.

24 Hume, 'The Natural History of Religion' in Richard Wollheim (ed.), *Hume on Religion*, London: Fontana 1966, p. 35.

25 Phillips, *Religion and the Hermeneutics of Contemplation*, p. 82.

26 Rush Rhees, 'Religion and Language' in Rhees, *On Religion and Philosophy*, ed. D. Z. Phillips assisted by Mario von der Ruhr, Cambridge: Cambridge University Press 1997, pp. 45–6.

27 Rhees, 'Religion and Language', p. 48.

28 I am grateful to Stephen T. Davis for voicing this concern in a seminar on The Problem of Evil which we co-taught at Claremont in 2001. I am

even more grateful to Richard Amesbury for pointing out what it was in my reading of Rhees that gave rise to Davis's misgivings.

29  John Cobb, 'The Problem of Evil and the Task of Ministry' in Davis, *Encountering Evil*, p. 185.

30  Rhees, 'Religion and language', pp. 46–7.

31  Rhees, 'Religion and language', p. 44.

# 9

# Faith and Expectation

## 1. *Dying to Expectations*

In the previous chapter, we saw the centrality of the notions of 'dying to the self' and 'becoming nothing before God' in the belief in God as the creator of all things. These notions manifest themselves in a variety of different contexts. It is not difficult to see, for example, how 'dying to the self' marks the difference between pure and impure acts of charity, between compassion and condescension in such contexts. Simone Weil writes:

> It is not surprising that a man who has bread should give a piece to someone who is starving. What is surprising is that he should be capable of doing so with so different a gesture from that with which we buy an object. Almsgiving when it is not supernatural is like a sort of purchase. It buys the sufferer.[1]

If we speak of 'dying to the self' when one is the sufferer, matters are rather different. The bewilderment sufferers may feel is not a matter of selfishness or self-aggrandizement, though the self is involved, hence the question, 'Why am *I* suffering? Why is this happening to *me*?' Dying to the self, being able to find God's will in the situation, is one way, not of answering the question, but of ceasing to ask it. What does this mean? By exploring this question further than we have done hitherto, we can deepen our understanding of a certain religious response to suffering.

At the end of Chapter 7, we saw the essential difference between an eternal covenant and a temporal covenant. The latter is understood as a kind of contract: if we do *x*, God will do *y*. As we have seen, that can lead to a kind of bewilderment of its own, ending, sometimes, in absurdity: we have done *x*, but God has not done *y*. The difference with an eternal covenant is that it offers a conception of human life in terms of which a believer in it meets *whatever* happens. Belief in 'the way of the gods', as we saw, can be such a covenant. It involved, unlike temporal contracts, recognizing that *anything* may happen to one, and that failure to recognize this is the sin of hubris.

There is a great deal in us that rebels against these religious responses to life. As Simone Weil said, 'Our personality is entirely dependent on external circumstances which have unlimited power to crush it. But we would rather die than admit this.'[2] Instead, we think that there will be checks and balances, a turn of good fortune to compensate for a turn for the worse.[3] Yet, even if this tendency is overcome, even if we can admit that belief in checks and balances in fortune, on our part, is an illusion, we can still believe in an alternative *moral* system of checks and balances in terms of which, it seems, we can meet *whatever* happens. In this way, even if we cannot rely on the course our lives will take, we can make moral sense of it, come what may. Simone Weil describes these *moral* checks and balances as follows:

> Every time that we put forth some effort and the equivalent of this effort does not come back to us in the form of some visible fruit, we have a sense of false balance and emptiness which makes us think that we have been cheated. The effort of suffering from some offence causes us to expect the punishment or apologies of the offender, the effort of doing good makes us expect the gratitude of the person we have helped.[4]

We can test the truth of Simone Weil's analysis, simply by thinking of those cases which occasion our indignation, by not providing the gratitude or apology we expect. How often we exclaim, 'He couldn't even say thank-you!' or 'He couldn't even apologize!' These expectations would be harshly misdescribed if one said that they were self-centred, or exercises in self-indulgence. Rather, they seem to be minimal moral expectations that operate, hopefully, in relations of common civility and decency. I do not think Simone Weil need be read as being averse to these expectations, or even as denying that, in certain circumstances, people have a right to them. What she *is* saying, is that, at this level, one is still dependent on a kind of temporal contract, though one of a special kind.

Up until now, we have treated a temporal contract as saying, 'If we do $x$, God will do $y$.' We soon have to face the fact that, despite $x$, $y$ does not happen. Instead $b$ (something bad) happens. The *moral*, temporal contract, simply put, says this, 'In this life, anything can happen, but if you do $g$ (something good), $gr.$ (gratitude) will occur as an acknowledgement of it; if $b$ (something bad) is done to you, $a$ (apology) will be offered to you as a result.' Once this moral, temporal contract is stated, we can see that, because of its temporal, contractual character, it will generate similar problems to the previous temporal, material contract in which, if we do $x$, God promises $y$. The previous problem was that though we do $x$, $y$ does not occur. The obvious problem with the moral temporal contract is that though $g$ occurs, $gr.$ does not occur, and though $b$ occurs, $a$ does not occur. If the sense of $g$ and $b$, respectively, depend on $gr.$ and $a$ occurring, what is to be said when they do not? For some, as we know, $g$ is rendered senseless. When charity does not prompt gratitude, people often say, 'That's the last time I'll do that. Don't rely on me again.'

Simone Weil also wants to talk of a different kind of love of the good which she equates with love of God. She calls it *a pure love of the eternal*, because it dies, not only to expectations of material good fortune, but also to moral expectations of gratitude or apology. A pure love of God does not depend on those moral expectations being realized, and the love of God need not be rendered pointless when they are not.

The bearing of the above on the problem of evil is obvious. No one is arguing against gratitude or apology when they are properly expressed, but it is possible for the sufferer still to find a point in the love of God when, for some reason or another, the world denies one the gratitude or apology that, morally, one may deserve. A relationship with God survives those denials when it is such that it does not depend on things being otherwise. The believer is called on to die to the expectations enshrined in temporal contracts, whether of a material or moral kind. This act of religious renunciation is not easy, and it is not an all-or-nothing affair in practice. One might say that no one achieves a pure love of God in all things. Nevertheless, in the context of the problem of evil, it is important to appreciate the character of such love, since it casts light on one sense in which God can be with a person in his or her suffering. God is with them if love of God has not been rendered pointless for them.

Before leaving this section of the chapter, I want to discuss a related, but different, example of the expectations that believers are called to die to in a pure love of God. In the two examples of temporal contracts we have considered, the self of the agent occupied a central role. In the case of the material temporal contract, if the agent did $x$, he expected $y$ at God's hand. If he obeyed God, he expected God's material protection. In the case of the moral, temporal contract, if the agent did $g$, or had $b$ done to him, he expected $gr.$ or $a$ done to him. If he did something good, he expected gratitude, although he did not do good in order to receive gratitude. If he is harmed, he expects apology.

In the case I want to consider now, the agent does not expect any material return from the world for any good done, nor does the agent expect gratitude from a person helped, or even an apology from the person who harms him or her. I am thinking of someone who is rare in that respect; a person who has renounced those expectations. Indeed, her life may be a life governed by renunciation and sacrifice. Yet, there is something she wants – she wants her love to reach its goal, and, in that sense, to succeed. What if the world does not grant it? I want to begin exploring this question with reference to a literary example, Edith Wharton's wonderful short story, 'Bunner Sisters'.[5] Ann Eliza Bunner and her younger sister, Evelina are of modest means, and keep a shop in a shabby New York basement from which they sell artificial flowers, bonnets and homemade preserves. Ann Eliza has always renounced her own needs to serve those of her younger sister.

When, however, she buys a clock for her for her birthday from Herman Ramy, who has opened a little shop in their square, she is attracted to him, and finds herself wanting something to be her own for the first time. Up to that moment, while she had thought that providence had never meant their shabby existence for her sister, she had never felt that way about herself. Unfortunately, when her younger sister comes into contact with Ramy, Ann Eliza sees that she, too, is attracted to him. She finds this sad, but unsurprising. To her amazement, however, it is to her, and not to Evelina, that Ramy proposes marriage. Knowing how hurt Evelina would be, she renounces her love for him. This renunciation is not without an element of the self-indulgence in sacrifice of which Simone Weil speaks.

To her dismay, Ann Eliza sees that Ramy is beginning to repay the attention Evelina has shown in him. By this time, she has begun to see flaws in Ramy's character, and she tries to warn Evelina against him. Her advice is cruelly rejected. Evelina, knowing nothing of the sacrifice she has made on her behalf, simply thinks that Ann Eliza is jealous of her chance for happiness. Evelina and Ramy marry. It is a huge blow to Ann Eliza to learn that they propose moving to St. Louis. She does not know how she can face her loneliness. Yet, once again, she puts Evelina first, and even uses some of her meagre money to finance their trip.

From time to time, Ann Eliza has bad news of the marriage. Her worst fears about Ramy are confirmed. When Evelina finally does come home, having lost a baby, and having suffered from Ramy's drug addiction, it is to blame Ann Eliza for having introduced her to him in the first place. Desperately ill, Evelina has come home to die. She has no idea that Ann Eliza has suffered, saying to her, 'You don't know what life's like – you don't know anything about it – sitting here safe all the while in this peaceful place.'

At least, it seems, Ann Eliza can look after the sister she loves in her last days, but even this is not to be. To Ann Eliza's horror, Evelina has become a Catholic. She is under the influence of a priest, who offers her the consolation that she will be reunited with her baby after death. Ann Eliza is cut off from all close contact with her sister. In her funeral, as 'a passive spectator, [she] beheld with stony indifference this last negation of her past'.

Ann Eliza finds her faith undermined. But what undermines it? Not the absence of the world's rewards – that goes without saying. Not the absence of moral recognition by others either. No, it is undermined by something deeper:

> Self-effacement for the good of others had always seemed to her both natural and necessary, but then she had taken it for granted that it implied the securing of that good. Now she perceived that to refuse the gifts of life does not assure their transmission to those for whom they have been surrendered; and her familiar heaven was unpeopled.[6]

Ann Eliza thought that, somehow or other, God would see to it that goodness would be transmitted to its intended beneficiary. If God *is* love, and God is all-powerful, isn't that what one would expect? And yet, as Edith Wharton's powerful story shows, love is not always transmitted to the object it seeks. What tempts us to think otherwise? We came across part of the answer early in the book, in the confused attempt to ascribe something called 'all power' to God.[7] As a result of this attempt, it can be thought that God has two separate attributes, love and the power to make it effective. Once that assumption is made, one inherits one form of the problem of evil. If God has the power and the love, if he is both able and willing, whence evil? And the hunt for morally sufficient reasons for not exercising his power begins, with the familiar consequences we have noted.

Things look very different if we take seriously the conclusions reached in the last section of the previous chapter on 'God's Grammatical Predicates'. What if religion means what it says, that God *is* love, no more and no less? It would follow that God does not have two separate attributes, power and love, but that the only power God has or is, *is* the power of love. Recall Rowan Williams's remark quoted in Chapter 7, section 2: 'God's action has been held, in orthodox Christian thought, to be identical with God's being – that is, what God does is nothing other than

God's being actively real.'[8] Love has no power external to itself to guarantee its success.

The good that Ann Eliza seeks is in the hands of God, but the radical freedom of human beings entails the possibility that it may be rejected. Does the love lose its point when that happens? A pure love of God has to die to this expectation too, the expectation that love offered will be love received. Of course, in Edith Wharton's story, that does not happen. Despite her self-sacrifice for her sister, the fact that it is not transmitted to its object, unpeoples her familiar heaven.

By what right do I refer to dying to this expectation, one seemingly more extreme than dying to the moral expectations we discussed earlier? I can do so only because, at the heart of Christianity, there is a story of one who is said to be able to save, but who was a man of sorrows and acquainted with grief, and who dies the death of a common criminal, with spittle on his face. 'He came unto his own, and his own received him not' (John 1.11). I can do so, only because, in the Judaic concept of the Suffering Servant, we hear that, 'He is despised and rejected of men . . . and we hid as it were our faces from him; he was despised, and we esteemed him not' (Isaiah 53.3). In these central paradigms, we are shown what can happen to the love of God, and it happens precisely because of what that love tries to be in a world such as this. Love cannot intervene to stop it. That is why we hear the harsh, but deep reality: 'Yet it pleased the Lord to bruise him; he hath put him to grief' (Isaiah 53.10), and 'He that spared not his own Son, but delivered him up for us all' (Romans 8.32). Yet, in seeing what can happen to love, that love may offer an eternal covenant which the world cannot touch. At the same time as being told that God's Servant is brought to grief, and that the Son of God is rejected by his own, we are given, in the paradigms I am referring to, a remarkable description of the coming of the Suffering Servant: 'How beautiful upon the mountains are the feet of him that bringeth good tidings, that publisheth peace . . . that saith unto Zion, Thy God reigneth' (Isaiah 52.7). And despite the fact that the Son of God was not received by his own when he came, we are also told, 'But as many as received him, to them gave he power to become the sons of God' (John 1.12).

What is regarded as beautiful and empowering, even when it is despised and bruised, is the pure love of God, one that involves dying to the expectations we have discussed. It is this love which is called beautiful. If it is manifested, no matter what the world does to it, it is called love of the beauty of the world. It is such a love that may sustain believers in their suffering. It may be thought that we are far away from the God of theodicies, who has the power to prevent any evil we mention, but who, apparently, also has morally sufficient reasons for not doing so. To which I can only reply: indeed we are.

## 2. Expectations and the Unthinkable

In the Holocaust and related horrendous evils, as we have already noted, there is not only a desire to destroy victims, but *to destroy their sense of the human*. If this is not achieved, the oppressors feel that something in their victims has escaped their grasp, something that the world cannot touch. That something is their dignity. By contrast, when we discussed dying to moral expectations of gratitude for good done and of apology for evil suffered, we were still thinking of that 'dying to the self' against a background of normal relations between human beings, where 'normality' includes familiar strengths and weaknesses. The same could be said of the expectation that good attempted should be transmitted to its intended beneficiary. No sense could be made of dying to this expectation, except against a background of normal endeavour, with its successes and disappointments. In short, both contexts involve the give and take of human life. In the Holocaust and related horrendous evils, an attempt is made to destroy this familiar background, in a context where the perpetrators have absolute control, a sovereign power, over their victims, who become subhuman in their sight.

These extremities create a problem of belief. In recognizing them we come to believe the unbelievable. This is not the paradox it may appear to be at first. If, in innumerable cases, I come to discover that what I thought was unthinkable is, in fact, thought, I have to give up my claim that it is unthinkable. But it is not always so in ethics and religion.[9] To call something 'unthinkable' is to express the extremity of what has been done. It is not to say it cannot be done. When this happens we say, 'What was done was unthinkable.' People do unthinkable things to each other. But there are gradations, even within this use of the term. The Holocaust is an expression of an extreme use of a term which is itself only used to refer to immoral extremities. That is why certain attempts to explain it, to capture it in more familiar categories, are resisted.

Viktor Frankl tried to maintain normal voluntaristic ethical categories to explain why people behaved in such different ways in the Nazi concentration camps, some like saints, others like swine. He advanced the following thesis: 'Man has both potentialities within himself: which one is actualised depends on decisions but not on condition.'[10] In this way, Frankl tries to retain the normal uses of 'choice', 'responsibility' and 'decision' within the conditions of the concentration camps. The point is not to deny that these normal uses ever applied, but to resist his too easy exaggeration. Frankl's thesis fails to recognize the extent to which the language of normality is disrupted and violated by the conditions within the concentration camps. Primo Levi has argued how, if the extreme elemental experiences of the concentration camps had continued, they would have needed a new language to express what happened there.

> Just as our hunger is not that feeling of missing a meal, so our way of being cold has need of a new word. We say 'hunger', we say 'tiredness', 'fear', 'pain', we say 'winter' and they are different things. They are free words, created and used by free men who lived in comfort and suffering in their homes. If the Lagers [camps] had lasted longer a new, harsh language would have been born; and only this language could express what it means to toil the whole day in the wind, with the temperature below freezing, wearing only a shirt, underpants, cloth jacket and trousers, and in one's body

nothing but weakness, hunger and knowledge of the end drawing near.[11]

It has been argued that corresponding to the disruption of the 'free' words of normal physical comfort and discomfort, is a disruption of the 'free' words of normal moral description, praise and blame. The following episode is related by Judith Sternberg Newman, a nurse, who was deported to Auschwitz from Breslau with 197 other Jewish women. Three weeks after their deportation, only 18 of them were still alive.

Two days after Christmas, a Jewish child was born on our block. How happy I was when I saw this tiny baby. It was a boy, and the mother had been told that he would be taken care of. Three hours later, I saw a small package wrapped in cheese cloth lying on a wooden bench. Suddenly it moved. A Jewish girl employed as a clerk came over, carrying a pan of cold water. She whispered to me 'Hush! Quiet! Go away!' But I remained, for I could not understand what she had in mind. She picked up the little package – it was the baby, of course – and it started to cry with a thin little voice. She took the infant and submerged its little body in the cold water. My heart beat wildly in agitation. I wanted to shout 'Murderess!' but I had to keep quiet and could not tell anyone. The baby swallowed and gurgled, its little voice chittering like a small bird, until its breath became shorter and shorter. The woman held its head in the water. After about eight minutes the breathing stopped. The woman picked it up, wrapped it up again, and put it with the other corpses. Then she said to me, 'We had to save the mother, otherwise she would have gone to the gas chamber'. This girl had learned well from the SS and had become a murderess herself.[12]

Commenting on this incident, Lawrence Langer writes:

How is one to pass judgement on such an episode, or relate it to the inner freedom celebrated by other commentators on the deathcamp experience? Does moral choice have any meaning here? The drama involves the helpless infant, whose fate is entirely in someone else's hands . . . the absent mother, who may or may not have approved of the action: the 'agent' who coolly sacrifices one life to preserve another, as a deed of naked necessity, without appeal, not of moral choice; and the author, sole witness to a crime that is simultaneously an act of charity and perhaps of literal secular salvation to the mother. Conventional vocabulary limps through a situation that allows no heroic response, no acceptable gesture of protest, no mode of action to permit *any* of the participants, including the absent mother, to retain a core of human dignity.[13]

What are we to make of a juxtaposition of Langer's remarks and Frankl's voluntaristic explanation of moral survival and perishing at the deathcamps? On the one hand, we find Frankl saying:

Psychological observations of the prisoners have shown that only men who allowed their inner hold on their moral and spiritual selves to subside eventually fell victim to the camp's degenerating influences.[14]

On the other hand, we have Langer's response:

How do we present this sanctimonious view to the woman who was forced to drown an infant to save the mother, or the other woman who could only stand by in silence? We have seen that when the environment in Auschwitz supported one person's life, it was often at the cost of another's death – not because victims made wrong choices, or no choices, but because dying was the 'purpose' of living in this particular environment: it was the nature of Auschwitz. The need to equate moral activity with continued existence and moral passivity with death reflects a desperate desire to retain some ethical coherence in a chaotic universe. But the 'decision to survive' is contradicted by the condition of 'choiceless choice',

and may betray nothing more than a misuse of what Primo
Levi called 'free words': using language to create value where
none exists.[15]

Both reactions trade in generalities. Frankl's voluntarism
reminds us of Swinburne's reluctance to admit that people can be
crushed by circumstances which we discussed in Part I, Chapter
3, section 8. Such voluntarism not only ignores the obvious in an
attempt to resist the conclusion that circumstances, such as the
Holocaust, show clearly, but also opens the door to the sin of
pride which makes a distiction between the weak who fall, and
the strong who have it in them not to. Such voluntarism often
speaks from 'free' surroundings which cannot be taken for
granted when 'the unthinkable' happens. When people go to
pieces in such circumstances, *must* we feel the necessity to judge
them? Where does grace and compassion fit in to the rush to
judgement in which some seem eager to engage, and which an
unthinking voluntarism makes unavoidable? As against *those*
tendencies Langer's reaction made me recall an incident at
Swansea's Philosophical Society, in a discussion of 'choice' and
'blame' in extreme situations such as those we have described.
One member of the Department said that, while he would not
condemn someone whose resolve is broken in such conditions,
he would condemn him to others in the hope that doing so would
increase their resolve, if similarly subjected to such pressures, not
to be broken in the same way. Rush Rhees responded, 'I don't
think I'd say that.' The other challenged him, 'Well, then, what
would you say about him?' Rhees replied, 'Good God, man, I
wouldn't say anything at all.'

Langer's response is much needed to combat the voluntarism
that often dominates discussion of the problem of evil. The term
'choiceless choices' is an apt reminder of what is facile in it.
Langer thinks, however, that the extremity of the situation in the
Holocaust calls for a new language, a 'vocabulary of annihilation
appropriate to the deathcamp experience'. He thinks that, in its
absence, 'we should at least be prepared to redefine the termin-
ology of transcendence – "dignity", "choice", "suffering", and

"spirit" – so that it conforms more closely to the way of being in places like Auschwitz'.[16] Though I sympathize with this reaction as a protest against an easy voluntarism and moralism in these extreme situations, I do not think a new language is needed. It is important to recognize that Frankl, albeit in a confused way, wants to leave room for *different* responses to horrendous evils in the camps. The problem with Langer's response is that it, too, trades in generalities. It is true that in the dire circumstances he describes, no room is left for any kind of ethical coherence. What of his description of the woman who kills the child as someone who 'coolly sacrifices one life to preserve another'? Does that 'coolness' make us uneasy? The nurse who witnesses it does not, as Langer says, call it a crime which, at the same time is 'an act of charity'. She says the woman had learned well from the SS, and become a murderess. Langer says that the child's mother may or not have approved of what was done. But, in that case, she is not devoid of moral sensibility or opinions. Is it difficult to think that she would have wanted to die instead of the child, or, if necessary, to die with it?

I am not prejudging what answers might have been given to these questions, but to point out that, even in horrendous circumstances, people's reactions varied. In accounting for them what we need is not a new language, different from our 'free' one, but a faithful depiction of the place of 'the unthinkable' in human experience. This can be done if the extremities of evil suffered are not falsified or tidied up, but are allowed to be their horrendous selves.

It has been perceptively pointed out that when one is made a victim of 'the unthinkable', it often involves what can fittingly be called a loss of trust in the world. For example, Jean Améry speaks movingly of torture in the Holocaust in these terms. What does this trust involve? Améry replies:

> the certainty that by reason of written or unwritten social contracts the other person will spare me – more precisely stated, that he will respect my physical, and with it also my metaphysical, being. The boundaries of my body are also the

boundaries of my self. My skin surface shields me against the external world. If I am to have trust, I must feel on it only what I *want* to feel.[17]

Améry, of course, does not deny that bad things happen to one in life, but, usually, they do so in a context of mutual aid, of checks and balances, which we have already discussed.

The expectation of help is as much a constitutional psychic element as is the struggle for existence. Just a moment, the mother says to her child who is moaning from pain, a hot-water bottle, a cup of tea is coming right away, we won't let you suffer so! I'll prescribe you a medicine, the doctor assures, it will help you. Even on the battlefield, the Red Cross ambulances find their way to the wounded man. In almost all situations in life where there is bodily injury there is also the expectation of help; the former is compensated by the latter.[18]

But, in torture, these expectations of mutual aid break down. One ceases to believe in them.

At the first blow, however, this trust in the world breaks down. The other person, *opposite* whom I exist physically in the world and *with* whom I can exist only as long as he does not touch my skin surface as border, forces his own corporeality on me with the first blow. He is on me and thereby destroys me. It is like a rape, a sexual act without the consent of one of the two partners.[19]

The absolute power enjoyed by the torturer means that there is no reciprocity, not even of the form 'an eye for an eye' in this context. The victim of torture is helpless; he or she is no longer at home in the world. This astonishing fact is difficult for the tortured one to accept. Améry describes this phenomenon as follows:

If from the experience of torture any knowledge at all remains that goes beyond the plain nightmarish, it is that of a great amazement and a foreignness in the world that cannot be compensated by any sort of subsequent human communication. Amazed, the tortured person experienced that in this world there can be the other as absolute sovereign, and sovereignty revealed itself as the power to inflict suffering and to destroy . . . Whoever has succumbed to torture can no longer feel at home in the world.[20]

That is the heart of the matter. The Nazis saw, and understood, that they represented 'a sovereign will', which challenged that of God and nature. Robert Jay Lifton puts the matter thus: 'the Nazis sought to take over the functions of nature (natural selection) and God (the Lord giveth and the Lord taketh away) in orchestrating their own "selections", their own version of human evolution'.[21]

In all three cases, nature, God and the Nazis, there was no question of justification, no answer to the question, 'Why? As Roth and Berenbaum point out:

> Paradoxically, the Holocaust was beyond the question 'Why?' because the minds that produced it thought they 'understood' why. They 'recognized' that one religion had superseded another. They 'comprehended' that one race was superior to every other. They 'saw' what nature's laws decreed, namely, that there was *lebensunwertes Leben* ('life unworthy of life'). Thus, they 'realized' who deserved to live and who deserved to die.[22]

The religion of the demonic is so unbelievable, so contrary to human expectations, that it was not always easy to get orders obeyed, even by those charged with their execution. One reason for the degradation of prisoners was to make them look less than human in the eyes of their guards. In an interview with Gitta Sereny, Franz Stangl, commandant of Treblinka gave the following harrowing, but illuminating reply:

> '*Why,*' I asked Stangl, '*if they were going to kill them anyway, what was the point of all the humiliation, why the cruelty?*'

'To condition those who actually had to carry out the policies', he said. 'To make it possible for them to do what they did.'[23]

## 3. *Witness in Extremis*

In discussing the ways in which believers are called on to die to certain expectations, we saw, in section 1, how purity in love of God can call for the renunciation of the expectation of gratitude for good works, of the expectation of apology for injury, and even for the renunciation of the expectation that good acts will benefit those for whom they are intended. In all three cases, the point is that love of God need not be rendered pointless by the defeat of such expectations.

But what of the expectations that die when people lose trust in the world? In fact, 'trust' is too weak a word to use for the destruction of the minimal respect for others. Is it not odd to say that, normally, we trust that people will not do to us what the Nazis did to their victims? If we want to capture normality, we should not say that we trust such things will not occur, but, rather, that the question of their possible occurrence *simply does not arise*. We do not know, believe, trust, assume or take for granted that such things will not occur. I repeat, normally, the matter does not arise. The fact that it does not arise is not a *presupposition* of our sense of the human. It is what is involved *in* our sense of the human. That is why, when the Holocaust did occur, it involved, for many of its victims, a sense of the destruction of the human. But when that happens, in the kinds of situation we have discussed, we do not feel any need to speak of a call to renounce the expectations that only became explicit when what was not even thought of occurs. Rather than rush to judgement, we feel pity for those who are crushed in such circumstances. A religious believer might simply commend them to the love and mercy of God. Someone might ask what doing that amounts to, and that is an issue to which we shall have to return.[24]

When one reflects on evils such as the Holocaust, it is tempting to see nothing more than the pity for those degraded and destroyed, for those who fell apart morally in those terrible circumstances. If this happens, we speak as though all victims of the Holocaust were robbed of choice, as though the compulsion they bore robbed all of them of any religious reactions that were untouched by the horrendous evils being witnessed and suffered. By 'untouched', I do not mean, of course, 'uninfluenced by'. Who could fail to be untouched by the Holocaust, in that sense, for good or ill? By religious reactions that were, for some, untouched by the Holocaust, I mean, those that did not lose their point in face of it. To ignore the fact that there were such reactions is to fail to do justice to those who showed them.

In an exchange with Elie Wiesel, Richard Rubenstein contrasts the anti-semitism of Ferdinand and Isabella of Spain in 1492 with the Holocaust. They gave the several thousand Jews in Spain three options.

> The first was to be baptized and become part of Christian Spain; the second was to leave the country if baptism was impossible . . . Ferdinand and Isabella had no interest in exterminating Jews simply because they were Jews. Their interest was in the creation of a Christian Spain, not the extermination of the Jews.
>
> The Jews had a third, tragic option: they could remain on Spanish soil as Jews, but they would be killed if they did so. Nevertheless, this option of extremity was not without dignity. Let us imagine a Jew saying to himself, 'I can neither leave this place which I love nor become a Christian'.
>
> By his decision such a man elected martyrdom. His death was freely chosen. It served as a witness both to his love of place and his Jewish faith. This is in stark contrast to what took place in the Nazi death camps. One of Hitler's greatest victories was that he deprived the Jews of *all* opportunity to be martyrs. There can be no martyrdom without free choice. In the camps it made no difference whether you were Dr. Edith Stein, who had become a Carmelite nun, or a Hasidic rabbi. All Jews were slaughtered without distinction. Even baptism

provided no escape. It must sadly be noted that the pathetic attempts of the Jewish community to see the six million as martyrs is a tragic albeit understandable misperception.[25]

There are a number of comments to be made on these remarks. First, there is a correction of fact that Elie Wiesel makes in response.

You say, Dick, that Hitler deprived the Jew of martyrdom. That is not true. Many Jews, especially the rabbis, could have saved their lives. In my town all the rabbis could have saved their lives, and do you know who wanted to save them? The priests. It's not the first time in history that they wanted alibis. The priests came to our rabbis – we had some thirty of them in our center – offering them refuge in the monastery, in the church. But, of course, what rabbi would choose it? I think there were two, out of at least fifty thousand rabbis in Eastern Europe, two who chose to escape individually. All the others preferred voluntarily, knowingly, to go with their Jews. How did these rabbis maintain their Jewishness and their humanity? *That* is the wonder! After all the system was so strong and the whole world was an accomplice.[26]

Wiesel does not offer any explanation of these choices by the rabbis. They occasion wonder in him, that is all. What we can say, in the context of the present discussion, is that the choices show that, for these rabbis, they had a point, despite what they entailed. Knowing that, they still made them. Love of God and of their fellow Jews was not rendered pointless. One could say that their love of their fellow Jews is an expression of their love of God.

Perhaps Rubenstein, in the light of these facts, would concede that he can no longer say that Jews were deprived of *all* opportunity to be martyrs. This is because some, like the rabbis, freely chose their fate. But, it might be said, those who exercised such freedom were a small minority. For millions, there was no freedom. They were simply herded, like cattle, to the camps and to their fate. Without the freedom enjoyed by the few, what sense can be made of a continuing love of God and humanity in them? Kierkegaard discusses the above question. He asks how, if suffering is unavoidable, there can be any place left for the will. Kierkegaard asks:

> Is not suffering something that one must be forced into against his will? If a man can be free of it, can he then will it, and if he is bound to it, can he be said to will it? . . . Yes, for many men it is almost an impossibility for them to unite freedom and suffering in the same thought.[27]

This seeming impossibility has to do with questions such as the following:

> Can anyone but one who is free of suffering, say, 'Put me in chains, I am not afraid'? Can even a prisoner say, 'Of my own free will I accept my imprisonment' – the very imprisonment which is already his condition? Here again the opinion of most men is that such a thing is impossible, and that therefore the condition of the sufferer is one of sighing despondency.[28]

If we are inclined to accept this conclusion, Kierkegaard has a question for us. He asks, 'But what then is patience?'[29] This use of the notion of patience may mislead us. Peter Winch has pointed out that it is essential to recognize that:

> [Kierkegaard] is not speaking of an attitude of quiescent acceptance of *avoidable* evils, but of an attitude which it is possible to adopt in the face of evils which are seen as *un*avoidable. And I think no questions are being begged concerning what evils are and what are not unavoidable; . . . Kierkegaardian patience is the *voluntary* acceptance of *unavoidable* suffering: both the inevitability of the suffering and the voluntariness of the acceptance are essential to it, and this is just what constitutes its paradoxical character.[30]

When Rubenstein says that martyrdom is the exercise of freedom, that exercise obviously involves *courage*. Kierkegaard wants to argue that what he means by 'patience' effects a greater miracle than 'courage'.

> Thus patience, if one may put it in this way, performs an even greater miracle than courage. Courage voluntarily chooses suffering that may be avoided; but patience achieves freedom in unavoidable suffering. By his courage, the free one voluntarily lets himself be caught, but by his patience the prisoner effects his freedom – although not in the sense that need make the jailer anxious or fearful.[31]

When Kierkegaard speaks of the jailer's fears, he is obviously referring to his fear of the prisoner escaping. The attitude of the prisoner to his imprisonment need not threaten that. But what if the purpose of the jailers is different. As Elie Wiesel says:

> What the Germans wanted to do was not only to exterminate the Jewish people physically; first of all, they wanted to exterminate them *spiritually* . . . The Germans wanted to deprave, to debase the Jew, to have him give up all values and dehumanize him. That was the first thing. Even the language in the camp – what kind of language was it? The most obscene language you could imagine, meant to create a climate, to impose an inhuman concept of man and of the universe upon the Jewish people.[32]

And the miracle was, that despite it all, in many cases this did not happen. As Wiesel says:

> What the Germans wanted to do to the Jewish people was to substitute themselves for the Jewish God. All the terminology, all the vocabulary testifies to that. And in spite of all, here were these men who remained human and who remained Jewish and went on praying to God.[33]

We have already noted the importance some prisoners attached to seemingly pointless activities, such as washing in dirty water, because in the observance of this order was the possibility, at least, of the retention of dignity. In one sense, given the excremental assault on them, dignity is the last word one would use to describe the prisoners. But by 'dignity', in this context, is meant that integrity which the external assaults have not touched.

The only dangers in these words is that they must not be used with an unearned generality. This dangerous generality is in Kierkegaard when he says:

> The outward impossibility of ridding oneself of suffering does not hinder the inward possibility of being able really to emancipate oneself within suffering – of one's own free will accepting suffering, as the patient one gives his consent by willing to accept suffering.[34]

The inward possibility of emancipation may or may not be hindered. There are circumstances of torture and tragedy that may make it impossible. All one can say is that, sometimes, perhaps often, it happens. But when it does happen, Wiesel wonders at it, for he regards it as a miracle. Also, when it happens, the jailer, who wants to break the spirit of his prisoner, has reason to be fearful, for his prisoner expresses something that he has been unable to touch. Someone may say that the prisoner is making a virtue out of a necessity, to which Kierkegaard replies:

> Undeniably he is making a virtue out of a necessity, that is just the secret, that is certainly a most accurate designation for what he does. He makes a virtue out of necessity. He brings a determination of freedom out of that which is determined as necessity. And it is just there that the healing power of the decision for the Eternal resides: that the sufferer may voluntarily accept the compulsory suffering.[35]

By 'patience', Kierkegaard means not being deflected from a sense of the importance of decency, love and compassion, despite external circumstances. The reason why the Holocaust is a limiting case, in this respect, is that it was a systematic attempt to destroy the very sense of those virtues in the Jewish people. But in many cases, it did not succeed.

> Why? Why did they do it? And what for? In whom could they believe? In man? This is what bewilders me and astonishes me: that they could still think of man and of God and of us, while they lived and died in an age in which both Jew and man were betrayed by man and God. This story of spiritual strength . . . of the Jew has to be told.[36]

There is still an unresolved tension, for Wiesel, between continuing to think of a God who, at the same time, is accused of betrayal. Are the references to the *same* God, or is the tension between *different conceptions* of God? It seems, sometimes, that one has this tension within the same biblical narrative. For example, in the story of Shadrach, Meshach and Abednego, their confidence in refusing to bow down to the golden image, as decreed by Nebuchadnezzar, is based on the expectation that, even if the king throws them into a fiery furnace, their God, whom they serve, is able to deliver them from the fiery furnace, and from the hands of the king. If the king puts them in the furnace, God will get them out unscathed. If *this* is part of one's conception of God, the ovens of the Holocaust indeed constitute a horrendous betrayal by God of his people.

In the narrative, however, there is a verse that stands in sharp contrast to the expectation of deliverance from the fiery furnace. It contains a conception of faith that does *not* depend on that outcome, since it addresses the possibility of its non-occurrence. The three men address the king, saying, 'But if not, be it known unto thee, O king, that we will not serve thy gods, nor worship the golden image which thou hast set up' (Daniel 3.18). In the event, the three men are put into the fiery furnace, but delivered from it.

> And the princes, governors, and captains, and the king's counsellors being gathered together, saw these men, upon whose

bodies the fire had no power, nor was an hair of their head singed, neither were their coats changed, nor the smell of fire had passed on them (Daniel 3.27).

Again, one need say no more about the contrast with the Holocaust where, despite the horrors suffered, there were those who showed what Kierkegaard calls 'patience', insofar as love of God and human dignity did not become pointless for them, and did not depend on their deliverance.[37]

There is another contrast between the story of the fiery furnace and what Kierkegaard is talking about. It does not make sense to speak of love of God, or the patient embracing of it as compelling, or being compelled. That is a central matter about which Process theologians are correct. Kierkegaard writes, 'For one can be forced into the narrow prison, one can be forced into lifelong sufferings, and necessity is the tyrant; but one cannot be forced into patience.'[38] Contrast these remarks with the reaction of Nebuchadnezzar to the deliverance of the three men:

> Therefore I make a decree. That every people, nation, and language, which speak anything amiss against the God of Shadrach, Meshach, and Abednego, shall be cut in pieces, and their houses shall be made a dunghill: because there is no other God that can deliver after this sort (Daniel 3.29).

As far as Nebuchadnezzar is concerned, God has won a power game with other gods. Anything they can do, he can do better. As Wiesel acknowledges in works like *Night*, faith in such a God died, for many, in the smoke of the camps. Anything that Nazis could do, God cannot do better. To think otherwise is another example of the foolishness (and, I would have thought, blasphemy), of attributing such power to God. At the end of the first section, we reminded ourselves of earlier conclusions about God's grammatical predicates. If God *is* love, God does not have two separate attributes, power and love. God's only power is the power of love.

In the story of the men in the fiery furnace, we are told that

Nebuchadnezzar says, when he looks into the furnace, 'Lo, I see four men loose, walking in the midst of the fire, and they have no hurt; and the form of the fourth is like the Son of God' (Daniel 3.25).

It would be obscene, of course, to say that the victims of the Holocaust suffered no real hurt. It is because of the fact that, *despite* the horrendous evil inflicted on them, many still prayed to God and preserved their dignity, that Wiesel finds in it a cause for wonder, wonder at the fact that they did not find it pointless to do so. Since that is true, would there not be a point in saying that they did not think they were alone, but that, rather, another stood with them whose form is like the Son of God? Notice, *I* am not saying that of them, but am seeking to do justice to the wonder of their witness.

In talking, in this section, of 'Witness in Extremis', one is conscious of walking a tightrope. One is in constant danger of falling off. We can see why if we try to relate what has been said to treatments of the problem of evil in contemporary analytic philosophy of religion. There, as we know, attempts are made to show that belief in an omnipotent, perfectly good God, is consistent with acknowledgement of evil. I do not know what it would mean to ask whether the Jewish witness Wiesel wonders at is consistent with the horrors of the camps. The witness is there. It says what it says, despite the surrounding horror. In the so-called solution to the logical problem of evil, on the other hand, God's non-intervention to prevent the Holocaust is justified in terms of the morally sufficient reasons he has for not doing so. The Holocaust, it is said, is cost effective in the divine plan! At the *eschaton*, every victim will look back and say that it was all worthwhile!

I am all too aware that this instrumentalist, consequentialist horror story may be applied to what I have been saying, as though I have been arguing that the religious human witness in the Holocaust, to which Wiesel refers, *justifies* its horrendous evils, and is even part of the reason God allows it to occur. Looking at the present philosophical scene, I fear that such misplaced attempts at *justification* will continue, even in philosophical and theological views that are not so crudely consequentialist as some of those I have criticized. For this reason, more needs to be said about them.

## Notes

1 Simone Weil, *Waiting for God*, New York: Putnam's Sons 1951, p. 147.

2 Simone Weil, *Waiting for God*, p. 224.

3 For a discussion of the groundless conviction that whereas misfortune happens to others, it *cannot* happen to oneself, see the discussion of Tolstoy's *The Death of Ivan Ilyich* in İlham Dilman and D. Z. Phillips, *Sense and Delusion*, London: Routledge and Kegan Paul 1971.

4 Simone Weil, *Waiting for God*, pp. 222–3.

5 I have discussed the story at greater length in 'Displaced Persons' in *From Fantasy to Faith*, Basingstoke: Macmillan 1991.

6 See Edith Wharton, 'Bunner Sisters' in *Madame de Treymes*, Virago 1984.

7 See Chapter 2, section 1.

8 Rowan Williams, 'Redeeming Sorrows' in D. Z. Phillips (ed.), *Religion and Morality*, Basingstoke: Macmillan 1996, p. 143.

9 See D. Z. Phillips, 'Minds, Persons and the Unthinkable' in *Minds and Persons*, Royal Institute Lecture Series, ed. Anthony O'Hear, Cambridge: Cambridge University Press 2003.

10 Viktor E. Frankl, *Man's Search for Meaning*, New York: Pocket Books 1963, pp. 212–13.

11 Primo Levi, *Survival in Auschwitz: The Nazi Assault on Humanity*, New York: Collier Books 1969, pp. 112–13.

12 Judith Sternberg Newman, *In the Hell of Auschwitz*, New York: Exposition Press 1963, pp. 42–3.

13 Lawrence L. Langer, 'The Dilemma of Choice in the Deathcamps' in John K. Roth and Michael Berenbaum (eds), *Holocaust: Religious and Philosophical Implications*, New York: Paragon House 1989, p. 225.

14 Frankl, *Man's Search for Meaning*, p. 110.

15 Langer, 'The Dilemma of Choice', p. 231.

16 Langer, 'The Dilemma of Choice', p. 231.

17 Jean Améry, *At the Mind's Limits*, Bloomington: Indiana University Press 1980, p. 28.

18 Améry, *Mind's Limits*, p. 28-9.

19 Améry, *Mind's Limits*, p. 28.

20 Améry, *Mind's Limits*, pp. 39–40.

21 Robert Jay Lifton, 'This World Is Not This World' in Roth and Berenbaum, *Holocaust: Religious and Philosophical Implications*, p. 197.

# Faith and Expectation

219

22 John K. Roth and Michael Berenbaum, 'Epilogue' in *Holocaust: Religious and Philosophical Implications*, p. 372.

23 Gitta Sereny, *Into That Darkness*, New York: McGraw–Hill 1974, p. 101.

24 See Chapter 11, section 4.

25 Richard L. Rubenstein and Elie Wiesel, 'An Exchange' in Roth and Berenbaum, *Holocaust: Religious and Philosophical Implications*, pp. 356–7.

26 Rubenstein and Wiesel, 'Exchange', p. 366.

27 Søren Kierkegaard, *Purity of Heart*, New York: Harper Torchbooks 1956, pp. 171–2.

28 Kierkegaard, *Purity of Heart*, p. 173.

29 Kierkegaard, *Purity of Heart*, p. 173.

30 Peter Winch, 'Can A Good Man Be Harmed?' in *Ethics and Action*, London: Routledge and Kegan Paul 1972, p. 205.

31 Kierkegaard, *Purity of Heart*, p. 173.

32 Rubenstein and Wiesel, 'Exchange', p. 366.

33 Rubenstein and Wiesel, 'Exchange', p. 366.

34 Kierkegaard, *Purity of Heart*, pp. 173–4.

35 Kierkegaard, *Purity of Heart*, p. 174.

36 Rubenstein and Wiesel, 'Exchange', p. 368.

37 I was brought to see this distinction in the biblical story by a sermon by J. R. Jones, 'Ac Onide' (But if not) in *Ac Onide*, Llandybie: Christopher Davies 1970.

38 Kierkegaard, *Purity of Heart*, p. 174.

# 10

# Sacrifice

## 1. Belief as Sacrifice

One way of summing up what was said in the previous chapter about 'dying to expectations' is to say that to believe in God is to worship him, and that worshipping him is wanting to make one's life a sacrifice to him. More needs to be said about this *religious* concept of sacrifice.

In the previous chapter we saw that it involves dying to the self. In section 1, we considered a number of examples. First, we mentioned the need to die to pride in actions such as an act of charity. Second, we discussed the different context of dying to the expectation that, no matter what happens to others, the world will smile on us. Third, we examined the need, in religion, even to die to moral expectations, the expectation of gratitude for good done or of apology for harm suffered. Fourth, we discussed the different case of dying to the expectation that good deeds will always succeed in benefiting those for whom they are intended. In this fourth context, love as expressed in the tradition of the Suffering Servant and the story of the crucifixion shows itself despite the scorn heaped on it by the world in all the ways mentioned. Yet, the coming of the Suffering Servant is called 'beautiful', and receiving the Crucified One is said to make those who do so sons of God.

In section 2 of the chapter we discussed attempts that are made to destroy an expectation of the human in people's dealings with one another. We saw the terrible attempts made to destroy every vestige of human dignity. We concluded that there was good reason to think that in the Holocaust an attempt was made to replace one religion by another, to replace the sovereignty of God with the sovereignty of the Nazi power over life and death.

In the third section of the chapter, we saw how, even in the deathcamps, there were those who bore witness to the things of God *in extremis*. We used Kierkegaard's notion of patience to illustrate this witness. Philosophically, there may be resistance to the idea that any freedom remains under the cruel yoke of such necessity; resistance to the idea that there can be a voluntary acceptance of the necessary. Yet, this resistance is a philosophical prejudice. Faced by dire necessities, there remains the question of how they are taken up into the lives of those who suffer them. The miracle was that the answer to this question, with respect to many in the deathcamps, was that necessities were taken up via their love of God. This did not happen always, of course. Indeed, as we said, there were circumstances that make it impossible to see how it could happen. But it *did* happen. There were those for whom the things of God did not lose their point. As with the men in the fiery furnace, it seems that they did not stand alone. Their lives, it may be said, became a sacrifice to God. But as soon as one says this, one is aware of how it can be misunderstood. That is why I said, at the outset of the section, that more needs to be said about it. I also said at the end of the previous chapter that a fatal instrumentalism may return to distort the whole picture.

In a critique of Stephen T. Davis's views on creation,[1] I put my point, perhaps misleadingly, by denying that God's gift of life is *for* anything. Davis, rightly, reminded me that, 'In both Judaism and Christianity, God gave human beings life for a purpose, viz., that they come to love and obey and glorify God in their lives.'[2]

It is important to remember, however, what I was concerned to deny. First, I wanted to deny that to make a sacrifice to God meant that one subjected oneself to a moral obstacle course he had designed because he wanted one to develop a certain moral character. Second, I wanted to deny that to make a sacrifice to God meant to satisfy his need for an egocentric glorification of himself by the only creatures who could provide it. I have no doubt that Davis is as opposed to the second construal of sacrifice as I am. But if the first construal of sacrifice is also to be rejected, how is making one's life a sacrifice to God to be understood?

In two essays, at least sixteen years apart, Rush Rhees shows how the notion of sacrifice can appear from very different points of view. In his first paper, he is critical of the egocentricity and servility a religious concept of sacrifice can be thought to imply.

> For religion turns men's deepest aspirations towards servility. Whatever it may say of another life, it is servitude and the impotence of the spirit that it fosters here. What it offers to the soul is consolation, but not freedom. There is no freedom in a life of propitiation and sacrifice. And there is no generosity in accepting one's lot.
>
> And the turning of everything into service of the master, making one's life an offering to him, goes with the emphasis on personal salvation. This is just the sort of egoistic concern about one's lot, that has to be overcome if freedom is to be possible at all.[3]

In the second paper, Rhees sees that religious sacrifice can be something different from propitiation, a giving something to God to get on the right side of him for selfish reasons. He sees that sacrificing one's life to God is the opposite of such servile egocentricity. It is done for God's sake, not one's own. Further, in this religious context, the idea of giving something to God which he needs would not even make sense. Rhees writes:

> If I sacrifice myself to make some scientific experiment possible – or if I sacrifice myself to save somebody from drowning – here there is something which depends upon the help I can give. I make something possible by my sacrifice which would not be possible otherwise. That is why it would be absurd to talk about sacrificing myself for God, in that sense.[4]

To make one's life a sacrifice to God would mean becoming nothing before him – ridding one's life from pride and selfishness, for example. It is their absence that gives glory to God. That is what glorifying him comes to. But this does not mean that, in that case, one is acting unselfishly *towards* God. Rhees says:

I am neither selfish nor unselfish towards God. That would make no sense. Certainly I may be selfish in my prayers, for instance. But that is not a selfishness *towards God.* A sinfulness towards God, maybe. But I can no more be selfish towards God than I can be generous to him.

If my life is a sacrifice to God, there is no unselfishness in that. There is, if my devotion is genuine, an abandonment of *pride* – a selflessness in *that* sense. And with that goes a love.[5]

Contrasting the different notions of sacrifice, Rhees brings out the grammar of *religious* sacrifice: ' "Let my life *be* a sacrifice to Thee": that is more the sense of it than 'Let me sacrifice myself for Thee' – which I think would be absurd.'[6]

To pray to love God is to pray to become nothing before him, to be free of the sins which separate people from that. To pray that God should not turn his face from one is not to say, 'Don't do that to me', but, rather, 'Don't let me become that.' That is why Rhees insists that making one's life a sacrifice to God is not like sacrificing oneself for some purpose, however important.

It is making my life a sacrifice: it is glorifying God.

We pray to God to accept this sacrifice. And if my life before God is nothing, my life is a sacrifice acceptable to God, is a glorification of God, has all the reality anything could have. That is why in becoming nothing before God it may approach God and to reality – and not otherwise.[7]

Even *in extremis*, people pray to suffer for God. Again, they are not praying to die for a cause. It is a prayer to love God *in* their suffering; a prayer which asks that that love should not become pointless even in the direst of circumstances. If the notion of God as Spirit is taken seriously, it is a prayer for that spirit of love and forgiveness not to forsake them. The prayer is a participation in that spirit; a practice of its presence. If the devotion is genuine, Rhees says, the believer comes into contact with that spiritual reality that is God. Religiously, it might be said that in genuine devotion, God speaks to God in human beings; to the extent that their devotion is genuine, God's spirit becomes theirs. He is said to dwell in them, and they in him. If this happens, they become his people, and he becomes their God.

If we look back at my discussion with Davis, and to his insistence that life has a purpose, namely, to glorify God, one ought to be able to see, in the light of Rhees' remarks, why I am anxious to avoid a means–ends relation in this context. It is not a matter of *finding out* what life is for, or what its meaning is. Still less is it finding out what I need to do to be saved. It is giving glory to God, that's all. Rhees writes:

> For the great saints, the love of God was not a matter of finding the meaning of life. If I do love God, then I pray that I may love him more perfectly. And I want to say: I cannot love God without offering my life to God. But it is turning things upside down to say that this is first and foremost a concern with the meaning of life; or even that it is a conviction that there is some meaning in life. Anyone to whom the love of God was important *because* it gave meaning to life, would be only imperfectly religious. For the religious person the love of God is important because of God. It cannot be for any other reason.[8]

The love of God will show itself in the way a believer loves his fellow human beings, so much so that the First Epistle of Saint John almost identifies these loves. It says, bluntly, 'If a man say, I love God, and hateth his brother, he is a liar' (1 John 4.12). Even in the dire circumstances of the Holocaust, those who prayed to God and strove to maintain human dignity expressed, in those prayers, the sacrificial love of God Rhees is talking of. Once again, the all-important thing is to love God, to find in that something that their tormentors could not touch. But it is important to get the emphasis right: it is not important *because* it cannot be touched. It is important, because it is love of God. It is tempting to say that, if it is of God, it *cannot* be touched, but that remark involves difficulties I shall discuss in section 3 of the chapter.

At the end of the present section, I want to show how giving what has been said an instrumentalist aspect can distort the whole picture. Note that Rhees is emphasizing that in making one's life a sacrifice to God, one approaches the reality of God – that is the *kind* of reality God has. God is not real in any other way – for example, as some kind of entity, or as pure consciousness. God's reality and God's divinity are one. God is a spiritual reality.

Yet, these insights can be negated in a moment if we claim, as many theodicists do, that God allows suffering *in order that* human beings should come into a certain relationship with him. He could do something about the sufferings if he wanted to, but doesn't, for these reasons. The whole picture changes into an instrumentalist nightmare, and a conception of God re-emerges as a creator who experiments with his creatures for his own glorification. We are back to a notion of worship as satisfying a need God has – an idea that, as Rhees says, is conceptually absurd and religiously blasphemous.

## 2. *The Persistence of Instrumentalism*

Having drawn attention to the fact of religious witness in the most dire of circumstances, it is still all too easy to give an instrumentalist analysis of that witness. It has been said that the destruction which has been visited on people, as seen in an extreme form in the Holocaust, is, nevertheless, a *creative* destruction, since it led to a quality of witness one would not have seen otherwise. It may even be said that a people were 'divinely chosen' to this end. The witness (the greater good) then becomes God's morally sufficient reason for allowing the destruction.

Instrumentalism may even affect the way in which philosophers and theologians protest against this way of thinking. On the one hand, they argue, as I have done, that the application of instrumentalist thinking here is completely misplaced. On the other hand, the argument continues by saying that no 'higher purpose' could justify the human waste involved in the destruction God is said to allow to bring it about. But if the first objection against this instrumentalism is taken seriously, this is the very kind of question that should not be entertained. Objectors are torn between objecting to the very idea of involving 'the higher purpose' and complaining that that purpose has not been effective.

Again, out of respect for the extent of the affliction suffered by human beings, many theologians have emphasized that the only response on God's part is silence. Any attempt, as in theodicies, to give a substantive account of God's reasons for allowing them has disastrous results. Having said that, however, instrumentalist reasoning can return in attempts to explain or to justify *why* God remains silent. This takes the form of the free-will defence which we have already discussed.[9]

God, it is said, has granted freedom to human beings. Once granted, that freedom cannot be interfered with. God must see how it develops. No doubt, it is said, he agonizes over the evils the freedom has led to. The argument then lapses into the contradictions we have already noted: complaining about the instrumentalism in the theology, while, at the same time, complaining about the ineffectiveness of the means chosen. There is no break here with thinking of God anthropomorphically.

God has no biography, no inner life, as an agent among agents, in which, on some days, he goes through agony, doubts, has second thoughts, regrets, and so on. As Rowan Williams points out, this way of thinking entails thinking of creation as a botched up attempt on God's part, deficient and incompetent in certain respects.[10] But, as we saw in Chapter 8, sections 2 and 3, on 'Outside the World' and 'Creation, Power and Freedom', God's relation to the world, the sense in which he is 'other than' the world, is itself a spiritual relation, not one of power and control. If one takes seriously the notion of God as Spirit, one sees, at the same time, that God can give no more and no less than what that Spirit is. If this notion is embraced, the 'cannot' in the claim that God cannot prevent the Holocaust would be seen as a grammatical or logical 'cannot'. It marks what cannot be said within a given conception of God. In that case, however, theologians and philosophers should not proceed to speculate as to the reasons why God has not done what now, after all, it appears, he could have done if he had wanted to. Their reluctance not to go down this road is due to the continued presence of the notion of an all-powerful God, which leads to questions about why that power has not been exercised to the full. This is the return of an old friend, the notion of 'all power' which analytic philosophers of religion like to call 'robust', but which, in fact, is unintelligible.[11] As long as one remains within its grip, the logical problem of evil will retain its misleading form, and the effort to find instrumentalist solutions to it will persist.

Having said what I have about God as Spirit, and what that spirit offers, this does not deny that someone may want to reject it, and wish things were otherwise. But this would not mean that *this* kind of critical rejection entails saying, 'Now, God should have done it differently,' or going on to correct him as though he had made a mistake! One may reject what a religious belief has to offer, but that *is* the offer, take it or leave it. Further, a personal rejection of what is offered, may be accompanied by a recognition that it *is* accepted, and goes deep with other people, and that it would be foolish to criticize it, as one would a confusion in a philosophical argument. Rush Rhees provides the following illustration of the point which I will quote at length. He is discussing what Wittgenstein meant when he said, 'I wouldn't dare criticize a man like Calvin.'

He might have said about Calvin's views, as he did say of the positions of certain Catholics (e.g. Miss Anscombe) that he, Wittgenstein, could never believe what they believed – or could never believe what Calvin seemed to believe. But this is not saying that Calvin was confused or was making mistakes. He would *criticize* Russell in logic, because he knew the criteria and the standards or requirements which were relevant to this. He would say also that he understood what Russell was trying to do. But he would not say any of this with regard to Calvin, I imagine.

For one thing, Calvin's views about religion and about ethics are not the sort of thing that *can* be discussed, in the sense in which questions in logic can. But more important: Wittgenstein would have said that Calvin was a man of great depth, I imagine: that Calvin saw problems and saw the weight of considerations pro and contra, by which Wittgenstein might feel attracted or repelled, but of which he did not feel able to say 'Yes, this is where your thinking on these matters ought to lead you' or 'this is superficial, and deeper thinking would turn you away from this'. . . .

It would be partly analogous if he had said he would never dare criticize the music of Mozart or Beethoven. On the other hand, I have heard him express his puzzlement or *annoyance* when listening to Beethoven's violin concerto: 'And now he goes back and repeats the whole theme again, . . . and then *again* . . .' – almost with an expression of disgust, because the thing *seemed* (to Wittgenstein then, anyway) so senseless. *And yet Wittgenstein would not have said that 'for these reasons he did not think the violin concerto was a great piece of music'.* Still less would he have said that Beethoven ought not to have written it in that way. He would never have had the slightest doubt that Beethoven knew what he was doing; although he, Wittgenstein, did not.

He said sometimes, too, that one wanted strongly to object to the world as it is, and to *complain*; and that sometimes it was right to do this. – I think he had something [like] the same idea as that which Kierkegaard expresses somewhere when he speaks in admiration of Job, and says that Job was right to voice his complaints: which does not mean that Kierkegaard was losing sight of the closing passages of *Job*, rather the contrary. But Kierkegaard was suggesting, if I remember, that nowadays people complain *too little* against God. And I guess he thought this tendency makes their religion half-hearted and hypocritical . . . I remember when someone began, half jokingly, 'You know, there is one thing God has arranged wrongly . . .' and Wittgenstein said (I probably have not the words correctly) with fervour: 'Oh, there are *many* things God has arranged wrongly . . .' – and he went on with clenched teeth. There was nothing blasphemous about this; no more, I think, than there is about Job's complaints. And Wittgenstein would have accepted the 'Where wast thou . . .?' passages at the end.[12]

Rhees is not denying, as is obvious in his paper, and throughout his book, that, sometimes, it is difficult to draw a sharp distinction between religious beliefs and philosophical theses, since confusions, akin to philosophical confusions, can enter into religious beliefs. That is partly why Wittgenstein says that certain religious beliefs can cause great harm. The present book, in what it criticizes, seeks to address such a situation. More will be said about it in the next section.

### 3. A Chosen People

One is faced by the difficult belief that the Holocaust is said to occur to God's chosen people. In Christianity, it is God's chosen one who is crucified. This is one of the religious beliefs that may lead us astray. Given the conception of God's omnipotence, his possession of 'all power', the notion of God's 'chosen people' is certainly problematic for now these events are not seen as random, but as deliberate stages in a plan.

Is this the only choice we are offered: determined or random? If we take the former option, we are led into the kind of picture of predestination that Wittgenstein says has caused great harm.

Suppose someone were taught: there is a being who, if you do such and such or live thus and thus, will take you to a place of everlasting torment after you die; most people end up there, a few get to a place of everlasting happiness. – This being has selected in advance those who are to go to the good place and, since only those who have lived a certain sort of life go to the place of torment, he has also arranged in advance for the rest to live like that.

What might be the effect of such a doctrine?

Well, it does not mention punishment, but rather a sort of

natural necessity. And if you were to present things to anyone in this light, he could only react with despair or incredulity to such a doctrine.

Teaching it could not constitute an ethical upbringing.[13]

Obviously, on such a view, both what the Nazis did to the Jews, and the prayers and retention of human dignity by many of their victims, would, alike, be simply natural necessities, since it would have been arranged, in advance, for *both* parties to behave like that. One could not speak of either atrocity or love of God. On the other hand, if one chooses the second option and calls the Holocaust a random, gruesome event, one simply severs it from the religious context that it has for many. But what is that context, or, at least, what is the context which has been sorely neglected in the discussions of this issue? Is it not the notion that the innocent are called on to suffer for the guilty? We are confronted by a religious notion of sacrifice.

*Called upon* – what does that mean? Does it mean *chosen by God*? But what does *that* mean if not the determinism that would make nonsense of any talk of 'sacrifice' at all? These questions take us back to the notion of covenant as contract that we discussed in Chapter 7, section 1 and contrasted with the notion of an eternal covenant, discussed in section 5 of that chapter. When the covenant is seen as a contract, the believer sees God's graces as a *right* to which he is entitled – hence the complaint against the Holocaust and other horrendous evils – what kind of grace could that possibly be?

But is there not in Isaiah and in the Gospels a rejection of this idea of a covenant as a contract and, hence, a different idea of redemption? To be a servant of God, as we have seen, is to want to love God. That love is not of this world. That is precisely why it may be called upon to suffer in the world. The sacrifice of worldliness may be called on to suffer by the world, precisely because of its reaction to such sacrifice. It is not that God first chooses a people and then, for reasons best known to himself, makes them suffer. Rather, it is *when* people suffer for God, *when* their love of God brings suffering on them, that they are

God's chosen people. This is not a bestowal of a grace or a calling at any particular time, but the terms of an eternal covenant that reveals what it is to serve God *at any time*. Rhees thinks that this is what goes deep in the notion of predestination and of God's elect. Rhees says it is a way of emphasizing

that God's grace is eternal, and that its bestowal is not an 'act' at a particular time and situation. It may have something akin to the remark that this Lamb was slaughtered at the beginning of the world. And perhaps: 'Before Abraham was, I am.'[14]

The trouble comes from thinking of eternity in temporal terms, as that which is *before* time, when everything is fixed in advance etc., so leading to the reading of predestination which, as Wittgenstein showed, leads to insuperable difficulties.

Rhees points out that the notion of an eternal, as opposed to temporal contract is found in both Judaism and Christianity, which is not to deny that other notions of covenant compete with it and prove an obstacle to it.

Rejection of the very early idea of a Covenant between God and his people. I cannot count myself in God's grace, cannot count myself as chosen, just because I am of the seed of Abraham. – I think there may be something of this in Isaiah as well, with his new conception of what it means to be the chosen people: to be the *suffering* people. And if St. Paul used a phrase that is translated by 'election' . . . I suppose the idea is the same as that of '*chosen* people' . . .
[. . .]
Is not part of the emphasis in the Gospels on a different notion of Redemption? – expressed also in such sayings as 'My Kingdom is not of this world' of which there is some premonition in Isaiah's point that earthly suffering is not a sign that one is abandoned by God, rather the contrary . . .[15]

Isaiah was pointing out that it is the very love of God, the service of God, that may call on one to suffer, and Jesus said that those who followed him would have to take up a cross. The story

of the coming of the Suffering Servant, and the story of the
crucifixion thus form the parameters for the understanding of
what it means to be chosen of God – to be God's chosen people.

## 4. Can Believers be Harmed?

There is a tradition which says that the innocent cannot be
touched. There is also a counter-tradition which regards that
claim as, not so much false, as incredible. Faced by the Holocaust, and other horrendous evils, how can it be anything other
than a sick joke? The difficulty with that reaction is that it asks
us to believe something equally incredible, namely, that those
who say that the innocent cannot be touched, are unaware of the
existence of such evils. Obviously, they are aware of them, and
yet say what they do. What can they mean?

It is obvious that Kierkegaard is aware of horrendous evils. He
is also aware that there is no correlation between seeking to serve
God and the fortune and misfortune the world may mete out to
one. But there is no contradiction between the latter happening
and loving God. On the contrary, it can happen despite or
because of one's love of God. Kierkegaard writes:

> To be sure the world has power. It can lay many a burden
> upon the innocent one. It can make his life sour and laborious
> for him. It can rob him of his life.[16]

But, having said this, Kierkegaard also says:

> But even if the world gathered all its strength, there is one
> thing it is not able to do, it can no more punish an innocent one
> than it can put a dead person to death.[17]

Socrates speaks in a similar way in the *Apology*:

> Wherefore, O judges, be of good cheer about death, and know
> of a certainty, that no evil can happen to a good man, either in
> life or after death. He and his are not neglected by the gods.[18]

Wittgenstein, in his 'Lecture on Ethics', says:

> I will mention another experience straight away which I also
> know and which others of you might be acquainted with: it is,
> what one might call, the experience of feeling *absolutely* safe.
> I mean the state of mind in which one is inclined to say 'I am
> safe, nothing can injure me whatever happens.'[19]

We have said enough to recognize that we are back with the
Kierkegaardian notion of patience that we discussed in Chapter
9, section 3. Christian patience is being able to love God and the
good despite what the world does to one; not to think that they
have become pointless because of the evils which may befall one.
To be able, on the contrary, to find those evils informed by that
love. In that way, the suffering becomes sacrificial. For example
in the collection *Dying We Live*, we have last letters to loved
ones by those about to be executed by the Gestapo. I choose
simply one example of letters by Kim Malthe-Brunn, a cabin boy
and seaman aged 22, executed by the Gestapo in 1945. In a
farewell letter to his mother he writes:

> I have traveled a road that I have never regretted. I have never
> evaded the dictate of my heart, and now things seem to fall
> into place. I am not old, I should not be dying, yet it seems so
> natural to me, so simple. It is only the abrupt manner of it that
> frightens us at first. The time is short, I cannot properly
> explain it, but my soul is perfectly at rest . . .[20]

Again, in a farewell letter to his girlfriend he writes:

> I think of Socrates. Read about him – you will find Plato telling
> about what I am now experiencing.[21]

At this stage, however, a serious difficulty must be faced. Can
examples such as these stand in face of the Holocaust and other
horrendous evils, where circumstances are such, the suffering
inflicted so great, that it makes little sense to think of someone

saying 'my soul is perfectly at rest' or finding things falling into place in a natural and simple way. Peter Winch comments:

> I have the impression in reading Kierkegaard's *Purity of Heart* that he is not always willing to concede to affliction the power to overcome even the Good . . . On the other hand, Kierkegaard's insistence that the ethical requires completion by the religious is surely the result of the pressure of just this sort of point.[22]

Part of the difficulty comes from the minor role played by the notion of sacrifice in Kierkegaard's *Purity of Heart*, and hence by the notion of grace too. Socrates' confidence that he would face his death with equanimity and Wittgenstein's conviction that he is absolutely safe illustrate the lack. Contrast their confidence with Simone Weil's treatment of a similar confidence expressed by Peter before he denied Christ. Simone Weil, strikingly, states that Peter denied Christ, not when he broke his promise, but when he made it, for it showed a false confidence that did not recognize its dependence on grace. She writes:

> for it was supposing the source of faithfulness to be in himself and not in grace. Happily, as he was chosen, this denial became manifest to all and to himself. How many more there are who make similar boasts – and they never understand!
> (May all my denials become manifest. May they also be of rare occurrence.)[23]

In another expression of the same reflection:

> since it was to suppose the source of loyalty to be in oneself, and not in grace. Since he was of the elect, this denial fortunately became clear. But in other cases, people's boasts may come true and be apparently confirmed, and they never understand.
> How grateful I ought to be that I was born incapable even of picking grapes without the help of grace![24]

It is not difficult to see how certain remarks in *Purity of Heart* would lead one to think that Kierkegaard is displaying the same false confidence found in Peter. For example, this might be thought when he writes, 'When the good man truly stands on the other side of the boundary line inside the fortification of eternity, he is strong, stronger than the whole world. He is strongest of all at the time when he seems to be overcome.'[25]

Neither is it difficult to see that these words ring hollow when one considers how affliction crushed so many victims of the Holocaust. To say, as Kierkegaard does, that they are the strongest of all at the time when they are overcome seems a sick joke. That is why some theologians, while wanting to draw connections between the Suffering Servant, the crucifixion and the Holocaust, nevertheless insist that it is obscene to talk of the love of God in the presence of burning children. The only response that makes sense is to attempt, however hopeless it may be, to save the children. There are fears of the quietism that may result from a notion of self-sacrifice, one that will avoid doing what needs to be done; a failure to detect a difference between an unavoidable evil, and one that was possibly avoidable. But, as we have said, no questions are being begged about that even in our earlier discussion of Kierkegaard's distinction between courage and patience. Courage was the voluntary acceptance of evil that can be avoided, but patience is the voluntary acceptance of unavoidable evil. If the emphasis on 'doing something about people's sufferings' is one that prompts people to be alert to the constant threat of the demonic, while it has much to say about avoidable evils, it appears dumb in face of unavoidable evils. The problem in Kierkegaard's notion of 'patience' is that it envisages the sufferer always being sustained by a sacrificial love, whatever the suffering. This, too, seems vacuous in face of that suffering where the possibility of that sustenance is itself destroyed by affliction. What are we to say of the child not pulled out of the pit, whose face is not cleaned and whose body is not healed? To say that this *should* not happen does not address the fact that it *does*. To say that injustice should not occur does not address extreme affliction, involving injustice which crushes a person.

The question is whether it is an obscenity to speak of God's love in such circumstances. Kierkegaard's notion of 'patience' does not address this question. There are times, however, when he speaks in a way that begins to address it.

> And even if all the world rose up in tumult and even if everything were thrown into confusion: the limit is nevertheless there. And on the one side of it with the innocent ones is justice; and on the other side toward the world is an eternal impossibility of punishing an innocent one. Even if the world wishes to annihilate an innocent man and put him out of the way, it cannot put the limit out of the way, even though it be invisible. (Perhaps it is just on that account.) Even in the moment of his sacrificial death, the limit is there: then it stretches itself with the strength of eternity, then it cleaves itself with eternity's all-encompassing depth.[26]

This gets closer to the relation of divine love to extreme affliction. It does not speak of a person being sustained in a sacrificial love, but of annihilation, including annihilation, presumably, of any sense of that love. Yet, Kierkegaard wants to say, the limit is still there, though invisible, adding – *perhaps it is just on that account*. The question then, becomes; what is this invisible limit, which may not even be visible to the sufferer? I no longer think that the way I have responded to this question previously is satisfactory. I had attempted to respond to the following comments by Wiesel:

> No. I think the word 'triumph', unfortunately, does not apply to anything relevant to the Holocaust. There was no triumph. I think Man was defeated there. The Jew in some way came out in a better way, because he is used to suffering and because of historic situations that he has known. It happened that he was not the executioner, he was the victim. And in those times it was better to be victim than executioner. But no one triumphed. It was triumph for nobody – for man or for God either. Therefore we have this strange, strange feeling of

helplessness . . . But something went wrong with creation. Maybe the angel of Death, to use a cabbalistic expression, substituted himself for God then.[27]

I responded:

No doubt 'triumph' is the wrong word, but it does not follow that no one could want to speak of God as present even in situations such as this. To witness absolute evil, and to see it as such, is to feel at the same time that an absolute good is being outraged, desecrated. Wiesel says that in the Holocaust it was better to be victim than executioner. That conviction is found down the centuries. Socrates said it was better to suffer wrong than to do wrong. The absolute good does not triumph when violated by absolute wrong: it suffers. It can offer no explanation, no end to which the evil is a means. On such matters, it is dumb; it simply is what it is in its suffering. For the religious believers I have in mind, God and absolute good are one. If absolute good can suffer, so can God.[28]

I then went on to suggest that what I was talking about is expressed in the Suffering Servant and in the crucifixion, but I do not think I had seen how. Moreover, in speaking of God suffering, I seem to have left out the *human being* who suffers.[29] I had concentrated on *our* view of the sufferer. What I hope I have come to see is that what needs to be said *is* to be found in the Jewish conception of the Suffering Servant and in the story of Christ's Passion.

The Suffering Servant is said to be 'struck for the sins of all men', and is said to be 'despised and forsaken of men'. The Suffering Servant, as a creature, is stripped naked of all human consolations. If this is thought of as some kind of policy-decision taken by God for our good, the instrumentalist horror story returns. What we are given, rather, is a revelation of a creature *in extremis*, who simply reaches out from the midst of an uncomprehending affliction.

Rubenstein and Roth do not see the Passion in this light

because, *contrasting* it with the Holocaust, they are tempted by a view that attributes a voluntaristic policy to the incarnation and the crucifixion: 'In the crucifixion, God descends to the world, takes human form, and voluntarily gives up human life to save a world of undeserving sinners.'[30]

This is contrasted with the hideous suffering imposed 'upon millions of frail, frightened and undeserving human beings' in the Holocaust. The divine act appears as a controlled experiment or policy. But does this capture the agony of Christ's passion? Simone Weil does so by insisting on a distinction between the suffering of the martyrs and the suffering of Christ. Rush Rhees finds this distinction one of the deepest aspects of her work. It is the one I do not think I did justice to in my previous remarks.

There is no doubt that Weil admired the martyrs, of course, and recognizes that their martyrdom need not be something they sought. Her point is not to deny that. Nevertheless, she wants to emphasize that their sufferings are not the same as the sufferings of Christ. Importantly, they did not feel separated from God in their martyrdom. With Christ's Passion, it is different – and that is important. He is stripped of all consolation. God comes to earth to show how, in his creation, compassion should be felt towards his creatures. He can show this only by becoming a man who is subjected to the most extreme suffering, *including feeling abandoned by God*. This is different from the martyrs. If one emphasizes only the sacrifice of Jesus, one might imagine doing this oneself in some act of sacrificial love. But though Jesus is a willing victim, he is also *broken*, and that cannot be a matter of the will. This is the point of Weil's deep remark:

> Those who think of the crucifixion only in terms of sacrifice erase the mystery and bitterness through which it brings salvation. To desire martyrdom is to desire far too little. The cross is infinitely more than martyrdom.[31]

Rhees comments:

> And – I suppose to explain the expression 'the mystery and the bitterness which brings salvation' – she adds: 'The *irreducible*

character of the suffering' – meaning, I suppose, the suffering which cannot be brought lower – 'which makes it impossible to keep from horror as soon as one is subjected to it, is designed to arrest the will, as absurdity arrests the intelligence, and as the absence or non-existence arrest love. Until, when he has reached the limit of human faculties, a man reaches out his arms, stops, looks and waits.

'The looking and the waiting – this is the attitude towards beauty. As long as you can still think, will, desire, beauty will not appear.'[32]

It is in this extreme affliction that the dependence of the creature is revealed. In reaching out, the only reciprocating touch is a compassion for the human condition *as such*. To have that compassion is to know God. But in the Suffering Servant and in the Passion, both the radical dependence on grace and the need for compassion are revealed through the infliction of extreme suffering on God's Suffering Servant and on his Son. Some have objected to Weil's use of 'beauty' in this connection, but, for her, as Rhees says, that 'beauty' is linked with a dependence on grace and a need for justice and compassion – a love of the beauty of the world – but it is evoked through the sacrifice and affliction of the Suffering Servant and Christ.[33] It is in that sense that we are told that, by their stripes, we are healed.

This is why, Rhees emphasizes, following Christ is not like following the teachings or example of a good man.

For none of us can be God incarnate. God crucified and God risen again. I cannot myself see any sense in speaking of following Christ, apart from the eucharist. If someone says that it is in the eucharist that we are followers of Christ, then I can understand him, at least partly. Put it otherwise: the crucifixion was not simply the killing of an innocent man. The crucifixion was the sacrifice of the lamb of God to take away the sins of the world. Now in what sense can I follow Christ in *that*? There is a sense in the doctrine of the eucharist, but I cannot see any otherwise. And that sense of 'following' is a particularly religious one.[34]

Kierkegaard discusses the difference between learning from Socrates and learning from Christ.[35] However foolish it would be to think one might be like Socrates, it might make sense for someone to try. And whatever Socrates teaches me, he himself is not the lesson, important though his character as a teacher may be. But Christ *is* the lesson. To learn from Christ, and from his Passion in particular, is to accept one's radical contingency and dependence on grace, and to see creation itself as an act of grace and compassion. To follow Christ would be to follow him *in* that. We are back with the notion of an eternal covenant, a conception of human life given once and for all, but whose application in the details of daily life cannot be laid down in advance in any systematic way. Theologically, I suspect, this means agreeing with those who see God's will as identical with his essence – eternal, immutable and impassable – 'the Lamb of God slain from the foundation of the world' (Revelation 3.18).[36]

## 5. *Purity and its Danger*

At the end of the previous section we mentioned the difference between following Socrates and following Christ; how the latter cannot be understood as an attempt to emulate the standards of a good man. To follow Christ is to follow him *in* his Passion. In worship, this means following Christ in the Eucharist. It means wanting to love God in the sense of wanting to be a vehicle for his self-less compassion, but realizing that whether this wish is granted itself depends on grace. It is important to recognize that for much of our lives we do not want this. Instead, the 'I' intrudes or dominates us in such a way that it makes love of God impossible. That is why we call some people great saints. It is because of the way their lives show them to be selfless vehicles of compassion. In this section I simply want to consider one remarkable prayer by Simone Weil in which she prays to be a vehicle for God's love. It is not a prayer many people would pray. It is more remarkable than Saint Peter Claver's prayer to become a leper, like those he ministered to, though that is remarkable enough. Weil's prayer is a prayer for senility, though it is important to emphasize that she insists that she should not seek for this in any way. But if, through God's will, this should happen, and through it, something of one's utter dependence on grace could be revealed, she would regard it as a privilege to be such a vehicle of revelation. Part of the idea is that the 'I' in her would then be annihilated, the 'I' which comes between us and God.

I am aware that readers will react very differently to this prayer. I should not be surprised if some find it immeasurably deep, while others find it even evil. I want to consider two different reactions to the prayer by Rhees, because they illustrate both a depth and beauty one may find in the prayer, but, also, some dangers it may lead to – dangers that Rhees finds, at times, in Weil's thought. Weil's prayer is connected with a remarkable confession she makes, namely, that every time she thinks of the crucifixion of Christ, she commits the sin of envy!

Rhees says of the prayer, that it asks:

with the terrible sincerity which much of her writing has – 'that I may be insensible to every sort of grief and of joy, and incapable of love for anyone, for any thing, not even for myself, like old people who are completely paralysed and insane'. She goes on at some length, and makes the whole thing deeply beautiful.[37]

Here is some of the prayer:

Example of prayer.
 Saying to God:
 Father, in the name of Christ, grant me this:
 That, just as with someone who is completely paralysed, my will may find no expression in bodily movement, however rudimentary. That, like someone who is totally blind, deaf, and deprived of the three other senses, I may be incapable of having any sensations whatever. That, like a village idiot who does not know how to count or read, has never even learnt to speak, I may be unable to string together even the simplest thoughts.

That I may be insensible to every sort of grief and of joy, and incapable of any love for anyone, for any thing, not even for myself, like a silly old fool.

Father, in the name of Christ, do grant me this. That my body may move with perfect suppleness, or stand still with perfect rigidity, and in unswerving conformity to your will. That my hearing, sight, taste, smell, touch, may receive the perfectly faithful stamp of your creation. That my mind may, in the fullness of lucidity, combine all its ideas in perfect conformity with your truth. That I may experience, as intensely and purely as possible, the whole spectrum of sorrow and joy. That my love for God may be a flame, completely consumed by God's love. That all this may be forced from me, consumed by God, transformed in the body of Christ, and fed to the unfortunate whose bodies and souls lack any kind of nourishment. And that I may be a paralysed, blind, deaf, and senile old fool.

[. . .]

Father, since you are the Good and I am the inadequate, take this body and soul from me and make them your own, and for all eternity let not remain anything of me but this appropriation – or rather: nothingness – itself.

Such words can have any real virtue only if they are dictated by the Holy Spirit. One may not ask for such things by one's own will. It is a point one reaches in spite of oneself. In spite of oneself, one consents to it. One does not consent voluntarily. One consents with a violence exercised by one's entire soul. But the consent is entire and without reserve, given by a single movement of one's whole being.

Is it from this that the metaphor of marriage comes? The relation between God and the soul is like that of a husband with a wife who is still a virgin, on their wedding night. Marriage is a violation by consent. And similarly the union of the soul with God. The soul feels cold, and does not feel that it loves God. It does not itself know whether if it did not love it would not consent. The conjugal union turns the human personality into a simple intermediary between its flesh and God.

Other souls love God as a woman loves her lover. But the loves of lovers are not everlasting. Only man and wife are one single flesh for ever.

(But all these spiritual phenomena are completely beyond my grasp. I know nothing about them. They are reserved for those beings who, to begin with, possess the elementary moral virtues. I am speaking off the top of my hat here. In spite of this, I am not even capable of sincerely telling myself that I am doing so.)[38]

Rhees not only emphasizes that she does not think she ought to seek to realize her prayer, but that her remarks in the closing parenthesis are typical of her humility. She is concerned, throughout the prayer, with the pride in wanting to be someone, and she is praying, as against this, for a nudity and purity which is its opposite. Her passionate desire for such purity is impressive, but it also has its dangers.

Rhees goes as far as to say that there is evil in what she says. He calls it a deep evil. Why does he say this of someone while making the qualification, 'I say this although I admire her and her life as I have hardly admired anyone'?[39]

One reason he gives is that he thinks that her desire to cut herself off from all attachment, in a desire to be nothing before God, can lead to a flight from responsibility and an ignoring of the dependence others may have on you.

More importantly, Rhees says that in her emphasis on the way in which 'I' comes between us and God, she seems to want to eliminate it, almost as though a blot on God's creation would be removed by doing so. Rhees is surely right in saying that this is a false reading of humility. Part of seeing what one's dependence on grace means is to accept one's weaknesses, realizing that they are here to stay. Of course, this has dangers of its own – a self-deceiving contentment in what can be changed with effort, or thinking that because one keeps sinning in the same old way, the next time one does so doesn't matter. Nevertheless, it is important to recognize those characteristics in one that are not going to change. One might say that accepting that, in humility, is an integral part of the recognition that one is a sinner who stands in need of mercy.

We must remember that Weil was deeply moved by the afflictions of others, such as workers in a factory suffering privation and humiliation. Her concern for them would be free of vanity. On the other hand, though she did have friends, for the most part she seems to have shunned close relationships, and did not open herself up to the hurts and shortcomings such relationships involve. She is ashamed, as many people would be, of shortcomings in her love, for example, pride and possessiveness. But, at other times, the very fact that loving a particular person will inevitably involve such shortcomings, from time to time, makes her want to call this *kind* of love a case of 'loving wrongly'. Rhees says this, again, seems to indicate a lack of acceptance of our finitude. He says that *recognizing* that such love has these shortcomings, or is open to them,

> is important in connection with *humility* before God, it is [that is, this *kind* of love] not something of which I ought to be ashamed in the sense in which I ought to be ashamed of the cowardice or the pettiness I showed on this and that occasion.[40]

Because of the lack of recognition of the difficulties involved in the kind of situations Rhees is discussing (in much of what she *says*, at least), Rhees concludes that she does not seem to be acquainted with the kind of despair concerning them which we find in Kierkegaard or Lenau. If one regards a certain *kind* of loving as a 'wrong way of loving', one is unlikely to give much attention to the despair which can occur *in* that kind of loving.

I urge the reader to read this section with caution and not to draw wild generalizations about Simone Weil from it. All I have done is to draw attention to a conception of purity before God which is immensely deep, but which, *if* it is developed in certain directions, can lead to evils which Rhees also regarded as deep.[41]

# Notes

1. D. Z. Phillips, 'Critique of Stephen T. Davis' in Stephen T. Davis (ed.), *Encountering Evil*, Louisville: Westminster John Knox Press 2001, pp. 89–90.
2. Stephen T. Davis, 'Rejoinder' in Davis, *Encountering Evil*, p. 103.
3. Rush Rhees, 'Religion, life and meaning A' in Rhees, *On Religion and Philosophy*, ed. D. Z. Phillips, assisted by Mario von der Ruhr, Cambridge: Cambridge University Press 1997, p. 170.
4. Rhees, 'Religion, life and meaning B' in *On Religion and Philosophy*, p. 176.
5. Rhees, 'Religion, life and meaning B' p. 176.
6. Rhees, 'Religion, life and meaning B' p. 176.
7. Rhees, 'Religion, life and meaning B' pp. 176–7.
8. Rhees, 'Religion, life and meaning B' p. 192.
9. See Part I: Chapter 4.
10. Rowan Williams, 'Redeeming Sorrows' in D. Z. Phillips (ed.), *Religion and Morality*, Basingstoke: Macmillan 1996, p. 142.
11. See Part I: Chapters 1 and 2.
12. Rhees, 'Election and Judgement' in *On Religion and Philosophy*, pp. 248–50.
13. Ludwig Wittgenstein, *Culture and Value*, Oxford: Blackwell 1984, p. 81e.
14. Rhees, 'Election and Judgement', p. 247.
15. Rhees, 'Election and Judgement', pp. 245–6.
16. Søren Kierkegaard, *Purity of Heart*, New York: Harper Books 1956, p. 97.
17. Kierkegaard, *Purity of Heart*, p. 97.
18. *Dialogues of Plato*, Vol. 1, trans. B. Jowett, Oxford: Clarendon Press MD CCC LXXV, 1875, *Apology*, p. 374.
19. Ludwig Wittgenstein, 'Lecture on Ethics' in *Philosophical Occasions*, ed. James Klagge and Alfred Nordman, Indianapolis: Hackett 1993, p. 41.
20. Hellmut Gollwitzer, Käthe Kuhn and Reinhold Schneider (eds), *Dying We Live*, London: Fontana Books 1960, pp. 84–5.
21. Gollwitzer, Kuhn and Schneider (eds), *Dying We Live*, p. 82.
22. Peter Winch, 'Ethical Reward and Punishment' in *Ethics and Action*, London: Routledge and Kegan Paul 1972, p. 207. Winch's whole essay is instructive on these issues.
23. Simone Weil, *Notebooks*, Vol. I, London: Routledge and Kegan Paul 1956, p. 148.
24. Simone Weil, *First and Last Notebooks*, Oxford: Oxford University Press 1970, p. 161.
25. Kierkegaard, *Purity of Heart*, p. 98.

26  Kierkegaard, *Purity of Heart*, p. 98.

27  Elie Wiesel, 'What is a Jew?' in Harry James Cargas (ed.), *Responses to Elie Wiesel*, New York: Persea Books 1978, p. 154.

28  D. Z. Phillips, 'Beyond the Call of Duty' in *From Fantasy to Faith*, Basingstoke: Macmillan 1991, p. 199.

29  This was true also of my contribution to the discussion of Marilyn McCord's paper, 'Evil and the God-Who-Does-Nothing-In-Particular' and Rowan Williams's response, 'Redeeming Sorrows' in Phillips, *Religion and Morality*. See 'Voices in Discussion', pp. 310–21. It is easy to identify the voices of the authors. My 'voice' is J. Here, at least, unlike my remarks in *From Fantasy to Faith*, I want to distinguish between Socrates' informed death and the agony of Christ's Passion.

30  Richard L. Rubenstein and John K. Roth, *Approaches to the Holocaust: Its Legacy*, Atlanta: John Knox Press, 1987, p. 307.

31  Simone Weil, *Gravity and Grace*, London: Routledge 1952, p. 80. The actual published version reads: 'Those who can only conceive of the crucifixion under the aspect of an offering do away with the salutary mystery and the salutary bitterness of it. To wish for martyrdom is far too little. The cross is infinitely more than martyrdom.' In Rhees's text cited below, and used in the quotation in the text, 'sacrifice' appears instead of 'offering'. He says that the latter almost kills the sense of the remark.

32  Rush Rhees, *Discussions of Simone Weil*, ed. D. Z. Phillips, assisted by Mario von der Ruhr, New York: SUNY Press 1999, pp. 173–4. It is through Rhees's discussion that I have come, hopefully, to appreciate a little more, at least, of the complexity and depth of these issues than I did before. The quotations from Weil come from other passages in *Gravity and Grace*.

33  See Rhees, *Discussions of Simone Weil*, p. 172.

34  Rush Rhees, 'Religion, life and meaning B', p. 193.

35  See Søren Kierkegaard, *Philosophical Fragments*, New Jersey: Princeton University Press 1985.

36  See the dispute on this issue between Rowan Williams and Marilyn McCord Adams, in Phillips, *Religion and Morality*.

37  Rhees, *Discussions of Simone Weil*, p. 108.

38  Translation by Mario von der Ruhr and Timothy Tessin from Simone Weil, *La Connaissance Surnaturelle*, Paris: Gallimard 1950, pp. 204–6.

39  Rhees, *Discussions of Simone Weil*, p. 110.

40  Rhees, *Discussions of Simone Weil*, p. 123.

41  I have already been discussing aspects of Rhees's much wider discussion in his chapter on 'Love' in *Discussions of Simone Weil*.

# Last Things

## 1. Last Judgement

Theodicists want happy endings. Their consequentialism in ethics makes such a demand inevitable. What is more, that demand, as we have seen, is deeply rooted in a need for compensation, a need for the books to be balanced in the end. It cannot be denied that there is a form of Christianity that caters to this need; that tells us that, in the end, God will give us what we want. So whatever happens, believers will be winners in the end. But the essential question is: what game do they take themselves to have won?

At its worst, the winner-takes-all religion seems to be a matter of backing the right horse. Don't back the Devil, because God has the last laugh. This seems to imply that there is no inherent reason for not backing the Devil. If he had the last laugh, presumably one would do so. But no one likes a loser, so God is backed instead.

In this kind of religion, God is a *means*, not an end. This truth is exposed if one suggests to adherents to such a religion that they are not going to 'win' in the sense envisaged. Their response is revealing, 'What! We don't get rewarded! I don't survive death? I won't be around to enjoy my crown at the end of the race, the glory I've been promised? In that case, tell me what's it all been for. Why have I bothered to obey the rules, struggled to keep commandments? I could have had a good time like the rest. I've been sold a dud deal. There's nothing to it after all.'

In some ways, these hopes, or hopes akin to them, find expression in some understandings of the tradition of belief in the

Second Coming, in which, it seems, Jesus returns to reign *on earth* in a kingdom which shall know no end. There are tensions enough in such a conception. If the kingdom is one that is established on earth, it seems to be understood as an historical event. But how can a historical kingdom have no end? Further, all this is supposed to happen 'at the end of time', as the consummation of all things, yet it is spoken of in temporal terms. Rather than pursue these formidable difficulties, it is more important, for our present purposes, to point out that much of this seems to be what Jesus preached *against*, when he said that his kingdom was not of this world. He is opposing the idea that eternity can be established on earth. Rather, what happens on earth is to be judged in the light of eternity.

This is connected with my opening remarks about the hope for an ultimate victory of the kind proclaimed in theodicies. The hope seems to be based on a conception of a reward understood, quite independently of God, insofar as the point of worshipping God depends on his ability to guarantee the reward. In the course of this book, I have talked of a religious inheritance, neglected, for the most part, in discussions of the problem of evil, where the *central* condition for passing into truth, is to die to the expectations that are of the essence of the popular religion I have described. Notice, the condition is one for passing into *truth*, since the expectations of popular religion for a balancing of the books in some future state are illusory. If death were faced properly, one would see that these expectations are not going to be fulfilled. That is precisely why the approach of death is so horrible for those who depend on them.

In the popular religion I have outlined, the point of worshipping God is found in the reward. In the religious inheritance I am contrasting it with, God is the point of worshipping God. That is why the hope of survival after death in a future state, logical difficulties apart, fails to do justice to that fact. Wittgenstein writes:

> Not only is there no guarantee of the temporal immortality of the human soul, that is to say of its eternal survival after death; but, in any case, this assumption completely fails to accom-

plish the purpose for which it has always been intended. Or is some riddle solved by my surviving for ever? Is not this eternal life itself as much of a riddle as our present life?[1]

Jesus tells those who believe in him that he is going to the Father to prepare a place for them. Thomas asks, 'Lord, we know not whither thou goest; and how can we know the way?' (John 14.5). Jesus does not reply by telling his disciples that they are at such an epistemic distance from God that the way cannot be obvious. He does not say that he is talking of some other realm or dimension of which we know little. His reply is one without hesitation: 'Jesus saith unto him, I am the way, the truth and the life' (John 14.6).

It is important to note that this reply is meant to clarify their puzzlement about his earlier remarks:

In my Father's house are many mansions: if it were not so, I would have told you. I go to prepare a place for you.

And if I go and prepare a place for you, I will come again, and receive you unto myself; that where I am, there ye may be also.

And whither I go ye know, and the way ye know (John 14.2–4).

As Thomas's question showed, Jesus was too hasty in thinking that his disciples understood, but, as his elucidation makes clear, he himself is the way to God. To be in Christ is to be in God. In other words, 'the place' being prepared must be understood in these terms. It has its sense in this spiritual context. This is 'the place' that is other than the world.[2] It is the only place promised – where God is, there also are those who dwell in him. To think of eternity as a place in any other sense is not only confused in itself, but fails to do justice to a religious notion of eternity. Kierkegaard has emphasized this point as follows:

let us understand one another; the journey of which we speak is not long . . . it is only a single step, a decisive step, and you, too, have emigrated, for the Eternal lies much nearer to you than any foreign country to the emigrant; and yet when you are there the change is infinitely greater. So then, go with God to God, continually take that one step more.[3]

Once these conclusions are embraced, it may be thought that the notion of the Last Judgement falls with the popular religious notions I have criticized. But this is not so, unless it is being thought of as a future event that *happens*, numerically, to be the last judgement – the one after the penultimate judgement. The special place occupied by the Last Judgement is due to the fact that it is a judgement about a human life when it is over. It is the judgement of eternity. Further, if the lessons of this chapter have been learned, together with those of previous discussions, it is a judgement concerning what can be said of a completed life given its relation to God. It is not a prediction about future events, but an eternal reality.

Most theodicists speak of the Last Judgement as though it were a prediction. For Swinburne, it is the time when we pay for our bad decisions and get rewarded for our good decisions. As we have seen, his voluntarism is such that Swinburne holds that we are free with respect to the big choice between good and evil. People are moulded by their bad choices to such an extent that they may be incapable of desiring the good. Since what they desire, on Swinburne's view, leads to constant frustration, the final verdict may be that it would be better if they did not exist. Even here, Swinburne argues that although this is not the state God desires for us, it is good that the damned are free to reject him. In opposition to Hick he writes:

Hick wants to claim that in the end we shall all through our own free choices become perfect: 'it seems morally (although still not logically) impossible that the infinite resourcefulness of infinite love working in unlimited time should be eternally frustrated, and the creature reject its own good, presented to it in an endless range of ways' (p. 380).[4] Maybe. If God always refuses to take no for an answer, we shall yield in the end. Yet if God is to give someone real freedom to reject him, he must after a finite time take no for an answer. To give us the choice to reject God, but never to allow that choice to be permanently executed, is not to give us a real choice at all.[5]

Marilyn Adams shares Hick's misgivings that God could be said to create a creature beyond the reach of his love. All evil is defeated by God. Apparently, there are post-mortem conversations. You may put your point of view to God, and then God puts his point of view to you. Once this happens, God's point of view is embraced, if not by its appeal, then by coercion. When asked whether Hitler could not get worse and worse after death, Adams replied:

> The experience of God after death will make it impossible not to embrace the new perspective he gives. I see no reason why the good it involves would not justify bringing its acceptance about by coercion. We often say that coercion is justified when something morally important is involved. Here we would be dealing with the source of highest value.[6]

Hick and Adams call themselves universalists in that they believe that everyone, in the end, is perfected in God. By contrast, Davis sees no warrant for such universalism in Christianity, and quotes Scripture to that effect. In response to Hick's view he says:

> I know from my experience of teaching Hick's theodicy in Philosophy of Religion courses that not all people are attracted to universalism. I have found that many of my Jewish students, for example, reject Hick's theory on the grounds that 'I don't want Hitler and the other Holocaust murderers to be present in heaven'. . . . As a matter of theological method, we cannot affirm a doctrine just because we would like it to be true. The plain teaching of scripture, I believe, is that some will be condemned to eternal separation from God.[7]

Davis goes on to offer some speculations about hell, including the observation:

> I believe the citizens of hell are there because they freely choose to be there. Unless one bows to God and makes God's will one's own, heaven is too much to bear and one chooses hell.[8]

I have to confess that I find this account of the voluntary choice of hell comic, as though its inhabitants simply found heaven not to their liking – too fancy a place, perhaps, where they felt positively uncomfortable. But I do not mean to isolate Davis for such criticism. I find writers to be hilariously anthropomorphic on this topic. Given what we have said about 'the eternal', it is not hard to see why. Writers continue to speak in temporal terms of a judgement that is eternal, and of developments relating to sin and virtue after death, when the conditions that give sense to such developments no longer obtain. We are talking about an eternal judgement on lives that are over; that is, we are asking what religion says about those lives in relation to the love of God that may or may not have been present in them. If one has understood what we have said about how coming to that love is to come to God's reality, one will realize that not even Adams's God could make this a matter of coercion.

Swinburne, Hick, Adams and Davis all take themselves to be making predictions about what will happen to people after they die. They make eternal judgement an event in time, a future event among others. By contrast, Wittgenstein did not want to treat damnation or judgement as *appendages* to the evil deed. Rush Rhees writes:

> 'Eternal damnation (of this man's soul) may be realized in a movement of time without any duration at all.' – Wittgenstein used to say this was one way, and a very *real* way of speaking of it. Cf. the notion of *signing a pact with the Devil* – in this life. Lenau's *Faust*: As soon as he has signed, his soul is utterly abandoned, cut off from God. – On the other hand I think he would have said that the 'future form' – 'I *shall* stand naked before my Judge' – was *generally* the more natural.

I want to suggest that we should *not* treat these two ways of speaking as incongruous or inconsistent.[9]

This last remark is extremely important. Whether one is talking of a pact with the Devil in this life or of an eternal judgement of a life when it is over, there is an *internal* relation between love of God and what we *mean* by reward and punishment in this context. The four writers tend to make them externally related to belief in God. The tension shows itself in Davis wishing that universalism were true, but finding no warrant for thinking so in Scripture. That wish seems to testify to a compassion in him which he cannot find in God – a sign I think that something has gone badly astray. As I have said before, to fear God's wrath is not to fear what God will do to one (the external view), but to fear what one will become (the internal view), namely, cut off from God. The question of eternal judgement, therefore, involves the question of who can be said, at the last, to be eternally cut off from God. It is the terribleness of saying this of anyone that universalism seeks to address in a misleading way.

Whereas Swinburne, Hick, Adams and Davis think they are disagreeing in their *predictions* about what is going to happen to people after they die, what in fact they are revealing, in what they say, is what *they* are prepared to say about people's lives when they are over. They are showing religious differences in their conceptions of eternal judgement on people's lives. This is shown, revealingly, in an imaginary exchange that Hick creates between Davis and himself.

Steve: But this idea that in further lives we shall all gradually grow spiritually towards an eventual universal 'salvation' is, surely, both speculative and, I'm sorry to say, quite unbiblical. The Bible teaches that 'some will be condemned to eternal separation from God'.

John: Frankly, I don't mind if it's unbiblical. To my mind the biblical eschatology, in for example the Book of Revelation, is itself speculative, as indeed are all conceptions of the final end. The question is, what speculation seems most probable? And it seems to me a reasonable expectation that in the infinite resourcefulness of infinite love working in unlimited time, God will eventually succeed in drawing us all into the divine Kingdom. However, I know that the fact that this is not a biblical teaching rules it out for you.

Steve: Yes, this lack of faithfulness to the Bible's my basic difficulty with all of you. None of you seems to feel 'any strong need to be guided in theology by scripture of Christian tradition', whereas I certainly do.

John: Yes, that's how it must seem from a conservative-evangelical point of view. But I think the rest of us see Christianity as a developing tradition, and one within which many different kinds of theological theory have emerged and will continue to emerge, going far beyond the presuppositions of the ancient world reflected in the Bible. And so we all in practice use the scriptures selectively – including, I'll bet, yourself. But of course that's a big subject.[10]

Hick speaks for me as a fellow symposiast in this exchange, but he should not do so. In this particular instance, my sympathies, generally speaking, are with 'Steve', though I deny his implication that I feel no need to be guided by Scripture of the Christian tradition, since that is what I am trying to elucidate. Scripture and Christian traditions, however, may be more of a mixed bag than Davis would allow, hence the need for the selectivity Hick refers to. On the other hand, I don't agree with Hick's claim that what the Bible says about eschatology is itself a speculative matter. The Bible offers *a conception of human life*. As we saw early on in the book, there is good reason to resist any arbitrary grammatical extensions of religious concepts free of any religious context.[11] Universalism is in danger of being such an extension.[12]

It is important to try to appreciate the concerns universalism tries to address, however misguidedly. It is concerned to deny an external conception of final rewards and punishments, where, as a *consequence* of loving God or separation from him, God bestows rewards or inflicts punishments on people after death.

Universalists cannot accept that such punishments should go on for ever. The problem is that they try to rectify the situation from within *the same* external conception of reward and punishment. They simply want to change the verdict. Their plea for mitigation or parole is *within* the same system.

What I want to show is that the weakness of universalism can be avoided, and so can external conceptions of eternal reward and punishment, if we emphasize, as we should, the internal relation between belief in God and the judgement of eternity.

## 2. Who are the Goats?

Even if we do emphasize the internal relation between belief in God and eternal judgement, religions speak of a separation, *even in these terms*, between the saved and the damned. But who are the damned? In the Gospel of Matthew we read: 'And before him shall be gathered all nations: he shall separate them one from another, as a shepherd divideth his sheep from the goats' (Matthew 25.32). Neither is there any doubt about the fate of the goats:

> And these shall go away into everlasting punishment: but the righteous into life eternal (*Matt.* 25:46).

But who are the goats? That question is said to be one that no human being can answer. It is not difficult to see why. We do not all start out on earth in the same circumstances, with the same resources, all, as it were, breasting the same starting tape to run a common race. Not only will the course we run not be free of obstacles, but the obstacles individuals have to face will not be the same for everyone. Even when they are the same, we do not all meet them in the same state, and their effect on us will vary enormously. Contingency will play an enormous role in all this, with respect to where we were at what time, what was just missed, or what was just met, for good or ill, through no fault of our own. Certainly, we make specific judgements about ourselves as good friends, husbands, wives, fathers, mothers and so on. But we are discussing an eternal judgement on the life of a person as such, where all the factors mentioned would have to be taken into account. How could any human being make such a judgement? This is the judgement which is said to be God's alone.

To want to know, on earth, who's who in the sight of God, is religiously condemned as itself being a denial of the dependence on grace we have discussed in Part II of this book. It would be an attempt to calculate who is, and who is not, deserving of eternal reward and punishment, whereas, as we have seen, for the believer, it is not a matter of desert at all. That is why it is said that those who think they have qualified, the first, will be last in the eternal judgement. The foremost sin is that of pride. The mistake of those who thought they were first, was not that they miscalculated, but that they wanted to calculate at all.[13] There is a story of a search conducted with a view to canonization, in which it was discovered that the person whose life was being examined had said of a criminal on the scaffold that he would surely go to hell. On the grounds of that one remark, canonization was denied.

Sometimes, Christianity has talked as though an outward sign was enough to show who the goats are in the eternal judgement – they are all those who are not Christians. This has puzzled many, since it would count as damned those whose lives have shown a spirit of compassion deeper than anything found in many Christians. In this respect, Rush Rhees refers to the lives of many of the Stoics and Cynics. If their lives are to be counted among 'the damned', then religion seems to be a matter of mere 'belief', in the sense of bearing the right label, or belonging to the right club. On the other hand, as Rhees points out, in the account of the Last Judgement in Matthew's Gospel, there are aspects that pull one in a very different direction. Those who have appropriated Christ's name, but have shown no compassion, are said to be damned, whereas those who have shown compassion, without explicit acknowledgement or even knowledge of Christ, are said to be children of his kingdom. This would link with the sense of 'Before Abraham was, I am', and 'The Lamb of God slain before the foundation of the world'. Simone Weil says, somewhere, that it is an intolerable thought that Christ is not present in suffering before the birth of Jesus.[14]

Swinburne completely misunderstands the spiritual import of Matthew's account of the division of the sheep and the goats in the account he gives of it.

> In the parable of the sheep and the goats at the Last Judgement, as related by St Matthew, the good are rewarded for feeding the hungry, visiting the sick, etc., in ignorance that the beneficiary of their acts was God himself. ('In so far as ye did it unto one of these my brethren, even these least, ye did it unto me', said the king.) And the bad are punished for their failures to act in similar ignorance. Their amazement at the punishment ('when saw we thee an hungered?' etc.) implies that if they had known who the potential beneficiary was, they would have fed him. Ignorance of God is a precondition here for the sheep making different choices from the goats.[15]

I do not want to repeat the discussion of Chapter 10, section 1 on 'Belief as Sacrifice', but Swinburne's conception of God as the *beneficiary* of our actions makes it salutary to remind ourselves of some of the central points made there. For example, I quoted Rhees's important distinction between making one's life a sacrifice to God and other forms of sacrifice.

> If I sacrifice myself to make some scientific experiment possible – or if I sacrifice myself to save somebody from drowning – here there is something which depends upon the help I can give. I make something possible by my sacrifice which would not be possible otherwise. That is why it would be absurd to talk about sacrificing myself for God, in that sense.[16]

God is not the *beneficiary* of bread given to the starving, since he is not hungry as they are. The sense in which giving bread to them is done 'unto God' is if the act of charity is done out of compassion, and does not buy the sufferer. My act of charity, so-called, may be tainted by selfishness in the form of self-esteem or condescension, in which case it is not done 'unto God'. That is why Rhees says of a *religious* conception of sacrifice: ' "Let my life *be* a sacrifice to Thee": that is more the sense of it than "Let me sacrifice myself for Thee" – which I think would be absurd.'[17]

Swinburne says that had the bad known that God was the potential beneficiary, they would have fed the hungry – his implication being that then they would have fared better in the Last Judgement. The story of the Last Judgement shows just the contrary – they would have been told to depart for want of any genuine compassion in them – a compassion that is said to be of God, or even Christ, even if *no* explicit acknowledgement of either is made. In Swinburne's account, the hungry and the oppressed are purchased, in that the point of heeding their needs is that God benefits by doing so, and that the giver will be rewarded in the hereafter by realizing that. This reduction of religion to transcendental prudence does not even capture the spirit of the simplest act of common decency. But neither does making one's everlasting happiness the point of religious belief, another consequence of religious consequentialism and utilitarianism. Rhees comments:

> But I think the great saints have rejected that notion. I am thinking of a poem that has been ascribed to St. Theresa, in which she is speaking to God, and says even if I could not hope as I do hope, I should still love as I love . . . And if you cannot understand what the Christian love of God is, then of course you cannot understand what the Christian takes his life to be.[18]

Yet, if we grant Rhees's point, this only increases the puzzle concerning who can be said to be the goats in the Day of Judgement, those worthy of eternal damnation. They are supposed to be those utterly bereft of any sense of God, but who are they? This may make us puzzled, as it does Rhees:

> This must make many wonder, 'Is he speaking of people who have *no* good in them at all? If even one single failure to show

the compassion one ought to have shown, is enough to bring this judgement on one . . . how many will there be who are *not* cursed? And if the goats are those who have *never* shown a glimmering of compassion for "one of the least of these" . . .?' I suppose we should have to add: 'who have never shown compassion, and have never repented of this.' Even so, I want to ask, 'Is it unthinkable that God, who understands how the goats have come to be what they are, should show compassion in some form towards them?'[19]

If we are asked to imagine the kind of persons who have never shown a glimmer of compassion, nor felt any remorse for not having done so, what comes to mind is the case of monsters, perpetrators of evil on a grand scale. They are rarely discussed in relation to the problem of evil. I do not mean that the evil they have done is not discussed. What we have said of discussions of the Holocaust shows that not to have been the case. Rather, I mean *the evil of being a monster*. In terms of theodicy, what good is supposed to come out of that? We have commented on the weakness of the argument that appeals to the fact that a world with the freedom of the will which allows one to choose to be a monster is a better world than one without such freedom.[20] Many have been puzzled by the mystery of evil manifested in the monstrous. François Mauriac quotes the following remarks from Baudelaire in his foreword to *Therese Desqueyroux*:

Life abounds in innocent monsters – Lord, my God! you, the Master; you, who has made Liberty and the Laws; you, the sovereign who does not interfere, the pardoning judge; you, who are bereft of reasons and causes, and who has perhaps implanted in my mind the taste of horror, in order to convert my heart, in the manner of a surgeon curing me with his blade; Lord, have mercy, have mercy on madmen and madwomen. O Creator! Can monsters exist in His eyes, who alone knows why they exist, how they have made themselves like that, and how they could have chosen not to have made themselves like that . . .[21]

Rhees asks, as we have seen, whether it is unthinkable that God should show compassion for monsters in some form. But in *what* form? For universalists, Hitler and his like are saved by being transformed, by coercion if necessary, by the presence of God in the hereafter. This has seemed to many to trivialize the evils they have perpetrated and to fail to do justice to their victims. Presumably, the students in Davis's class, who did not want Hitler to be in heaven, want him to suffer in hell. But if the suffering is understood in an external way, torment inflicted on the damned, one gets uneasy about the character of the one who is supposed to inflict or want this torment – remember, endless torment. Is not this, perhaps, the source of Davis's unease in wishing that damnation of souls did not occur, while accepting that it does? On the other hand, his attempt to sugar the pill by suggesting that Hitler and his like would simply not be at home in heaven, preferring to be in hell, hardly makes sense, given this picture of endless punishment.

I have argued against the external view of eternity and its rewards and punishments. Is there an eternal judgement for monsters that is not external, yet remains a punishment? Plato and Christianity, I believe, are one in thinking that there is.

In the *Gorgias*, Socrates argues that monsters, like Archelaus, are necessarily punished. Polus is amazed at this claim. It seems obvious to him that Archelaus has got away with his evil deeds. He has not been punished by the state; he has not regarded any misfortune in his life as a punishment from the gods for his misdeeds; and he has certainly felt no remorse for them. Yet, Plato says that he is *necessarily* punished. He is punished in a way that cannot be escaped – he is the object of divine pity.

When I have elucidated this notion in classes on the *Gorgias* for over 30 years, it has become increasingly difficult to convey this notion of punishment. The objection is that, on this view, there is no torment, no suffering experienced by Archelaus. Students want their pound of flesh. But, in doing so, are they not referring to worldly punishment, trying to make unavoidable what is essentially contingent? Perhaps that is why the most conservative theologians now hasten to assure us that hell's flames are symbolic. But eternal judgement cannot be avoided, because it is internally related to the soul of the damned. Hell is not a *consequence* of complete absence from God. It *is* that absence. What a terrible judgement on a life for all eternity! (Plato: fear not what can be done to the body, but fear what can be done to the soul.)

Warning of such an eternal judgement is given in the Gospels. I was privileged to be present on an occasion when I heard the warning delivered in a memorable sermon. It was in Warsaw, shortly before the Solidarity Revolution. I was attending a requiem mass for a student who had had his stomach kicked in by the police a year earlier. The police, of course, were not prosecuted. The doctors who tried, unsuccessfully, to save the student's life were too useful to prosecute. But the ambulance men, who happened to have come across the student, and had taken him to the hospital, were given long prison sentences for criminal negligence. It was said that they had killed the student by the improper way they had lifted him and carried him to hospital. I shall never forget the opening words of the priest's sermon. It is not unusual to hear those in rebellion say, 'I do not condone violence, but given the violence we have suffered, we must respond in kind, we must defend ourselves', etc. But that is not what the priest said. His first words, translated for me, were: 'Let us pray for murderers. Our brother is with the Lord. But there are those who are walking about with murder in their souls. What a terrible state to be in! Let us pray for murderers.' The authority in these words come from their being the judgement of eternity expressed in time – a warning of that judgement which talks of pity and punishment at the same time. The most pitiful and terrible thing would be for the murderer not to repent before death. The terribleness of dying an unrepentant murderer is the punishment. What a pitiful state for a soul to be in.


## 3. Death and Eternal Judgement

In the previous section, we discussed the notion of eternal judgement, its rewards and punishments, from a third-person perspective. In the present section, I want to discuss it from a first-person perspective. Once again, the discussion will illustrate the importance of recognizing the internal relation between love of God and eternal judgement.

It would be difficult to make sense of an eternal judgement without reference to a concern with one's life as a whole. This is not a concern that can be expressed by weighing up one's good and bad deeds in an attempt to reach a verdict. It is rather a concern with the purity or impurity of one's life; whether it has been a life of sacrifice as expressed in love of God. A desire for judgement is a desire for one's life to be seen in that light. This is a desire for 'answerability', and the emphasis is on God, not on oneself. It was in such a context that Wittgenstein came to see sense in the notion of the Last Judgement. Rhees writes:

> Wittgenstein said in conversation sometimes that he *could* understand how people could believe in a Last Judgement. There was something in the idea of 'being answerable for' what he had done, and for the kind of life he had lived; and also something (I think) in the idea of 'paying for it' – which seemed to him involved in his own value judgements on, or his own concern about, his actions and his life. – I think this went together with ideas which he expressed in the *Tractatus* and in the *Notebooks* before it. The idea that what I do (in those situations which call forth moral considerations) – what I do has a significance which 'goes beyond' the present circumstances, it has to be seen 'with the whole world as its background'. I am thinking of the way in which he spoke of 'absolute value' in the *Lecture on Ethics*, for instance.
>
> Those phrases make *me* think of: 'Heaven and Earth shall pass away, but my Words shall not pass away.' But I never heard Wittgenstein quote this in this connection, and he might say it was inappropriate.
>
> In this context I can imagine saying: 'The consequences of an evil deed are bottomless' (where of course 'consequences' does not mean what it meant for the utilitarians: it does *not* mean 'what effects the action has in the society in which it is

performed'). And when I do say this, I think I have some glimmer of what might be meant by Judgement.

He may have in mind something also of what Simone Weil speaks of often: that then the souls of all men will stand naked before God.[22]

What is it to want to stand naked before God? I want to explore this question in relation to Rhees's reflections on his own death, which are both personal and philosophical. To want to stand naked before God is to want his judgement, that is, to see one's life in the light of purity and perfection without self-deception or evasions. During life, the intrusion of the self makes this impossible. This is why 'facing death' in the right way is held to be a great hope. But to be such a hope, death must be used in the right way.

The wrong use of death is to think of it as a way out; as if, thereby, one could *escape* the evils one has done. A person, by committing suicide, may indeed escape arrest, but it would be confused to think he can escape dishonour in that way, even if his dishonourable deed remained unknown by anyone else. The religious analogue of the moral case is that God is not mocked. R. F. Holland brings out the confusion in the moral case as follows:

I once read of an officer with gambling debts who confusedly thought he had a moral reason, not against, but in favour of shooting himself. The note he left behind contained a remark to the effect that he was choosing death rather than dishonour (at the time of writing he had not yet been found out). Now that great maxim of the military ethic, 'death rather than dishonour', is exemplified by the conduct of the sentry who declines to leave his post when he could run away to safety but stays and carries out his duty although the consequence of doing so is death. Here the death and the dishonour are genuine alternatives – if he escapes the first he incurs the second, and if he embraces the first he avoids the second. But the case of the gambling officer is not like that at all. So far from being an alternative to the disgrace incurred by his inability to pay the debts, his death by suicide is rather a consequence of that disgrace. What he ends up with is both the death and the dishonour. There might or might not have been a way out of the dishonour had he stayed alive, but at least it is clear that killing himself is no way out of it. As Socrates observes, death is not an escape from everything: if it were, it would indeed be a boon to the wicked (*Phaedo*, 107c).[23]

A different case would be that in which a person welcomes death as an end to the degradations in his life. But that is *not* the sense in which Rhees is talking about death, in Christianity, as the hope for judgement.

> I know only that when I see my life for what it is – see myself for what I am: when I see how *incapable* I am of directing my *life* to anything holy – then the contemplation of death is the greatest *hope*. (And I do not mean this in a negative sense: that here at last will be an end of my own adding to my degradation.)[24]

The great hope for Rhees is not, of course, any reward or punishment, understood externally. The hope is the hope of glorifying God in his death, despite his low estimate of his own life. And that involves striving to see his life as it really is:

> That (even that) I should *know* the full depth of my depravity, and know it by the judgement of God. That I should be rid at least of the double-mindedness and self-deception that defiles my view as long as I live . . .
> God help me to keep a pure view of death: God help me to welcome whatever death is to be for my soul: God help me to keep from falsifying this.[25]

Given his estimate of his own life, Rhees asks whether those whom he regards as genuinely religious would deny him the possibility of seeking God in his death.

> Would a truly religious person object, and tell me that my death will be as evil – or as *godless* – as the life I have lived?[26]

He asks how one, such as he takes himself to be,[27] can become, in death, something more than he can be by his own efforts. His answer is that this is possible only if his life, with all its short-comings, is now seen, at death, as part of the majesty of the divine will; if his death is made an offering to God.

Unless death be an answer to *fiat voluntas tua*,[28] then it has nothing of the *nomen tuum*[29] either; that for which our *santificetur*[30] is an expression of thanks.[31]

We then have, from Rhees, a remarkable expression of what a longing for eternal judgement can come to.

It is partly that – even when I take seriously the *quantus tremor est futurus*[32]. . . – I know that with death I shall reach some-thing not myself. That – saving possible nonsense in this – even my damnation will have something divine about it.

. . . cum resurget creatura
judicanti responsura.[33]

As in the previous section, I have been concerned to emphasize the internal relation between love of God and eternal judgement, and to contrast it with external conceptions of such judgement. The central difference is between a concern that makes God the only reason for love of God, and concerns that make love of God the means to a good for oneself. Rhees is emphasizing that idol-atry in religion is precisely this tendency to look away from God to oneself. Death itself is misused when it is seen as the occasion when the believer is rewarded, in the external sense, for loving God. This is a form of idolatry. Rhees asks, 'Is this the tendency which finds its most vulgar expression in "That will be Glory for me"?'[34]

## 4. The Sacrificed and Eternity

In the first section of the chapter, I referred to the fact that theodicists want happy endings. If they are universalists, they want happy endings for everyone. In fact, in eternity, understood as a future mode of existence, everyone must end up in a state of perfection. In the course of the chapter, we have seen that eternity and the notion of eternal judgement cannot be so understood. Rather, they are spiritual realities, and the rewards and punishment associated with them must be understood in the same way. The rewards and punishments cannot be regarded as appendages to the completed lives of human beings. What is to be said of such lives is a judgement known only to God, but what *can* be said of them is internally related to the extent of the presence or absence of love of God in those lives. That being so, it *makes no sense* to say that the eternal judgement on saints and monsters will be the same. There will be those who will react to the eternal judgement on monsters being one of pity by demanding some suffering to be expressed by the monsters after death. If there is to be no such suffering, they feel that the monsters 'have got away with it'. To feel thus is to be discontent with the judgement of eternity and to want it replaced by a temporal, worldly conception of punishment.

At the other end of the spectrum, as it were, there is the demand for the sufferings of the innocent to be put right after death. If this does not happen, it is said to be *bad* news for them in a comparable way to the absence of suffering for monsters being *good* news for them. In these reactions, universalists and theological conservatives are as one in seeking temporal rewards and punishments, and showing a discontent with the judgement of eternity. I want to illustrate one aspect of this discontent by reference to Hick's reaction to the kind of view I have expressed in this book.

As we have seen, according to Hick's general picture, human life is a contest created by God for our moral development. He notes that at the end of a life, only few have made the grade God wants them to reach, hence the need for continued moral development after death. Given the standard is moral perfection, it is difficult to see how anyone makes the grade. That apart, it is clear that, on this view, coming to God is some kind of moral achievement, freeing oneself from the ego in a desire to serve others.

It will be clear that, on my view, Christianity clearly rejects the view of believers as high moral achievers, to be distinguished from others by the standards they attain. On the contrary, to be a Christian is to recognize that one is a sinner in constant need of grace. It is only through grace, through the recognition that life itself is an undeserved gift, that the Christian comes to anything approaching the love of God in his dealings with others. This can be illustrated by Rhees's reaction to a sermon he heard, in which Catholics were reprimanded for not being better examples to others, despite the fact that they possessed what others do not possess.

> I agree that the examples in the lives of people we know and meet are important – perhaps more important than anything else – in enabling most of us to overcome any evil at all in our lives. (Some of those who have been examples for me in this way have been Christians; others have not.)
> Must part of a Catholic's example lie in convincing the others that Catholics are different? Almost as though the outsiders should be brought to ask, 'What have they got that we haven't got?' I should be prone to remember such an example as 'Lord, we thank Thee that we are not as other men are'.
> You know as I do that many are put off religion by the suggestion that people who go to church are better than those who do not. (There is a story I like, that when someone objected to this to a young curate, the curate replied, 'Maybe they're worse, and that's why they go'.)[35]

Hick, by contrast, makes responding to one's own sufferings and to the sufferings of others, a moral achievement. After all, on his view, the attainment of such responses is the reason why God allows evils to exist. Responding to evil is the means to our moral development. He thinks that I recognize this, but refuse to go further. This is a problem for Hick because if the worship of God, or being with God, is a matter of making such responses, what of those who do not make them? Hick is not thinking of the monsters we discussed in the second section of this chapter, but of the victims of evils who are so crushed that the response becomes impossible for them. In these cases, evil has not become the opportunity for moral development which, on his view, it was meant to be. That is why he insists that this situation must be rectified after death in future lives.

It is as though Hick were saying, 'For Phillips, people meet evils by clinging to a love of God. But everyone does not. Therefore some possess something which others do not have. This is an unintended elitism on Phillips's part, and must be replaced by the eventual equality of all people with God.' The conditions that Hick thinks must obtain in order for people to respond to suffering in the ways I have described are worthy of comment. He refers to those who so respond as:

> the fortunate ones who are not chronically undernourished, and in living in fear of starvation . . . not trapped in abject poverty and desperately anxious for our own and our family's and community's short-term future . . . But to think that *all* men and women are free to join in this positive response would be like saying that the desperately poor and starving . . . are free to rise into serenity and inner peace. This would be true only in a cruelly ironic sense. In principle they can do so, but not in reality.[36]

I am so astonished at Hick's remarks that I feel I must have misunderstood him. First, I have said nothing about what *all* men and women are free to do in face of sufferings. In fact, one of my main criticisms of theodicies, especially those such as Swinburne's, is for their voluntaristic assumptions that people *are* always free to respond to sufferings in morally uplifting ways; that this is the purpose for which God allows such sufferings to occur; and their refusal to recognize that people can be crushed by their afflictions.[37]

Second, I said nothing to suggest that acceptance of suffering is always a matter of joy and serenity, though sometimes, as in the letter I quoted from *Dying We Live*, this serenity seems to be present.[38] Rather, I spoke of reactions to suffering that clung to belief, in the direst of circumstances, such as the Holocaust. In the light of that fact, I hope Hick would revise his description of

such responses as belonging to 'the fortunate ones'. I am thinking again of the prayer found on a piece of paper at Ravensbruck.
'And may the love that we have known be their forgiveness.' It
would be crazy to say that *anyone* in those circumstances was
free to pray that prayer. Think of Elie Wiesel's stories. Think of
the examples I have quoted in this book. All I am saying – and I
wonder at the fact – is that *someone did.*

Third, the most astonishing aspect of Hick's claim is that the
religious responses I have talked of are only possible for those
who enjoy a certain economic level of subsistence. Apparently,
they are not available for the starving and those in abject pover-
ty. Think of the condescension in *that*. Is Hick saying, 'Blessed
are the not so very poor, for only they can see God'? Is Hick saying, on his view, that the moral standards God hoped we would
achieve in this life are not going to be achieved by those below a
certain level of economic subsistence, and that, in that sense,
God has abandoned them in his life, but will get around to them
later after death? I do not think the level of economic subsistence
was very high in the Holocaust, but many did not abandon their
faith in God. Peter was a poor fisherman, perhaps below Hick's
required level of economic subsistence, but it is said of him that
he asked to be crucified upside down because he was unworthy
to die in the same way as his Lord.

Fourth, part of the trouble comes from Hick's instrumentalism, one endemic in theodicies that make suffering the *means*
and *justification* of life's sufferings. Christianity, in the main, forbids *seeking* suffering. Saints, such as Peter Claver, have prayed
for it. He wanted to become a leper like those among whom he
worked. Saint John of the Cross prayed to partake in the sufferings of Christ, and we have noted Simone Weil's incredible
prayer for senility. But, in all these cases, the prayers have
qualified their request by saying that it should be granted only if
it is God's will. Fulfilment should not be sought. Further, in none
of those cases would it be said that the experience of God,
through the sufferings, either justifies the suffering or is in any
way a compensation for them. This persistent instrumentalism is
difficult to get rid of.[39]

Because instrumentalism is present in Hick's thought, because suffering is the means to moral development, Hick has a major problem when that development does not occur. God's teaching programme has not worked. Despite the criticisms I have made of his remarks, he is right to call attention to those who are crushed by life's circumstances. But, given his instrumentalism, he wants this put right in a future life or lives after death. But this notion of 'putting things right', once again, distorts the character of eternal life and eternal judgement, and substitutes for it temporal conceptions of rewards and punishments.

By contrast, I have emphasized that what can be said of completed lives from the perspective of eternity is internally related to the relation of God to individual lives. The question to be faced, therefore, is this: what can be said, from the perspective of eternity, of those who have been crushed by life's circumstances? Whatever is said *must respect the historical particularity of the lives concerned.* To avoid that particularity is not only to indulge in a magical view of divine redemption, a 'God will fix it' view of eternity, but also to fail to respect the particular sufferings people have borne, some so horrendous that they have been crushed by them. These observations are not a matter of theological preference alone, since logical issues arise in connection with the alternatives most theodicies offer. We have been grappling with these throughout the course of the book. For example, in response to Marilyn Adams's notion of redemption in which an incommensurable goodness in God simply defeats evil, by coercion if necessary, Rowan Williams makes the following comments:

> But even if we allow such a minimal appeal to the post-mortem dimension, what we have to say is that the subject remains what he or she has become as a result of the experiences of this life; the possibilities that lie open are defined by a particular history . . . Otherwise, we should have to suppose that the post-mortem identity had suddenly ceased to be the identity constructed by this history and no other. This would resolve the problematic nature of destructive evil by a kind of eschato-

logical dissolution of the particular subject as such: in the light of eternity, the suffering of the abused child or the victim of torture is no more 'difficult' to heal than that of an academic who fails to get the job they wanted or a theatrical producer whose grant from the Arts Council has been halved.[40]

I know that Adams wants to avoid these implications. That is why she insists, as against Davis, that horrendous evils will not pale into insignificance in the light of the glory God has in store for us. But she insists that horrendous evils will be defeated. The problem is that, on her view, it is unclear how.[41]

In what sense can eternity 'heal' those crushed by life's circumstances? For some Christian philosophers, such as John K. Roth, the answer lies in the resurrection, which demonstrates that God can do all things. Of course, it also, for him, raises the question of why God hasn't done anything about sufferings earlier. Furthermore, whatever form the healing in eternity takes, he cannot see how God can be called perfectly good. Stephen T. Davis has no more idea than Roth as to why God has not intervened earlier, but believes, in a way he does not understand, that all suffering will, ultimately, be redeemed. As we have seen, Adams and Hick share the same hope. But if, as Williams rightly insists, the particularity of human lives is respected, what can 'putting things right' mean with respect to those crushed by suffering? Doesn't the desperate theological appeal to ignorance cover up a supposition that is logically incoherent?

Some appeal to the resurrection as the ultimate safety valve in the sky that redeems all afflictions. Not all Christian theologians, by any means, have thought so. They have not seen the crucifixion as a mistake (the bad news), which is put right in the resurrection (the good news). Rather, it is the crucified Christ who is said to be exalted, raised on high to sit on the right hand of God the Father. 'Raised' cannot be understood in any spatial sense, since as Hick recognizes, we are not spatially distant from God. If Christ is said to be raised on high, it would be manifestly absurd to ask 'How high?' And if Christ is said to ascend to his Father, it would also be absurd to ask where exactly that is. If we appreciate Kierkegaard's lesson, and see that 'eternity' is a spiritual category, then the concepts connected with it must also be understood in this way, namely, talk of being 'raised up', 'a glorious body' and of 'going to the Father'. The Passion shows us what love of God is, and it is in terms of it that the experiences of those crushed by suffering are to be understood from the perspective of eternity.

Some have objected to using the story of the Suffering Servant and the Passion of Christ in responding to those crushed by suffering, on the grounds that the voluntariness of the Servant and Christ cannot address the involuntary fate of the victims of affliction.[42] We saw, also, however, that such a view ignores the *involuntariness* in the fate of the Suffering Servant and Christ. One misses something essential if one treats them simply as marvellous examples of voluntary self-sacrifice. This leaves out the bitterness in the fact that they are *broken*. That cannot be understood as a voluntary acceptance by the will. Thus their fate, despised and rejected by men, speaks to the fate of those who are broken by affliction. In some Jewish and Christian traditions, we are shown what can happen to love. The crucified Christ is not resurrected with healed wounds. Those who taunt him on the Cross, urging him to save himself and thereby prove that he is the Son of God, fail to understand that the only omnipotence God has is the omnipotence of love. It is from such a love that the prayer for forgiveness for the oppressors comes from the Cross, 'Forgive them, Father, for they know not what they do.' But the price of such love is that it can be broken, sacrificed. And it is that sacrifice which is raised up, exalted, for all eternity.

In the course of the chapter, we have insisted that what can be said of human lives, from the perspective of eternity, cannot bypass the particularity of those lives, whether they be the lives of saints or monsters. The same is true of the lives of those crushed by life's adversities. Their fate must not be bypassed, since to do so is to betray it. At the outset of the book I mentioned the constant danger of such betrayal in writing of human suffering. At this point, it is essential to heed that caution.

We have emphasized that creation involves risk, including the risk that people can be crushed by circumstances. God does not (cannot) spare his own Son. Even the love of Christ is reduced to 'nothing' before God – 'My God, My God, why have you abandoned me?' The gift of life involves compassion for the gift, a compassion which realizes that in this life anything may happen to anyone, including God's Suffering Servant and Son.

An insidious instrumentalism will continue to make its appearance in the suggestion that God allows his Servant and Son to suffer thus *in order to* show us what love of God is. Once this is allowed, compassion for human life becomes the horror story I have objected to throughout the book.

Those who are crushed by life's afflictions are not going to enter a state where all this is to be put right. That is to seek an outcome other than the judgement of eternity. In that judgement, their story, which cannot be taken from them, is exalted, raised on high for all eternity, even though it is a story they cannot tell themselves.

I say that *they* have their story, rather than that *we* have it, to make an important final point. It is true that the lives of those sacrificed in life's adversities can show us what can happen to innocence and love, but the significance of what has happened to the afflicted does not depend on that. It depends on God. Even if no one knew their story – after all, how many stories do we really know? – its significance from an eternal perspective remains – it is still exalted, raised on high. That is the judgement of eternity on these completed lives. If anyone has understood, in the slightest, what I have been saying about eternal, as distinct from temporal judgement, reward and punishment, they will realize that believers are saying something very real for them when they say that even if the stories of the afflicted were forgotten by the whole world, God does not forget. Nearer than anyone, God listens.

I realize only too well that much of what I have said about eternity and its judgements will fall on deaf ears. To many it will seem that I have not been talking about anything real, not about anything that actually happens. This is because the sense of the eternal has been eroded in our culture, and the temporal has been transcendentalized as a pseudo-replacement for it. For me, evidence of this erosion is found in the sad fact that when we discuss the problem of evil, we do so in terms of what I have called our problematic philosophical inheritance. This is not simply a matter for intellectual regret. I said at the outset of the book that the problem of evil should be discussed with fear and trembling. This is because it is easy for us, as intellectuals, to add to the evil in the world by the ways in which we discuss it.

## Notes

1. Ludwig Wittgenstein, *Tractatus*, London: Routledge and Kegan Paul 1961, 6.4312.
2. See the discussions in Chapter 8.
3. Kierkegaard, *Purity of Heart*, New York: Harper Torchbooks 1956, p. 154.
4. John Hick, *Evil and the God of Love*, London: Macmillan 1966.
5. Richard Swinburne, *Providence and the Problem of Evil*, Oxford: Clarendon Press 1998, p. 257, n. 6.
6. 'Voices in Discussion' in D. Z. Phillips (ed.), *Religion and Morality*, Basingstoke: Macmillan 1996, pp. 320–1. The discussion is of Adams's paper, 'Evil and the God-Who-Does-Nothing-In-Particular' in the same volume. Adams is represented by voice F in the discussion. The printed discussion relies on the notes I took at the Claremont conference, but I am reasonably confident of the accuracy of the point of view expressed.
7. Stephen T. Davis, 'Critique of John Hick' in Stephen T. Davis (ed.), *Encountering Evil*, Louisville: Westminster John Knox Press 2001, p. 61.
8. Davis, 'Critique of John Hick', pp. 61–2.
9. Rush Rhees, 'Difficulties with Christianity' in Rhees, *On Religion and Philosophy*, ed. D. Z. Phillips, Cambridge: Cambridge University Press 1997, p. 359.
10. John Hick, 'Rejoinder' in Davis, *Encountering Evil*, pp. 68–9.
11. See Chapter 1, section 2.
12. There are, no doubt, forms of universalism other than the forms I criticize here. My remarks should be taken as applying only to examples I discuss.
13. For a marvellous treatment of a fall from such pride see Flannery O'Connor's short story, 'Revelation' in *The Complete Stories*, New York: Farrar, Straus and Giroux 1981. For my discussion of it see 'Who's Who' in *From Fantasy to Faith*, Basingstoke: Macmillan 1991.

14 For Rhees's discussion, to which I am indebted, see 'Election and Judgement' in *On Religion and Philosophy*.

15 Swinburne, *Providence*, p. 210.

16 Rhees, 'Religion, life and meaning B' in *On Religion and Philosophy*, p. 176.

17 Rhees, 'Religion, life and meaning B', p. 176.

18 Rhees, 'Religion, life and meaning B', p. 192.

19 Rhees, 'Election and judgement', p. 254.

20 See Chapter 4 on the free-will defence.

21 Quotation from Baudelaire, 'Madame Bastouri' in *Oeuvres complètes*, Paris: Laffont 1980, p. 208.

22 Rhees, 'Election and judgement', p. 255.

23 R. F. Holland, 'Suicide' in *Against Empiricism*, Oxford: Blackwell 1980, p. 147.

24 Rhees, 'Death and immortality' in *On Religion and Philosophy*, p. 235.

25 Rhees, 'Death and immortality', p. 236.

26 Rhees, 'Death and immortality', p. 235.

27 Needless to say, I do not share Rhees's judgement of himself. Far from it. But this is not, of course, to say that he was confused or mistaken in making that judgement.

28 'Thy will be done.'

29 'Thy name.'

30 'Hallowed be.'

31 Rhees, 'Death and immortality', p. 236.

32 'How great a terror there will be' (from 'Dies Irae', Requiem Mass).

33 'When creation rises again to answer the judge', Rhees, 'Death and immortality', pp. 235–6.

34 Rhees, 'Death and immortality', p. 237.

35 Rhees, 'Christianity and the growth of understanding' in *On Religion and Philosophy*, pp. 383–4.

36 John Hick, 'Transcendence and Truth' in D. Z. Phillips and Timothy Tessin (eds), *Religion Without Transcendence?* Basingstoke: Macmillan 1997, p. 45.

37 See Chapter 3.

38 See Chapter 10, section 4.

39 See Chapter 10, section 2.

40 Rowan Williams, 'Redeeming Sorrows' in Phillips, *Religion and Morality*, p. 139.

41 See Stephen T. Davis, 'Critique of John K. Roth', and Marilyn McCord Adams, 'Afterword' in Davis, *Encountering Evil*, pp. 23 and 197, respectively.

42 See Chapter 10, section 4.

# Index of Names

# Index of Subjects

Belief
  and affliction 236, 271–4
  as moral achievement 267
  as sacrifice 220–5, 237

Christianity
  as conception of human life 141–8,
    174, 227–9, 254
  and Christ's Passion 200–1, 237–8,
    240
  and Socrates 239–240
  and patience 212–7, 235–40

Covenant
  as contract 147–8, 150, 174, 230–2
  as eternal 159–62, 174, 230–2
  and Job 147

Creation
  as abdication 179–80
  as power 162, 177–80
  purpose of 221–2

Crucifixion and resurrection 271–4

Death
  and compensation 81–90
  and eternal judgement 261–5
  and memories 89–90
  and survival 85–90, 248–9

Dying
  to the self 182–6, 194, 267–9
  to love's expectations 197–9
  to moral expectations 195–6

Eschatology 70, 84, 118–9
  and ignorance 85–6, 122

Evil
  as logically necessary 51–6, 115
  as opportunity for character
    development 56–8, 115
  as opportunity for moral
    responsibility 58–60, 115
  as opportunity for causal initiatives
    60–3, 115
  as opportunity for admirable
    responses 63–6, 115
  as opportunity for admirable
    endurance 66–71, 115
  as result of bad choices 71–7, 115
  as less than it seems 77–8, 115
  as not unlimited 78–81, 115
  and compensation after death
    81–90, 115
  and existential problems xi–xv
  and logical problems xi–xv, 3–5
  responses to and theory xv–xxi

Faith
  and expectations 194–219
  and the terrible 201–9
  in extremis 209–11, 217

Free-Will 54–5, 74–5
  and action 27–32
  and divine non-intervention 106–8
  as a good 95–7, 116

Free-Will Defence 95–109, 116

Geometry 172–3

God
  and caprice 134–6
  and consequentialism 35–46, 76–7,
    217, 247–8